M000275922

$39.95
NEW

This Compost

This Compost

ECOLOGICAL IMPERATIVES IN AMERICAN POETRY

Jed Rasula

THE UNIVERSITY OF GEORGIA PRESS
ATHENS AND LONDON

Athens, Georgia 30602

Designed by Betty Palmer McDaniel
Set in 10 on 14 JansonMT by BookComp
Printed and bound by Maple-Vail
The paper in this book meets the guidelines for permanence and durability of the Committee on Production Guidelines for Book Longevity of the Council on Library Resources.

Printed in the United States of America
02 03 04 05 06 C 5 4 3 2 1

Library of Congress Cataloging-in-Publication Data
Rasula, Jed.
This compost : ecological imperatives in American poetry / Jed Rasula.
p. cm.
Includes bibliographical references and index.
ISBN 0-8203-2366-7 (hardcover : alk. paper)
1. American poetry—History and criticism. 2. Nature in literature. 3. Environmental protection in literature. 4. Nature conservation in literature. 5. Ecology in literature. I. Title.
PS310.N3 R37 2002
811.009'355—dc21 2002000856

British Library Cataloging-in-Publication Data available

IN MEMORY OF MENTORS

Mike Erwin

Harvey Brown

Mark Ruddick

Of course the old questions, why are we here?, why do we exist in the flask of visible circumstance?

Only to have the animal stolen from us?, only to have our most intimate fervour destroyed?

WILL ALEXANDER, *Towards the Primeval Lightning Field*

for a meniscus tension of exhumation
swells the page—
fugue and segue, modicums of {wonder / wander}
for the {locus / logos}

all along the shifting {boundary / bounty}

RACHEL BLAU DUPLESSIS, *Drafts*

One being climbs up inside another
for the revolution in art.

JOANNE KYGER, *Just Space*

Contents

Preface

This Compost combines several functions in one. It is an anthology of sorts, concentrating on the Black Mountain lineage in modern American poetry, though with plenty of related extracts going back to Whitman and Dickinson. But anthologies invariably reflect judgments of taste, and *This Compost* neither argues the priority of, nor attempts to canonize, a particular set of poets. Insofar as I take poetry to be something more than the exercise of aesthetic self-expression, there are tacit limits to the poets included here. Robert Creeley reports Allen Ginsberg urging, "You don't really have to worry about writing a good poem any more, you can write what you want to" (Faas, 187). While Creeley overestimates will, the peculiar energy I find in the poets in *This Compost* is their willingness to work outside prevailing literary sensibility. Often the very look of the poems discloses a sculptural address, or a kinetic choreography attentive to organism, not decorum. As a compendium of extracts, this book does not validate aesthetic claims commonly made in literary criticism so much as document a stance toward the living planet, a stance these poets share with many people who know nothing of poetry.

Despite its length, *This Compost* is also an essay. There are no chapters as such; rather, the headings indicate *topoi* in the old rhetorical sense: sites of excavation and deliberation. While they are arranged to be read chronologically, the method is somewhat circular, so the reader will find certain *topoi* recurring in a seasonal rotation. Footnotes appear at the bottom of the page because I write that way; I favor a bifocal prospect, atavistic residue perhaps of hunting and tracking instincts. Ed Sanders says "A footnote is a dangling data-cluster" and compares it to a mobile by Alexander Calder. I like the quadruped diagram Sanders provides ("The Art of the Elegant Footnote," in *Thirsting for Peace in a Raging Century*, 162).

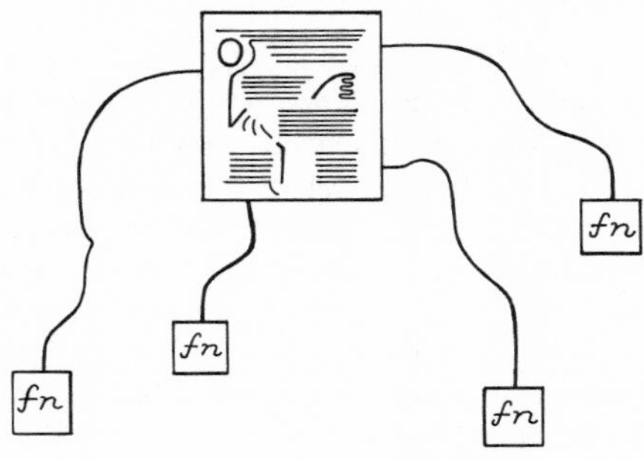

As an exercise in ecological solidarity with the materials it conveys, *This Compost* practices what it preaches in that most of the citations of poetry are not identified in the text, but blended into polyphonic configurations. Sometimes what is given as a single poetic citation is assembled from several poets or poems—although different extracts are always indicated by a marker (~) at the right-hand margin. All sources from books of poetry are clearly identified at the end of the book, in the citations chapter (pp. 201–2). Quoted prose, on the other hand, is identified parenthetically in the text. (Citation from prose poems complicates matters; but if no reference is given in the text, you can bet it's a prose poem referenced in the citations chapter.) I have taken the liberty of not citing pre-twentieth-century work by page number, since there are so many editions. But the originals—from Emerson's prose, Whitman's poetry, or early modern authors like Thomas Browne—tend to be concise or conveniently divided. So extracts from Whitman are identified by section numbers (in the numbering of Whitman's final "deathbed" edition), and in the case of prose writers I provide chapter or section indicators.

The origins of my citational practice are also the origins of *This Compost* in that I initially noticed thematic congruencies specific to some primary books published in 1960—*The Distances* by Charles Olson and *The Opening of the Field* by Robert Duncan—which led to comparisons with work by Jack Spicer and Louis Zukofsky, among others. The notion of "composition by field" carried obvious implications of compost, which led me to the concept of "necropoetics" developed here by way of Whitman. The notion of a "compost library" arose when I began carefully placing certain extracts side by side without authorial distinction. It's worth recalling that this tactic was also indebted to those influential if too easily misconstrued essays by Roland Barthes ("The Death of the Author") and Michel Foucault ("What Is an Author?"), along with the notion of intertextuality developed by Julia Kristeva and Barthes.* Eventually, I recognized the implications for a body of poetry written *in* and *for* a community, however loosely defined. Readership was tan-

* These long-familiar works had a tremendously fertilizing impact for certain communities of American poets as they were translated. Barthes's *The Pleasure of the Text* was the subject of a symposium (in the older Greek sense of a quasi-Bacchanale) in my magazine *Wch Way* (1975). "The Death of the Author" appeared in Stephen Heath's collection of essays by Barthes, *Image, Music, Text,* in 1977, the same year that Donald Bouchard's selection of essays and interviews by Foucault, *Language, Counter-Memory, Practice,* brought "What Is an Author?" into English. The alignment of poetic practice with continental theory is rightly associated with Language poetry, but the discursive foreground of "composition by field" is essential. In fact, figures like Derrida were being discussed at the Ethnopoetics conference at the University of Wisconsin in Milwaukee in 1975 well in advance of academic assimilation.

tamount to collaboration; authorship, in turn, extended far beyond specific acts of writing.

The bibliography includes titles cited or mentioned in the text. Additional titles appear in the biographical glossary, which consists of thumbnail sketches of the poets most prominent in *This Compost.* The resources used here vary considerably, having much to do with the span of time during which *This Compost* was written. At the outset, in 1980, there were no standard editions of most of the work I deal with here*—and some of it was still appearing in little magazines—but in the intervening decades they have proliferated (University of California Press doing the lion's share, issuing *The Maximus Poems, "A,"* Creeley's *Collected Poems,* and numerous other titles by Olson, Zukofsky, and Creeley). I have been able to make use of these and some other definitive collections (like those of Robinson Jeffers [Stanford] and William Carlos Williams [New Directions]), but it proved too much to keep adapting to all the reissues and new editions as they appeared. So, as much as I appreciate the editorial labors of Ben Friedlander and Donald Allen, I have not cited from their edition of Olson's *Collected Prose* (which, in any case, omits many texts central to *This Compost*); nor have I gone beyond the 1972 edition of Pound's *Cantos.* I deliberately chose some earlier versions of "Image-Nations" by Robin Blaser over those included in his magnum opus, *The Holy Forest* (readers will find the appropriate distinctions in the citations). And I decided to stick with *In Cold Hell, in Thicket* and *The Distances* as a way of emphasizing Olson's own arrangement of the poems, despite the fine chronological presentation in the *Collected.*

This Compost is not altogether a scholarly project. It represents instead an intersection of communities. It might be regarded as an instance of "poet's prose," on the model of Robert Duncan's copious "H. D. Book," and my ongoing participation in an extensive network of poets has informed the project at every step. It also bears traces of involvement in the milieu of archetypal psychology, culminating at a 1981 conference in Buffalo where the Jungians were treated to memorable readings by Creeley and Duncan. I might also trace the book's origins to a radio program I hosted in Los Angeles on the Pacifica station KPFK (fm) from 1979 to 1981, osten-

* Nor was there much in the way of scholarship. Michael Palmer has talked about his experience in the 1960s, looking into work by Pound, Williams, Zukofsky, and others without benefit of academic guidance: "I was reading 'in the dark,' which was very exciting" (Gardner, 274). The situation hadn't changed much a decade later; and while there has been a relative mushrooming of scholarly work in the past twenty years (significantly aided by *Sagetrieb*), there has also been a corresponding decline in pedagogic attention to poetry as such.

sibly a book review format that evolved into a lecture series. On the first program I reviewed Zukofsky's newly published *"A."* I didn't cover much poetry (*Hades in Manganese* by Clayton Eshleman and *Ark: The Foundations* by Ronald Johnson were the only ones besides *"A"*); instead, I delved into the historical and political spectrum that *This Compost* draws on. Among the many books I "reviewed" on KPFK were *The Dream and the Underworld* by James Hillman, *Keepers of the Game* by Calvin Martin, *Iron Cages* by Ronald Takaki, *Discoverers, Settlers, Explorers* by Wayne Franklin, *The Economics of the Imagination* by Kurt Heinzelman, *American Hieroglyphics* by John Irwin, *Beyond Geography* by Frederick Turner, *The Real Work* by Gary Snyder, *The Geography of the Imagination* by Guy Davenport, *Extinction* by Paul and Anne Ehrlich, *Laying Waste: The Poisoning of America by Toxic Chemicals* by Michael Brown, *The Age of Surveillance* by Frank Donner, *The Legacy of Malthus* by Allan Chase, and *Empire as a Way of Life* by William A. Williams. Not all of the above ended up being cited in *This Compost,* but they guided drafts and suggested the territory.

Acknowledgments

For early interest and support I am indebted to Charles Bernstein, Burton Hatlen, and James Hillman, who published extracts in *L=A=N=G=U=A=G=E/Open Letter* (1982), *Sagetrieb* (1982 and 1983), and the Jungian annual of archetypal psychology *Spring* (1979). Other material from *This Compost* was published by Barrett Watten and Lyn Hejinian in *Poetics Journal* (1982), Andrew Benson in *Adz* (1983), and Paul Naylor, who made a handy selection for *Facture* (2000) and also offered crucial guidance for final revisions. I owe special thanks to Lyn Hejinian for advice about the title and to Bob Grenier for giving it to me straight. Harvey Brown offered invaluable scrutiny of my first draft in 1981, and Mark Ruddick provided the setting for the second draft. Readers for the University of Georgia Press offered welcome encouragement, and I'm indebted to the precision of their suggestions about bringing the manuscript to completion. Barbara Ras's heartening reception of the manuscript presages a notably smooth path to production at the University of Georgia Press, particularly under the watchful eye of Jon Davies.

Financial assistance from the Advisory Research Council of Queen's University, along with some funds from a Social Science and Humanities Research Council of Canada grant, expedited completion of the manuscript. To that end, the assistance of Nathan Brown was particularly valuable.

This Compost could not have been written without years of exchange with many of the poets it discusses. Their friendship and generosity enhanced this book in countless ways (not least in access to manuscripts long before they were published). I regret that too many of them are no longer alive to accept this long-delayed record of my thanks: Robert Duncan, Jack Clarke, Ronald Johnson, Paul Metcalf, George Butterick and Lee Hickman. Exemplary companions, for whom in every immediate sense I wrote the book, are Don Byrd, Chuck Stein, Gerrit Lansing, Ken Irby, Andrew Schelling, Nate Mackey, Will Alexander, Jerry and Diane Rothenberg, Clayton and Caryl Eshleman. I would also mention Duncan McNaughton, Robert Creeley, Robert Bertholf, Michael McClure, Robin Blaser, Jackson Mac Low, Bruce Andrews, Mike Boughn, James Hillman: tutelary spirits along the way. The sustaining ground from beginning to end has been shared with Suzi Wong and Sonja and Hilda Rasula.

This Compost

Introduction

"All our literatures are leavings," writes Gary Snyder (*Practice of the Wild,* 112), recycling Thoreau's remark "Decayed literature makes the richest of all soils," which he wrote in his journal after observing that "while we are clearing the forest in our westward progress, we are accumulating a forest of books in our rear, as wild and unexplored as any of nature's primitive wildernesses" (16 March 1852). While Thoreau's reading in the classics marked him as a Harvard man for his contemporaries, his instincts were not scholastic, but ecological. *Walden,* that prospectus of wild moods, is a compost of rhetorical jubilation Thoreau prepared with geophysical patience. The years he spent writing *Walden* are testimony to a composting sensibility: attuned to the rhythms by which literary models decayed and enriched the soil, Thoreau was prepared for his own notebook entries (the ready mulch of chronicle) to fertilize and incubate the book that was latent in them. Fittingly, Thoreau's resources included Walter Whiter's *Etymologicon Universale* (1822), its two fat tomes proclaiming with manic industry that all words derive from references to earth, or with reference to the activity of handling it. Thoreau's palpable delight in the Homeric battle of the ants is not just pleasure in the rhetorical inversion, but reverence for microcosms rendered visible in the scale of human prejudice, revisiting old paradigms of what Melville called our mortal inter-indebtedness; "indeed what reason may not goe to Schoole to the wisedome of Bees, Ants, and Spiders?" Thomas Browne wonders (*Religio Medici,* para. 15). "Thus there are two bookes from whence I collect my Divinity," he declares: "besides that written one of God, another of his servant Nature, that universall and publik Manuscript, that lies expans'd unto the eyes of all: those that never saw him in the one, have discovered him in the other: This was the Scripture and Theology of the Heathens . . . [who] knew better how to joyne and reade these mysticall letters, than wee Christians, who cast a more carelesse eye on these common Hieroglyphicks, and disdain to suck Divinity from the flowers of nature" (para. 16). Thoreau shared a comparable reverence for the pagan hieroglyphic divinity of the natural world.

A nineteenth-century agricultural milieu and a sixteenth-century theological recapitulation of the great chain of being are not the only settings in which thoughts of compost might arise. Eugene Jolas, the polyglot metropolitan editor of the avant-garde journal *transition* (in which Joyce's *Finnegans Wake* was serialized), advocated on behalf of a rectified "vertigral" imagination, "subobjective" and "inter-racial," with a corollary in poetics: "The 'poem' must change into a *mantic* *compost* which organizes the expanding consciousness of 'the expanding universe' " ("Workshop," 100). For Jolas, compost is not conceptually restricted to the decay of organic matter; it affords a commanding prospect of correspondences, resonant parallelisms, glimpses of independent figures participating in a fortuitous isomorphism.*

"A rhyme in one of our sonnets should not be less pleasing than the iterated nodes of a sheashell, or the resembling difference of a group of flowers," wrote Emerson in "The Poet." Whitman promptly echoed the injunction in his preface to the 1855 *Leaves of Grass:* "The rhyme and uniformity of perfect poems show the free growth of metrical laws and bud from them as unerringly and loosely as lilacs or roses"—shedding, along the way, Emerson's attachment to rhyme as an identifying trait of poetry. Whitman then goes on to offer a prescriptive manual of applications for his book:

> This is what you shall do: Love the earth and sun and the animals, despise riches, give alms to every one that asks, stand up for the stupid and crazy, devote your income and labor to others, hate tyrants, argue not concerning God, have patience and indulgence toward the people, take off your hat to nothing known or unknown or to any man or number of men, go freely with powerful uneducated persons and with the young and with the mothers of families, read these leaves in the open air every season of every year of your life, reexamine all you have been told at school or church or in any book, dismiss whatever insults your own soul, and your very flesh shall be a great poem and have the richest fluency not only in its words but in the silent lines of its lips and face and between the lashes of your eyes and in every motion and joint of your body.

Carefully placed in the deepest recess of this compendium is Whitman's insistence that his poems be read outdoors. When, in "The Lesson of a Tree"—one of the entries in *Specimen Days*—he recommends arboreal articulation as antidote to human chatter, the botanical affiliation of his "leaves" is evident.

The composting sensibility awakened by the outdoor setting is an adamant feature of Whitman's sense of education. In the late (1888) "Backward Glance O'er Travel'd Roads," Whitman reminisces on his "outdoor influences"—citing, in this category, the works of Homer, Æschylus, Sophocles, Shakespeare, Dante, the

* For a broad contextualization of Jolas's Romantic Modernism, see my anthology *Imagining Language,* coedited with Steve McCaffery.

Nibelungenlied, and "the ancient Hindoo poems": "it makes such difference *where* you read," he notes. "I have wonder'd since why I was not overwhelm'd by those mighty masters. Likely because I read them . . . in the full presence of Nature, under the sun, with the far-spreading landscape and vistas, or the sea rolling in." Whitman of course makes a rhetorical point that equates the grand masters with the great outdoors, and he offers a tacit invitation to read *Leaves of Grass* before a panoramic scene by Frederic Church or Albert Biertstadt, American painters of the geophysical sublime. But Whitman admits a more endearingly domestic sort of outdoors episode as well in a memorable icon of the writer at work in *Specimen Days,* in which "a drove of young hogs rooting in soft ground near the oak under which I sit . . . come sniffing near me, and then scamper away, with grunts"—a scene further elaborated by "the clear notes of the quail" and "the quiver of leaf-shadows over the paper as I write"; "the swift darting of many sand-swallows coming and going" and "the odor of the cedar and oak, so palpable, as evening approaches." There is an easy and equitable transition here in which the parenthetical definition of Nature as "the only complete, actual poem" in *Democratic Vistas* is not an instance of literary Romanticism, but a pledge of allegiance to what Gregory Bateson called the ecology of mind. "The individual mind is immanent but not only in the body," writes Bateson in a passage verging on the "cosmic consciousness" announced by Whitman's Ontario devotee Dr. Bucke. "It is immanent also in pathways and messages outside the body; and there is a larger Mind of which the individual mind is only a subsystem" (*Steps to an Ecology of Mind,* 467). Karl Kroeber gives a precise corollary in his celebration of the English Romantic poets' anticipation of modern ecology. "The unity of an ecosystem . . . is not something sensorily perceptible, even though it is determinative of our sensory experience," he observes. "An ecosystem, finally, although very complicated, is also something very specific. So it is understandable that the romantics emphasized the importance of complex integral unities of being whose wholeness could only be *imagined*" (*Ecological Literary Criticism,* 58). "Wholeness" is an overdetermined word, so it might be better to speak of long-range views or the bigger picture. Succinctly put by Wendell Berry, "We live in eternity while we live in time. It is only by imagination that we know this" (*Standing by Words,* 90).

Calling on the imagination as a resource of ecological understanding means calling on poetry in a truly re-creational capacity, one that redefines "recreation" as original participation, much as Coleridge sought a poetry that would propagate a continuum initiated by the divine fiat. Such a prospect has gone in and out of focus during the past two centuries, but its reemergence under the countenance of a so-called "Black Mountain" school was historically congruent with, and sometimes affiliated with, the interdisciplinary matrix gathered around what Norbert Wiener named "cybernetics." Systems theory is a more general term for it, and recently the focus has been on self-organization as a property observable in systems at different thresholds of organic integrity and sapience. Henri Atlan defines a field of interanimating tendencies converging on "the possibility of the emergence of newness, of the unpredicted"—which is the aspiration of the poetics informing *This Compost.* "It is at this junction, which makes time creative, that we see appear, as a *shadow,* what we could call a self-*unconsciousness,* not necessarily human. And we can reach this junction by three different paths: one which explores the organizational role of randomness; another which explores the role of the creation of meaning; and a third, that of the autonomy of the self, which brings together 'the knower, the known, and knowledge' " (Atlan 127). These paths can be followed in reflecting on poetry as well. Randomness, for instance, was first solicited as an object of poetic aspiration by Stéphane Mallarmé, whose *Un coup de dés* was the inaugural text of open form (preceded, however, by the serial practices of Whitman and Dickinson). Atlan's second path, the creation of meaning, is relevant to poetry in obvious ways, but it's important to construe it in the extrasemantic sense that poetry re-creates language. It is not confined to the role of performative arabesque, dilation on a space previously (or even evidently) convened. In this capacity it is informed by the principle of structural coupling outlined by the biologists Humberto Maturana and Francisco Varela: "We work out our lives in mutual linguistic coupling, not because language permits us to reveal ourselves but because we are constituted in language in a continuous becoming that we bring forth with others" (*Tree of Knowledge,* 235). Atlan's third path, which envisions a conjunction of subject-object-act as constitutive of an autonomous self, is more expressively subsumed under the principle of autopoeisis, in which "values are not objects but moiré patterns which emerge from the superimposition of opposites" (William Irwin Thompson, *Gaia,* 28).* The *self* that becomes evident in the occasion of autopoeisis is not the preestablished "speaker"—the enunciative rational ego—which we have been accustomed to identify in the poem. It's not easy, of course, to peremptorily cancel or refuse the accumulated authority of poetry's resident voice-over. The struggle to do so continues to precipitate squalls and squalor in which a hideous proprietary

* A thoroughgoing attempt to rethink Western thought from the point of view of autopoeisis is Don Byrd's *The Poetics of the Common Knowledge,* a book intricately involved with the poets and poetics engaged in *This Compost.*

vocabulary anatomizes "modernist" from "postmodernist" tendencies. But in the milieu of *This Compost* these terminological considerations are beside the point. This is not to deny their validity under certain conditions, in some discussions, but to insist on the nondenominational value, as it were, of what Aldo Leopold affirmed as a need "to preserve the element of Unknown Places" (*The River*, 125). He was referring to wilderness, but (and in fact because of that) poetry necessarily belongs to such places.*

In his late essay, "Poetry To-day in America—Shakspere—The Future" (1881), Walt Whitman reiterated a charge he had been making for a quarter century, that "the overwhelming mass of poetic works, as now absorb'd into human character, exerts a certain constipating, repressing, in-door, and artificial influence." The derogatory characterization of the "in-door" here need not be taken literally: the "Omen in the Bone" (no. 532) and the "Contusion of the Husk" (no. 1135) of which the domestic Emily Dickinson writes are admonitions to regard any settled stance as another constipated hindrance to the adventure of enlargement, along with the lubrications of what Whitman called "adhesiveness." Between them, Dickinson and Whitman typify *literal* versions of indoor and outdoor life; but at the same time, the poetic wilderness they share reveals the ineptitude of the literal. They embody a profound compulsion to find the measure of poetry in "orbic traits" (Whitman)—"For Earths, grow thick as / Berries, in my native town," Dickinson writes. "My Basket holds — just — Firmaments — / Those — dangle easy — on my arm, / But smaller bundles — Cram" (no. 352). Whitman's prospect in "Democratic Vistas" seems germane to Dickinson as well: arguing the need for "a new Literature, perhaps a new Metaphysics, certainly a new Poetry," he clarifies that he does not mean "the smooth walks, trimmed hedges, posys and nightingales of the English poets, but the whole orb, with its geological history, the cosmos,

* Such an assertion may not seem self-evident, but insofar as it is, it reveals a tacit alliance of the project of *This Compost* with that of ethnopoetics, which Jerome Rothenberg defines as "the reinterpretation of the poetic past, the recurrent question of a primitive-civilized dichotomy (particularly in its post-Platonic, Western manifestations), the idea of a visionary poetics and of the shaman as a paradigmatic proto-poet, the idea of a great subculture and of the persistence of an oral poetics in all of the 'higher' civilizations, the concept of wilderness and of the role of the poet as a defender of biological and psychological diversity, the issue of the monoculture and the issue of cultural imperialism, the question of communal and individual expression in traditional societies, the relation of culture and language to mental processes, the divergence of oral and written cultures (and their projected reconciliation), and the reemergence of suppressed and rejected forms and images (the goddess, the trickster, the human universe, etc.)" ("Pre-Face" to *Symposium of the Whole*, xvi).

carrying fire and snow, that rolls through the illimitable areas, light as a feather, though weighing billions of tons."

If we take this orbic mass as the geophysical phantom of an ever-impending "new Poetry," where are we to find it today? A glance at the bulk of modern poetry suggests a calamitous abandonment of the legacy imposed—enabled—by Whitman and Dickinson. The situation is hardly recent, of course. Even the major impetus of high modernism advanced without reference to Whitman and Dickinson (except for Pound's testy acknowledgement of his male forebear, and William Carlos Williams's willingness to stake out a claim for "antipoetry" in *Spring and All* as affording a "co-extention with the universe" [*Collected Poems,* 1:177, 192]). The self-proclaimed "post-modernism" of Randall Jarrell, John Berryman, Robert Lowell, and Richard Wilbur—sanctioned for American poetry by Auden's move to New York in 1940—revitalized the "smooth walks" and "trimmed hedges." Lowell was a dissimulator, of course, since even as he embodied the urbane persona of metrical order he clawed his way up the heap of reputations with the rapaciousness of a raccoon. But his debonair persona lent credibility to hosts of lesser epigones, and to read through much of the verse of the 1950s is to think (as Whitman did ninety years earlier) that "To prune, gather, trim, conform, and ever cram and stuff, and be genteel and proper, is the pressure of our days."

This Compost searches out another order of poetry, one which literary politics has made it misleading to call "open," so I prefer to indicate its temper by way of George Santayana, who complained that European philosophical systems "are egotistical; directly or indirectly they are anthropocentric, and inspired by the conceited notion that man, or human reason, or the human distinction between good and evil, is the center and pivot of the universe. That is what the mountains and the woods should make you at last ashamed to assert" ("Genteel Tradition," 106). The corollary, of course, is that mountains and woods—*Mountains and Rivers Without End* (Snyder)—actually compel certain assertions concerning "a defense of cosmos, not scenery" (Oelschlaeger, "Wilderness, Civilization, and Language," 273). By the same measure it is poetry, not poets—the system, not the signet—that is in need of attention and nurture.*

* The damage wrought by careerism in modern American poetry is documented in my study *The American Poetry Wax Museum.* As Robert Duncan remarked long ago, the commodification of values extends even to poetry. The quick fix, the easy target, the vapid solution are as eligible for poetic as for press conference recitation. An apparent growth in the popularity of poetry readings in the 1990s is not necessarily salutary. Philip Lamantia derided a poet who "thinks poetry's at his beck and call" (*Meadowlark West,* 21), and John

"Ecology is the science of communities, and the ecological conscience is therefore the ethics of community life," wrote Aldo Leopold in 1947 (*The River,* 340). I would describe poetry as ecology in the community of words. Curt Meine has noted Leopold's turn, late in his life (when he was writing *Sand County Almanac*), to the prospect that "perception now had *survival value;* aesthetic sensitivity, as partially redefined by the new science [ecology], was *useful*" ("Utility of Preservation," 150).* In 1978 Neil Evernden urged that "Environmentalism without aesthetics is merely regional planning" ("Beyond Ecology," 103). In the same year, William Rueckert (notably a follower of Kenneth Burke) proposed a model of the poem as "stored energy, a formal turbulence." "Poems are part of the energy pathways which sustain life," he wrote. "Poems are a verbal equivalent of fossil fuel (stored energy), but they are a renewable source of energy" ("Literature and Ecology," 108). It's an optimistic assumption. While I do not give much credence to familiar models of artistic decadence and decline, I do think of poems as ecosystems, precariously adjusted to the surrounding biomass, and concur with Gary Snyder's view of poetry (articulated as early as 1967) as "ecological survival technique" (*Earth House Hold,* 117). The nutritive sensibility, envisioned as an environmental continuum encompassing biotic as well as cultural communities, has recently prompted Snyder to speak of languages as "naturally evolved wild systems": "language does not impose order on a chaotic universe, but reflects its own wildness back" (*Place in Space,* 174)—a lovely thought that brings to mind Emily Dickinson's image of "a Panther in the Glove" (no. 244). The image is a stark reminder of hidden claws, the core of menace informing even while potentially undermining our personae. It is these "less familiar energies of the wild world, and their analogs in the imagination, [which] have given us ecologies of the mind," writes Snyder (*Practice of the Wild,* 111). He also notes that "in spite of years of personhood, we remain unpredictable even to our own selves"—and this unpredictability is the mark of our wildness, " 'wild' [being] a name for the way that phenomena continually actualize themselves" (*Place in Space,* 173, 168).

Clarke complained, "Poets are so comfy, they can't see anymore these nasty / historical habits, e.g., Capitalism as any other than / simple evil, as though some lucky slung stone would bring / down the giant" (*In the Analogy,* 201).

* Leopold colorfully characterized national parks as hospitals for treating cases of "esthetic rickets" (*The River,* 216). The more serious underlying premise of ecological aesthetics, expressed in 1925 in Leopold's proposition for considering wilderness a form of land use, is "the assumption that enlarging the range of individual experience is as important as enlarging the number of individuals" (142).

Poetry is a kind of echo-location.* But since its medium is language, its repertoire of echoes is bewilderingly diverse. The greediest of gifts, the most beneficent of appropriations, poetry is language disclosed as paradox, where naming does not re-present but dissolves and then reforms creation, where the speaker too is dissolved into the act of speech and reemerges, *alieniloquiam,* as another, a reader or listener who is in turn displaced from self-assurance, forced to take up residence in the strange. Poetry is this strangely familiar realm of estrangements, its uncanniness preternaturally arousing a maximum alertness, but an alertness achieved paradoxically, by dissolving the resources of intellection and identity. I don't mean to be mystifying; the point is to abide by that "practice of the wild" evoked by Snyder. Such practice is invariably and necessarily collective, and that is what this book is about. *This Compost* goes about its business by pragmatically realizing its issues in its design. It is written in units of variable length, but tending to brevity, the sequence of which is determined by imaginal,† not logical considerations; its argument is hologrammatic, not hypotactic—that is, not hierarchically disposed, but radically egalitarian. Its parts are its wholes and vice versa. If holes are found in the "argument," all the better—they're for burrowing, for warmth and intimacy.

* The thought is indebted to Calvin Martin: "One of the great insights of hunter societies is that words and artifice of specific place and place-beings (animal and plant) constitute humanity's primary instruments of self-location, the computation of where, in the deepest sense, one is in the biosphere, using words and artifice that have accurately touched the place and these elder beings. For mankind is fundamentally an echo-locator, like our distant relatives the porpoise and the bat" (*In the Spirit of the Earth,* 103).

† My use of the term *imaginal,* here and throughout, follows James Hillman's proposal that we "read all the documents and fragments of myth left from antiquity . . . as accounts or witnesses of the imaginal" (*Re-Visioning Psychology,* 30). The imaginal is distinct from *imagination* (a faculty) and *the imaginary* (a product of that faculty) in that it names a realm superseding individual volition. Hillman remarks, "My so-called personality is a persona through which soul speaks" (51), soul being an event of creative imagination ("soul-making can be most succinctly defined as the individuation of imaginal reality" [Hillman, *Archetypal Psychology,* 27]). Hillman's perspective on the imaginal ultimately derives from Henry Corbin, whose essay "Mundus Imaginalis, or the Imaginary and the Imaginal" Hillman published in *Spring 1972.* In *Creative Imagination in the Sufism of Ibn 'Arabi,* Corbin provides a succinct evocation of the terrain (although *imaginal* is not in his vocabulary): "We wish to stress on the one hand the notion of the *Imagination* as the *magical* production of an *image,* the very type and model of magical action, or of all action as such, but especially of creative action; and, on the other hand, the notion of the image as a body (a *magical* body, a *mental* body), in which are incarnated the thought and will of the soul" (179); and, to return to Hillman, "we too are ultimately a composition of images, our person the personification of their life in the soul" (*Re-Visioning Psychology,* 41).

This Compost takes seriously the prospect of an "opening of the field," which was worked out in the quasi-collaborative enthusiasms of Charles Olson, Robert Creeley, and Robert Duncan, but which radiates out from there into that nexus of fellow poets Creeley refers to as "The Company" (in his *Collected Essays*), taking *company* in a more expansive sense to include those like Robinson Jeffers, Muriel Rukeyser, and Kenneth Rexroth, who tend to fall outside customary genealogies. The key organizing principle is the trope, in several senses: trope *as* trope or turning (which I relate to the Lucretian *clinamen* or swerve), trope as linguistic cousin to the tropic as geographic situation, and trope as poetry's composting medium. As a trope, the "field" extends much farther back, of course, so Whitman plays a significant role. *Leaves of Grass* is a prototype for the long poem of the twentieth century, as Dickinson's fascicles (however belatedly discovered) serve as precedent for the modern serial poem. *This Compost* is in part a rumination on three of the most imposing of long poems—*The Cantos, "A,"* and *The Maximus Poems*—though they are not accorded equal attention. The point is not nominative, however. By dissociating the name of the poets from many of the citations, I wanted to restore to the poetics at hand that solidarity in anonymity which is the deep issue of planetary time, for that *is* the "issue" in several senses of the poetry of *This Compost.*

The senses *are* several, confirming our attraction to sensory multiplicity as well as multiple meanings. Had Wordsworth been Thoreau, he might have been keen to the pun in his line "we lay waste our lives, getting and spending," since our lives *are* matter (mattered) by begetting (in the archaic expression, to "get" with child), and the majority of our expenditures are bodily "waste." Poetry is a space in which we're implicitly invited to deliberate on—and make hay with—the puns that calibrate our existence, our mortal exigency. Paul Shepard describes the ethos of hunter-gatherers in terms that are not restricted to the Paleolithic: "The lifelong theme is 'learning to give away' what was a gift received in the first place" ("Post-Historic Primitivism," 70). Wendell Berry gives a concise version as "the paradox that one can become whole only by the responsible acceptance of one's partiality" (*Recollected Essays,* 303). "I am a fragment, and this is a fragment of me," declares Emerson of his own essay ("Experience"). The dictum recurs in another formulation: "We are symbols and inhabit symbols" ("The Poet"), an insight founded on the root meaning of symbol, *sum-ballein,* thrown together. When we think of something "thrown together," like a quick meal, it is usually in a derogatory sense; but we tend to think of symbols as products of deliberation. Heidegger characterizes Dasein by way of a neologism, "Geworfenheit," or "thrownness," by which he means not that we are outcasts, fallen figures expelled from some ancestral wonderland, but that our arrival into a terrestrial life is a forcible event. Watching the birth of my first daughter I had the sense that this wet intensity had been projected from a great distance, she arrived with such force; and how could it be otherwise? Starting out as a zygote nine months earlier, she had swollen like a tropical storm to the incredible magnitude of seven pounds, a concrete reminder that "While we live our bodies are moving particles of the earth" (Berry, *Recollected Essays,* 269). Both she and her sister have grown from infants to women while I was writing this book, and I too have changed with everything around me; but certain challenges persist: the need of long-term views, the need to reckon our own wild natures into any consideration of "nature" as such; and certain pleasures continue to abound, especially the pleasure of good company, the manifold lure of the elements, the tingle of every night and day.

Gilgamesh

The barren sand opened up to British archaeologist Sir Austen Henry Layard in 1845, as he tapped into two millennia of unguessed literacy:

> . . . papyrus
> jungle sandhill splayed-wedge wader damsel
> crane . . .

The papyrus had long since decayed (taking with it perhaps the major literature of the time, since the most esteemed Mesopotamian texts were inscribed on elegant parchment rather than on the crude though durable clay tablets); but some twenty-thousand tablets of "splayed-wedge" script went to the British Museum, where the work of deciphering and translating eventually captured public interest in pages of the *Daily Telegraph* in 1886. Over twenty-five hundred years had passed since these tablets were kept in baskets on shelves, in cataloged order. This library of Assurbanipal was destroyed in 612 B.C. when Chaldeans and Medes overran the city of Ninevah, whose walls were broad enough for chariot tracks. The books were shelved according to subject in a series of rooms; one of the rooms was devoted to legend and mythology—ancient at that time by as much as two thousand years—in which was kept an Akkadian rendition of an old Sumerian poem, *The Epic of Gilgamesh.*

The invocation "Praise! . . gill . . gam . . mesh . ." is recorded by Louis Zukofsky (a late member of the tribe of Israelites that has its roots in Assurbanipal's time), composting Levantine mythology in 1973. By that time his text, for nearly fifty years called simply *"A,"* had begun to resemble "an ancient manuscript" with "hints of syntax, but key words or phrases obliterated by tears or worm holes. There are too many words or not enough" (Byrd, "Getting Ready to Read 'A,'" 291). Access to *Gilgamesh* is now limited to twelve Akkadian tablets from Assurbanipal's library—thirty-six hundred lines—and a scattering of older versions in Babylonian, Sumerian, Hittite, and Hurrian fragments, all of which we read toward an unavailable "complete poem" that our Greco-Hebraic literary sensibilities attempt to project, an epic by patchwork.

Charles Olson's project in *The Maximus Poems* is to reactivate such particles of archaic texts in a terrain that engages wreaderly energies in their full proprioceptive stamina, overcoming the restrictions implicit in generic frames.* His theory of

* "Wreading" is my neologism for the collaborative momentum initiated by certain texts, like *The Maximus Poems,* in which the reader is enlisted *as* an agent of the writing. Recip-

projective verse at this level is wreading or inhabiting the text as the poem comes to inhabit Olson himself, and he ends up pacing roads in Gloucester, Massachusetts, attempting to identify everything as if it were a text (and a text a map), as if crossing a street were to pace off one line of the poem, as if going around the block made a trope, a turn, a verse. The labor becomes a spiritual exercise, convening a heavenly city in which the earth's own geography is divinity, out of which the figures of mythology from around the world are liable at any moment to extrude, like Ge in the Gravelly Hill poem (*Maximus Poems*, 330–32). The surface of the earth is itself a parchment, and to scratch the surface is almost certainly to come across a prior attribution for everything discovered. A life already in momentum. All there is to be found has been lost and recovered before. Recycled, composted. But once the crypt is unearthed, or the *ka'ba* circumambulated in Gloucester streets, the space is available for such acts of psychic reclamation as the plowing of a poem allows (its "verses" turns at the edge of a field). Zukofsky chose for *"A"* 23 conditions as immutable as mortality and the accidents of archaeological exhumation. His Gilgamesh is narrated with harsh ellipses into four pages of five-line stanzas, each line consisting of five words: a pregnant example of a sediment that measures "the sifting of human creations"—which is how William James defined the humanities ("Social Value," 1243).

Readers of the *Daily Telegraph* were thrilled by the discovery of an old text that gave credence to the biblical flood; *Gilgamesh* was an event for Victorians because it fit into the library of the Christian epoch. Scholars would later come to value it as an epic because they could ascribe "heroic proportions" to Gilgamesh's quest for eternal life. But for Zukofsky near the end of his own life, Gilgamesh preceded Heraclitus in the perception that both the sleeping and the dead are doing the world's work:

> I outlived a flood to
> be called everlasting, to know
> distant partings of tidal river,
> asleep and dead grow alike.

To read *"A"* is to become an adept of the compost library. In a text that wakes the dead, Gilgamesh comes forward to speak and display himself after all this time. Zukofsky writes as if already dead himself, where the companions are far more plentiful than in life. They are all animated and hot, as it always is in compost.

---

rocally, the writer discloses his or her own readerly orientation (albeit in ways that vary from work to work).

Ain't pleasant to work at the compost,
but the niches are empty,
and the eye will terribly blaze from the triangle
when the lion god
                    at last
                                        steps forth by day.

The library

The Romantic phase of English poetry is separated from that later branch we know as American by nothing less than the recovery of half the total span of the Western literary record. Champollion's decipherment of the Rosetta stone in the 1820s, and the subsequent popularization of prebiblical civilizations, created the unique conditions in which a distinctively American literature arose. Emerson, Thoreau, Melville, Hawthorne, Poe, and Whitman can be read as inaugurating an imaginal bibliographic recovery of the oldest written records (see Irwin).* It's interesting to imagine that the now clear distinction between English and American writing may have been blurred if Keats and Shelley had lived long enough to follow the same archaeological research that mesmerized Whitman and his fellow

* The enthusiasm for hieroglyphics persisted. Pound started incorporating Egyptian writing in *The Cantos* after his daughter married an Egyptologist; Vachel Lindsay was obsessed with Egyptology, offering a "Primer Lesson on Hieroglyphics" in his 1926 poetry collection *Going-to-the-Stars*. Also found there is a paean, "Celestial Flowers of Glacier Park," profusely illustrated with fanciful hieroglyphs like "The Mountain Carpet":

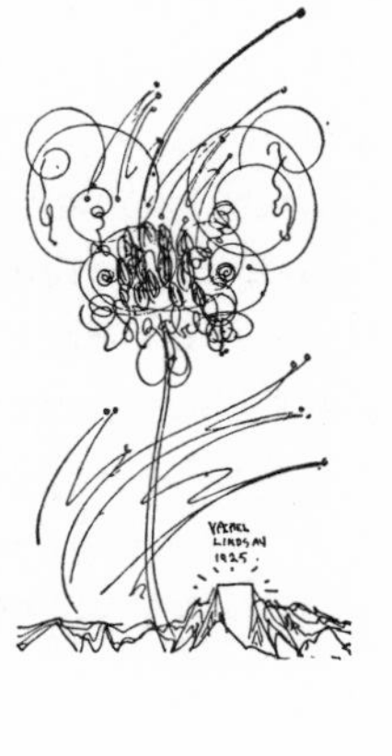

Americans. Romanticism across Europe was stimulated by this first wave of archaeological and philological recoveries of the past. The tradition of English poetry is abundant with superinscriptions on, and rewritings of, this legacy. Coleridge's "Kubla Khan" and Shelley's "Ozymandias" and visions of Zoroaster are first animations from the new vista of the compost library—available to them, however, only in a mirage of anticipation.

American poetry is the first full opening of a field of archaic, scattered, incomplete, and scarcely surmised literacies from that compost library unearthed in the nineteenth century. The general atmosphere of hieroglyphics, undeciphered scripts, and the mystery of unimagined antiquities now recovered is what makes the America of Whitman's generation a Renaissance, much as the recovery and circulation of Hellenistic materials constituted a European Renaissance four hundred years earlier; and it's what gives force to Thoreau's remark, "Decayed literature makes the richest of all soils" (*The Journal,* 16 March 1852). As Jack Spicer remarks, "As things decay they bring their equivalents into being." Out of an Asiatic antiquity as old as any in the West, Confucius's word was disseminated for half a century by Ezra Pound. Zukofsky's Gilgamesh and *Catullus:* compost library, hothouse for his *80 Flowers.* Olson's Hesiod and "Song of Ullikummi" (read to honor Pound's presence at the Spoletto festival in 1965): compost library. From that heat there have been notable recoveries by Olson's students, like *Origins: Creation Texts from the Ancient Mediterranean* by Charles Doria and Harris Lenowitz, and Charles Boer's *Homeric Hymns.* The recovery of the compost library extends in all directions through the ground of American poetry, as poets become signatories of distant texts: Jerome Rothenberg's large anthologies flower (as the word means) at the heart of this practice; David Meltzer's anthology of Kabbalah; Ed Sanders's Egypt; Nathaniel Mackey's African Dogon ("a nomadic calligraphy, wandering, spinning off dark incalculable rhythms, its overtones humming like a compost of entanglement" [Alexander, 700]); Nathaniel Tarn's Meso-America; Paul Metcalf's American vernaculars; Susan Howe's colonial New England captivity narratives; Gary Snyder's and Kenneth Rexroth's China and Japan; the India of Snyder, Ginsberg, Anne Waldman, and Andrew Schelling; Clayton Eshleman's Paleolothic Dordogne; Paul Blackburn's Provence and the Provençal vestiges of Gallo-Roman antiquity for Gustaf Sobin—these are all integral to a poetics of the archaic, restored exercises of *Homo projectivis* (Sobin, *Luminous Debris,* 20). And through the same attentions a different Greece and Rome have come into view in Olson, kofsky, and (via H.D.'s *corpus hermeticum*) Robert Duncan, Robert Kelly, Guy port, and Anne Waldman. Even the kitsch statuary of the ancient Near East in Albert Goldbarth's "junktique" catalogs resonate with the "mantic compost" of Eugene Jolas.

Uniquely indebted to this condition of filtration and infiltration is *The Tablets* by Armand Schwerner, which purports to be a scholarly edition of archaic tablet inscriptions, with extensive ellipses, bracketed guesses at missing words, notes and professional citations accompanying a text uniquely suited to this labor of recovered antiquity in American poetry. Tablet X reduces the project to a decisive minimum:

TABLET X

```
............................................++++++++++++
++++++++++++++++++++++++++++++++++++
++++++++++++++++
++++++++++++++++
++++++++++++++++
+++.........................................⊕⊕⊕⊕⊕⊕⊕⊕
...............++++++++..........+++++++++++++
++++++...........++++++..........++++++++++++++
................................................................
.........................................⊕⊕⊕⊕⊕⊕⊕⊕⊕⊕⊕⊕
+++++++++++++++++.......+++++++++++
+++++++[the the]+++++++
+++++++++++++++++
+++++++++++++++++
+++++++++++++++++
++++++.......++++++.......++++++......++++++
..........................................................
.......................................................
.......
...............
.......................
..........................++
.....................................++++++++++
```

In his notes for *The Tablets,* Schwerner suggests the gist of his project in these lines by Zukofsky: "My poetics has old ochre in it / On walls of a civilized cave" (*The Tablets,* 139). The doubling of the archaic shadow projected over a contemporary poem deepens the lines into the ominous voice of Mesopotamian injunctions:

> go into all the places you're frightened of
> and forget why you came, like the dead.

Likewise, Heraclitus: "We assume a new being in death: we become protectors of the living and the dead" (Davenport translation, 22).

Out there somewhere
a shrine for the old ones,
the dust of the old bones,
        old songs and tales.

What we ate—who ate what—
        how we all prevailed.

American writing itself appears to be contingent on the reclamation of the compost library. Libraries as we know them—with subject classifications and arrangements, procedures for withdrawing or examining the holdings, which are conscientiously diverse—are as old as cities. Sumerians, Babylonians, Assyrians, and Egyptians had libraries. The Greeks had them relatively late (and, as legend has it, only at the behest of tyrants). From the bulk of Mesopotamian texts available, it is clear that *archives*—as opposed to libraries—were administrative practicalities, part of the bureaucracy in its maintenance of land deeds, contracts, inventory reports, and so on. What we would regard as literature occupied the same limited portion of public documents five thousand years ago as it does now. Sometime between 3000 and 2000 B.C. there arose libraries as distinct from archives, the difference being that an archive preserves all the relevant documentation on a given topic, or for a specific purpose—such as authenticating the history of a dynasty—whereas a library proposes in its very arrangement a field of material yet to come, for purposes unknown. Early religions were characteristically archival, and books such as the Bible are anthologies constituting an archive. The conflict between the archive of the Bible and the library of Hellenistic heritage is one of the more interesting tensions carried out in monastic life between the early Christian era and the Italian Renaissance. The spirit of the library is not hierarchy, but endless proliferation.* Matthew Arnold suggests as much in his famous distinction between Hellenistic expansive free play of consciousness and Hebraic (in which he includes Christian) conscientiousness and devotion: "The uppermost idea with Hellenism is to see things as they really are; the uppermost idea with Hebraism is conduct and obedience" (*Culture and Anarchy,* chap. 4).

From the earliest times, however, the open-ended organization of the library carried an implacable suggestiveness. Script could, by analogy, contaminate everything. The bones of sacrifices are "the oldest approaches to a sort of writing"

* See the Introduction to Jack Goody, ed., *Literacy in Traditional Societies* for a general survey, and "The Consequences of Literacy" by Jack Goody and Ian Watt in the same volume for an intensive examination.

(Richardson, 138); the early Assyrian palaces were regarded as *the books* of the history of the king's reign; and now we imagine DNA to be a script of biological destiny. To the Chaldeans, *chaos* meant "without books." The book and the library were some of the earliest symbolic distinctions the urban bureaucratic mind placed between itself and the deep past. Archives could claim completion and authority by association with religious dogma and military power, but libraries by nature resist culmination: there's only more and more, or further to dig. A natural phenomenon. In the compost library books have a way of collapsing into each other, not in the improvements of more "authoritative" editions or versions, but by constant recycling.

Not one   but many energies shape the field.
It is a vortex.   It is a compost.

"[T]here is a mound," writes A. R. Ammons, "in the poet's mind dead language is hauled / off to and burned down on, the energy held and // shaped into new turns and clusters." Ronald Johnson ventilates *Paradise Lost* by removing most of the words of Milton's poem, retaining others in a ventilated scenario (each word remains in its original location) that exemplifies composting poetry:

heaven's fire

From wing to wing, and

Words interwove with
mortal
Matchless,

change
of mind,

In Johnson's treatment of Milton, the words have changed their mind.

Johnson had been primed in the ventilation method by his friend Jonathan Williams (working with Havelock Ellis's *Studies in the Psychology of Sex*), who summons Olson, Zukofsky, Davenport, and others as instigators of the practice. "I would affirm that 'poems' are but the *deified* prosaic speech of plain men and women; that 'art' is in raising the common to grace . . . [and] that the poet is 'the guy* who puts things together'" ("Excavations from the Case-Histories of

* Not necessarily, and increasingly otherwise. For a fetching medley of American vernaculars—raising the common to grace in the deified speech of men and women—see the book-length poem *Deepstep Come Shining* by C. D. Wright (a woman).

Havelock Ellis," *Loco Logo-Daedalist in Situ*). Williams specializes in putting together captivating morsels of the living vernacular (as in his "Selected Listings from the Western Carolina Telephone Company's Directory," which includes Gentry Crisp, O. U. Muse, Zero Webb, and Hope Strong—a feat matched by Metcalf's *Zip Odes* [*Collected Works,* 2:126–81]); it's characteristic that his appetite encompasses print as readily as speech, as three of his books *(An Ear in Bartram's Tree, The Loco Logo-Daedalist in Situ,* and *Elite/Elate Poems)* amass 120 epigraphs, including this choice dictum from Albert Einstein: "Everything should be as simple as it is, but not simpler" ("In Lieu of a Preface," *Loco Logo-Daedalist in Situ*).

Poets have often been committed readers, but modern American poetry has been a resuscitation of reading into wreading, or nosing into the compost library.* Before Pound and Olson, we have no instances of poets whose reading itself becomes the manifest fulcrum of their commitment to poetry. If there is a precedent, it is Coleridge in his notebooks, which are themselves only opened to their poetic potential by an uncanny resemblance to Olson's practice in *The Maximus Poems. The Cantos* are not only intricately involved with the use of other texts, but are a massive exhortation to be aware of a specific library. Some of the earlier Cantos are re-presentational (Chinese history is digested from de Mailla's thirteen-volume history in French), but later sections implore the reader to examine Alexander Del Mar, John Heydon, Apollonius, *The Sacred Edict* of Kang Hsi, and much more. These later Cantos become a textual counterpart to the literary modernism that Pound had a great hand in establishing; and part of the symmetry latent in his life's work is a singular proposition to his readers, as if to say: you heeded my appraisals of Joyce, Eliot, Lewis, Gaudier, Williams, Frost, cummings, Hemingway, and others, now follow my leads into economics, history of law, pantheistic ceremony, and so on. Pound's adversary position in the literary world of his time has continued in the reluctant academic dissemination of the critical injunctions implicated in his poetic practice. In an institutional (archival) framework stressing the primacy of

* Lest the term "poet" prejudicially exclude a writer like Paul Metcalf, it is meant honorifically. Metcalf is usually regarded as a prose writer, but as Guy Davenport insists in his Introduction to the *Collected Works,* "Paul Metcalf is a great reader. . . . Metcalf's reading is to find things which he puts together in patterns. Such was the working method of Plutarch, Montaigne, Burton, all of whose books are new contexts for other voices" (ii). This ostensibly prose lineage is a filtration system for the compost library. Because of Metcalf's close association with Charles Olson, his projects offer resonant intrications of geophysical strata with historical events: see especially *Patagoni, The Middle Passage, Apalache,* and *Waters of Potowmack.*

the text itself, Pound's work keeps grossly forwarding a library. There is no shortcut. "The greatest barrier is probably set up by teachers who know a little more than the public, who want to exploit their fractional knowledge, and who are thoroughly opposed to making the least effort to learn anything more" (*ABC of Reading,* 35). Howard McCord remarks in *Gnomonology,* "the classics are becoming *occult,* as the Bible has been for centuries." There is a distinction between recommended books—Pound as critic and arbiter of the library—and the mass of materials that breaks across the prow of *The Cantos.* With Olson, however, having the advantage of Pound's precedent, it's all the same. Olson's reading is intrinsic to a frame of mind that makes no distinction between reading and writing. It's all wreading. We read passages of *The Maximus Poems* without the slightest suspicion that the text is closely paraphrasing other material. *My condition is this embodiment*—this is what the text implies for such materials. And if a text that is identifiably by Hesiod is embedded in *Maximus IV, V, VI,* there is no need of cues to alert the reader to a bibliographic event, as Hesiod in such a context—in the gravity of so inner an inherence—cannot appear *as Hesiod* because he's no longer alive to make the claim. His appearance is abbreviated into "Olson," who comes to share the same *logos,* and both exit together into that enlarged capacity, Maximus.

Olson takes a step beyond Pound in realizing the compost library as the materiality germane to his own work and therefore the embodiment of his concerns. Olson is no advocate for the library; he is inseparable from it. *The Maximus Poems* greet the eyes like tattered papyrus, frayed tablet; the organization and distribution of the words, beginning with the second volume, invite the consideration that the visible text is hedged all about with invisible text. As Olson's writing extended restlessly to whatever was at hand, the reduction of that writing to a *book* comes to seem more and more precarious and arbitrary. The writing on the windowsill in his Gloucester apartment returns us to the Assyrian palace, at once codex and domicile. It also compels attention back to those earliest depositories of human creativity, the cave walls of the Paleolithic, which in their record of thousands of years of overlaid application are the primal image of *what the mind looks like* projected over time. The dominant animal content seems singular only in retrospect, as our eyes condense the theme into a momentary obsession. But the truth is that those images are the most sustained objects of study recorded, and the singularity of that persistence challenges our oculocentrism, which identifies image at shutter speed, 125th of a second.

Image *is* a limit. But what is opened up between images—in the unsettling flicker on a movie screen—is motion. So there are limits, and

Limits
are what any of us
are inside of.

But as Emerson insists in "Circles," "The only sin is limitation." "We can afford to allow the limitation," he clarifies in "Fate," "if we know it is the meter of the growing man." Meter: measure of expansion. Literacy in the compost library is just such an actualization that it takes the psyche to be real, its actions to be consequent, and life as expansive. "Perhaps it is the role of art to put us in complicity with things as they happen," writes Lyn Hejinian (*Language of Inquiry*, 391). "Life recognized as happening restores event," says Olson ("Chiasma," 41), whose aspiration is to overcome the commercialism lamented at the beginning of *The Maximus Poems*, to be restored to the unmistakable: the consequential reality of generative human event.

Generation

In a few months of North Carolina spring in 1953 Charles Olson came to articulate fully the shift from the productive to the generative.

> The generative is, in fact, the weather of existence, of all of it, of every act, as well as those biological dominant acts which engage us all.
>
> Generation can be seen literally to be *the climate* of our being as decisively as the *place* of it is that internal environment we call our selves, the individual ("Chiasma," 36).

To his poet's sense, one word discloses three: actions are generative, as weather is (he values the Cro-Magnon for "not letting this weather of life fog on them"); generation is the climate of propagation—in which individuals are generated, and in which they pass the world on to the next "generation." The generative nurture implicit in the early Neolithic development of animal husbandry and agriculture is attributed by Lewis Mumford to a rising matriarchal urbanism: generation as womanly modification, particularly in the invention of receptacles. "Under woman's dominance, the neolithic period is pre-eminently one of containers: it is an age of stone and pottery utensils, of vases, jars, vats, cisterns, bins, barns, granaries, houses, not least great collective containers, like irrigation ditches and villages" (*City in History*, 16).* The labor of generation, under the dispensation of the matriarch, consolidates vessels of all sorts; in the urbanized setting of statecraft and priesthood, the symbolic amplitude of containers is expanded to the generative devices of social institution. "Each generation could now leave its deposit of ideal forms and images: shrines, temples, palaces" and of course writing (69).

Olson's vocabulary is saturated with the masculinist inflections symptomatic of the American midcentury—which has given rise to peremptory dismissals of his work—but his struggle to ascertain the primordial dimension of public accountability transcends the parochial chauvinism of his own jargon.† In an initial gesture, Olson takes care to distinguish birth and death from the life of the individual, since "Those false termini, birth & death as a man's, are thrown down. And a man's pillars are seen to be his acts, his several acts as long as he lives, not that he was born (that was his mother's act) or that he also dies—which is nature's" ("Chiasma," 41). Olson's "act" is Emerson's "event": "The event is the print of your form. It fits you like your skin" ("Fate"). But the actor in a "Human Universe" (in Olson's essay) is variably extensive. The botany and geography Olson knew from Edgar Anderson and Carl Sauer fortified his sense that landscape is contingent on human peregrination. Civilization is at once complete control and remote control (control only in the sense of being generative of consequences—the "willy nilly" of "Human Universe," the helplessness with which man arrogates the world to himself as raw material, what Heidegger names *zuhanden,* or *to hand*). Under the prompting of the occasion—now reduced to a moment, yet altogether momentous—"his job becomes quite another: to raise himself" ("Chiasma," 41) (for Williams, too: "somehow a man must lift himself / again— / again is the magic word"):

> . . . as there is always
> a thing he can do, he can raise himself, he raises
> on a reed he raises his

—the possessive pronoun (deliberately suspended by Olson) gestures to an event, a coming-to-be, which is always in process, never finalized, for

* Mumford emphasizes the symbolic dimension of protective enclosures as markedly feminine. Indeed, "House and village, eventually the town itself, are woman writ large" (*City in History*, 13).

† Sandra Alcosser evokes the period flavor: "Charles Olson's 'I, Maximus / a metal hot from boiling water' might have been the lyric sung on the backlot of the body shop where I grew up—paint fumes, grease pans, sparks flying—surrounded by Serbs, Germans, Hungarians returned from the Second World War, men who saw themselves, no matter how confusing, in direct lineage from the gods" (*Except by Nature*, 32).

. . . he
is already also
moving off
into the soil, on to his own bones

—where he is raised as voice:

Or, if it is me, what
he has to say.

And a voice so raised is "raised" also in the sense of coming to maturity.

The lines above are from the title poem of Olson's first substantial collection, *In Cold Hell, in Thicket,* published in March 1953 in Mallorca by Robert Creeley. Also in March, at Black Mountain College in the mountains of North Carolina, Olson was preparing an Institute in the New Sciences of Man for which he tried to get Jung, Carl Sauer, and Christopher Hawkes and ended up having Marie-Louise von Franz and Robert Braidwood (who discovered the Neolithic settlement of Jarmo). Olson's own lectures in anticipation of the Institute, delivered from February to March 1953, were the distillation of "what he has to say," from which a massive run of *Maximus Poems* sprang, civil Athena from the brow of Zeus (81 of the 160 pages of the first volume of *The Maximus Poems* were written April to May of 1953, a watershed comparable to Rilke's composition of *Duino Elegies* and *Sonnets to Orpheus*).

The civic concern is preeminent. As the world in the view that the city proposes is all eye—"polis is / eyes"—there is a sense of witnessing that Olson through these early months of 1953 wanted to see *enacted,* as theatrical (he insisted theatre was not script but the specific action witnessed when actors and audience gathered). Olson linked Greek drama, with its three tragedies and fourth *satyros,* to spectacles performed for ten thousand years in view of those painted Paleolithic walls, a force he saw persisting as late as the *Odyssey* ("Chiasma," 92). It is *this* human universe he specifies as the mythological:

> The *mythological* was the way I had come, finally, to put the sense I had that each of us obeyed and acted in and by a space upon facts by way of a series of multiple stances which, so far as I could see—so far as I can see—had not been admitted or investigated in any way adequate to their dimensions in us, and by way of all of us, outside us, the—human landscape (97).

Because of the gestural clarity of Olson's "push" at this point, *The Maximus Poems* did not succumb to that decorative rehearsal of myths endemic to poetry of the

1950s. The engagement with the generative arrived at in the "Chiasma" lectures is civic and psychological: "only by obeying the total self in all its idiosyncratic direction is morality & concord established, both for the individual & by the total of the individuals, in the society" (40). And, in a reformulation of the premise underlying *The Maximus Poems*—and specifying its particular political ground: "Because of the agora America is, was, from the start, the moral struggle" (*Maximus Poems*, 62).

The tropics, & the trope

For many generations "America" was sheer verbal invention: a provocation of the advertising circular and the conceptual challenge of a newly discovered realm. But " 'Discovery' was a double concept, since it referred both to the act of finding and to the later act of revealing what had been found" (Franklin, 182). In calling many of his Maximus poems "letters," Olson wedges himself into that exploratory stance in which each notation redefines the utility of perception. "[O]ne real center in American experience has been the isolated self"—recalling Olson's "Isolated person in Gloucester, Massachusetts, I, Maximus, address you"—"which is given some connection to presumed communities (and thereby an identity) by its engrossment of America as an elaborate, even arcane, sign of where it stands and what it means" (Franklin, 183). America is the name for what language does in the world. As long as there is a struggle for freedom within language, that struggle will be tropical inasmuch as it solicits its occasion from *language in heat.* The trope of this struggle (or rutting) makes it, if not American, at least *of* the Americas (rendering South American Spanish and Portuguese, along with North American French and English, so distinct from their transatlantic origins). "For, in the end, America has been a series of competing stories told by figures who ought to have seen their community precisely in their parallel efforts at narrative persuasion, in their exuberance of faith, their diligence of speech" (Franklin, 203).*

The discovery of America was an accidental by-product of a European ambition to open trade routes to the Orient. Despite massive evidence to the contrary,

* This turning, this *tropikos,* meaning "turn" or "belonging to a turn," also comes to mean "figure of speech" in Greek *tropos* and Latin *tropus.* Another series of permutations places this business of troping firmly in the hands of poets: late Latin *tropare,* "to versify," becomes *trovare* in Italian, *trovar* in Spanish, *trouver* in French: "to find, devise, invent or make up poetry." The Provençal form, *trobar,* gives us the agent, *troubador.*

Columbus felt certain that the land of the Great Khan and the Emerald City was just over the ridge, down the river, or farther along the shore. This conviction was excited by a cartographic coincidence: on Columbus's maps, the south coast of Cuba bore a superficial similarity to the Chinese province of Mangi, east of the long-sought Malay Peninsula ("the Golden Chersonese"), regarded as the ultimate trading zone. On his second voyage Columbus explored the Cuban coastline until he reached the point where the Malay Peninsula was presumed to bear southward. Rather than confirm this by continuing his exploration, the admiral opted instead to return to Spain. Under threat of severe bodily punishment and heavy fines, in the presence of the fleet scribe, the crew was forced to take an oath that the coast they had explored could not possibly belong to an island because of its size. Columbus also compelled assent to the fantasy that "a few leagues hence, sailing along this coast land would be found where civilized people exist, and who know of the world" (O'Gorman, 89).

Columbus's desperate commitment to the Orient reflects a Eurocentric appetite for expansion, a craving for contact with others who "know of the world," but whose knowledge would confirm Europe's estimate of its own centrality. The rotundity of the globe, after all, was a recent postulate. The antipodes and the infernal regions—given the fact of such a world—were now places to be encountered on the way home, not eccentric zones to which an aberrant course might lead. By the same token, such desirable places as the Golden Chersonese might as readily be encountered en route. Diversity and difference, the sheer fact of otherness, were henceforth to be raw material for self-affirmation.

History tends to be perceived as either topological (Greece, Rome, British Empire) or typological (monarchy, oligarchy, democracy);* but Columbus stands at the inaugural moment of a different kind of history. He didn't discover America, he *troped* America. Expecting India, he called the Caribbean peoples Indians, and the islands themselves came to be known as the West Indies. He was so obsessed with the Great Khan of China that he heard the islanders' tribal name Carib as "canib" (from which we get "cannibal"), or agents of the Khan.

Four centuries after Columbus's celebrated tropism, Walt Whitman found him-

* Not only history, but poetry too has its *topos* and *tropos:* "In poetry, a place is *where* something is *known,* but a figure or trope is *when* something is willed or desired. A Classical or Enlightenment 'commonplace' is where something is already known, but a Romantic or Post-Enlightenment 'place' is a more inventive and indeed a Gnostic 'knowing,' a knowing in which one *sees* what Walter Benjamin called the *aura.* In the *aura* what is known knows the knower" (Bloom, 69).

self still alive to celebrate the year of the Columbiad, 1892, in "A Thought of Columbus":

> Thousands and thousands of miles hence, and now four centuries back,
> A mortal impulse thrilling its brain cell,
> Reck'd or unreck'd, the birth can no longer be postpon'd:
> A phantom of the moment, mystic, stalking, sudden,
> Only a silent thought, yet toppling down of more than walls of brass or stone.
> (A flutter at the darkness' edge as if old Time's and Space's secret near
> revealing.)

America is resolved in a "phantom of the moment," a thought in one man's mind, a trope that comes to tyrannize the rounded world. The globe troped in a single thrilled brain cell does indeed "flutter at the darkness' edge" like the predawn sky at Alamogordo, moments before yet another *new world* blazed forth in 1945, "toppling down of more than walls of brass or stone."

To follow the turn of that initial trope of a "New World" is to begin to hear the actual *place* of this world as tropical, in and of the tropics: fecund, hot, multiple. When Europeans came to settle the American shores, they were prepared to endure a spiritual and physical wilderness, to void its tropes by means of their own blinding revelations. They erred in presuming revelation could immunize them from the tropic difference of a new world. Olson's kingfishers are emblematic of New World settlers: "as they are fed and grow, this nest of excrement and decayed fish becomes a dripping, fetid mass." Echoing Heraclitus, he names the tropic claim:

> To be in different states without a change
> is not a possibility.

"The Kingfishers" revisits a site memorialized by Joseph Conrad, who documented that fundamental inability of Europeans to thrive in such circumstances. His characters come apart in the heat, the cadaverous living remnants of imperial ravages in tropical outposts, helpless avatars of the "fetid mass" of their own civilization *in extremis.*

Place nourishes transformation. Each place is *a* place, with its own bio-anatomy of stability and transfiguration. *A* place is not "anywhere": it is always *here.* This is what the European settlement of the Americas refused to concede, and such imaginative parsimony was the principle by which Columbus troped Caribs into Indians. Tzvetan Todorov notes that by imposing themselves militarily on native populations, the European conquistadors "destroyed their own capacity to integrate themselves into the world." By this he means that a particular hermeneutic circle was closed: just as global circumnavigation returns all travelers home in the end, military authority ensures that all communications are returned to sender, secured in the language of domination.

> [T]here exist two major forms of communication, one between man and man, the other between man and the world. . . . We are accustomed to conceiving of communication as only interhuman, for since the "world" is not a subject, our dialogue with it is quite asymmetrical (if there is any such dialogue at all) (*Conquest of America*, 97).

The world viewed as unresponsive object forecloses earth as place or home from any but the most mercantile considerations. The manifest resistance of America's places to such calculation appeared to the settlers in the form of Indians. These people were not recognized as "natives" because their habitation of the land didn't conform to European habits of soil dependency. They were therefore disposable: human weeds impeding cultivation. But as Todorov suggests, the main strike against them was the innate bias of their own communication axis, which privileged dialogue with an articulate natural world over interhuman exchange. European travelers returned home with enslaved Americans in tow, to be displayed in the metropole as pure ciphers of difference, parts of speech bereft of context, living verbs shorn of scholastic declensions. They were not solicited for what they might know, but exhibited as mute artifacts, *tableaux vivant.* By this means Europeans spurned the tropological lesson that the world in another's language is another world. Rather than being an animate environment, the "New World" was simply a less defiled—if more unruly—version of the Old World.

Wallace Stevens's Crispin is a figure of the colonial imagination wrestling a space for itself out of tropic wilderness. "The Comedian as the Letter C" opens with a proposition: "Nota: man is the intelligence of his soil, / The sovereign ghost." "It was a flourishing tropic he required"—so as to offset the lunar perversity in which he had previously sought "the blissful liaison, / Between himself and his environment, / Which was, and is, chief motive, first delight." As he encounters "the fecund minimum" in the tropics, Crispin readjusts his principle: "Nota: his soil is man's intelligence. / That's better. That's worth crossing seas to find." Yet this is but the Satanic temptation of man conceived as steward of earth, restlessly seeking "A still new continent in which to dwell," because "the purpose of his pilgrimage / . . . [is] to drive away / The shadow of his fellows from the skies."

As the poem goes on, the Satanic momentum is accelerated by prepositional duplicities. Stevens reveals poetry to be not verse but *verso* of language, the other side of its coin of sense—sensed and *incensed* in its unhinged coign.

> Beauty is natures coyn, must not be hoorded,
> But must be currant, and the good thereof
> Consists in mutual and partaken bliss,
> Unsavoury in th'injoyment of it self;
> If you let slip time, like a neglected rose
> It withers on the stalk with languish't head.
> Beauty is natures brag, and must be shown . . .

In lines like these from *Comus,* Milton is of the devil's party, as Blake remarked. But the occasion is reopened, in effect, by Stevens, ventilated in the New World tropic where any given thought or perception or sign can be imposed, or transposed, onto another place. Tropical poetry is a language proposing in itself an omnipresent relevance "transcending all limit and privacy" (as Emerson put it). Ominous, omnivorous, tropical poetry teaches a biodegradable thinking, a thought for composing beings, for being decomposed and recomposed, for being composed (with equilibrium, staying cool), for being compost (heating up). The poem's plot is no sequence of narrative events, but a garden plot that makes its protean heap a biodegradable mask of regeneration. Poetry is the immense reserve of language, a claim on underground and underworld where a new prospect is grounded.

The heterological nature of words, redoubled by grammatical ambiguities, is quintessentially tropical, rich in tropism: a struggle between veracity and voracity. This, more than anything, is the world Crispin comes to inhabit, a "Green barbarism turning paradigm" in his "flourishing tropic . . . an abundant zone, / Prickly and obdurate, dense, harmonious" like the poems of Stevens's own *Harmonium.* The fate—"All din and gobble"—that befalls Crispin in his final costume as fatalist is "Delivered with a deluging onwardness." The deluge engulfing earth is not aquatic but human, with Crispin's heirs at the helm, the sea of humanity "Making gulped potions from obstreperous drops." The accumulated wisdom of the sage or patriarch issues in the gurgle of babes. Within the market economy designated "literature," poetry occupies the position of this comedic trope; and in order to *embody* the tropic, the language of poems has had to retain some figure of the human, a composite portrait that the economy of literature anachronistically retains as the author, but which the texts realize as a still wet palette of tints and smears, the unauthored ground of erasures and geomorphic drift. Poetry is biodegradable thought, "the honey bearing chaos of high summer."

Conrad's Kurtz in *Heart of Darkness* hears the voices of the muses whisper out of that tropic he has come to master; "But the wilderness had found him out early, and had taken on him a terrible vengeance for the fantastic invasion. I think it had whispered to him things about himself which he did not know, things of which he had no conception till he took counsel with this great solitude—and the whisper had proved irresistibly fascinating. It echoed loudly within him because he was hollow at the core." Kurtz is no poet, so he can't live with that hollowness. But poets know that such a cavity can be a drum for sounding rhythm, a ham bone or basin to catch the Muse's thunder as it lets down "gigantic quavers of its voice." The hollow is not only the life of the poet, but can even endure domestication: the comedian as the letter C is a recomposition (by phonemic transference) of Kurtz (though not going so far as to include that Old World "K" of Kafka's golem-haunted imagination): Kurtz as Crispin, a "connoisseur of elemental fate" whose poetic destiny is to domesticate the great solitude with a fund of tropisms. Crispin's "blissful liaison, / Between himself and his environment" becomes as well Stevens's own mock rehearsal for his lifework, which was (combining Milton with Mallarmé) to make the world into the final poem, to render all the world's significations tropological. That this is also the propensity of market economy is worth noting; but the gold standard or any other model of currency exchange legislates a specific model, the heliotropism which Derrida charts in philosophical rhetoric in "White Mythology," and which persists in the idealist alliance of king-phallus-capital-logos. Stevens, on the other hand, like Dickinson before him, openly toys with the posturings of idealism by absorbing the materialist priorities of a composting dispensation into a ground of thought where the reality will not be mutilated by the report. "The plum survives its poems"; and "The wheel survives the myths. / The fire eye in the clouds survives the gods." "The wheel, the lever, the incline, / May survive, and perhaps, / The alphabet."

Cinders

Gradual adjustment to the rugged sylvan dimension of a New World enabled settlers to rejoice in the "bee-loud glade"; but for the natives, the sound of the bees had a more ominous connotation.

. . . the movement of men was to the west,

as the slow advance

of bees

through the woods

meant to the Indians

in a year, an axe would be heard.

Each coffin hollowed out

as a canoe. Each set backwards on a river,

underground.

It has not much been told from the perspective of those who suffered first epidemic and then actual invasion—the microbial assault that spread far more rapidly and pervasively than their human hosts.* For some, like Susan Howe, reflecting on early colonial history, "In the machinery of injustice / my whole being is Vision"—where Vision is the "understory of anotherword." The understory expanded from microbial to colonial agents, culminating in the state-sanctioned exterminating vendetta of "relocation" to which tribes like the Apache were subjected after the Civil War. Ed Dorn tellingly writes,

They were sentenced to observe
the destruction of their World
The revolutionary implications
are interesting

They embody a state
which our still encircled world
looks toward from the past.

Wherever we find that "the share of language is a yearning," in Kenneth Irby's words, America is at hand with its abrasive testimony.

* The precontact population of North and South America combined is estimated to have been between seventy-five and a hundred million people, of whom 95 percent succumbed to diseases transmitted by the European invaders (Stannard, 268). For a multifaceted account of these "virgin soil epidemics," see Alfred W. Crosby, *Germs, Seeds, and Animals: Studies in Ecological History.*

How long did it last, that Paradise?
never longer than it took those French to travel North along the coast
to Maine

. . . .

April to May 1524—the open welcome of the New World
willingness all eager to embrace
took one toke from those who only wanted to go *East* for riches
and the shit was shot.

W. S. Merwin's "one-armed explorer / [who] could touch only half of the country"—having lost his hand—"groped on / for the virgin land // and found where it had been."

. . . the alien world, the new world about him, that might have been Paradise
but was before his eyes already cleard back in a holocaust of burning Indians,
trees and grasslands,
reduced to his real estate, his projects of exploitation and profitable wastes . . .

~

Here is a map of our country:
here is the Sea of Indifference, glazed with salt
This is the haunted river flowing from brow to groin
we dare not taste its water
This is the desert where missiles are planted like corms
This is the breadbasket of foreclosed farms
This is the birthplace of the rockabilly boy

~

The magic we have is that we do not believe in magic
and will not retreat.

~

. . . one's forced
considering America,
to a single truth: the newness

the first men knew was almost
from the start dirtied
by second comers. About seven years
and you can carry cinders
in your hand for what

America was worth

~

7 years & you cld carry cinders in yr hand
for what the country was worth broken
on the body
                    on the wheel of a new
body
        a new social body

~

A noise in the head of the prince. A noise that travels a long ways
Past chances, broken pieces of lumber,
"Time future," the golden head said,
"Time present. Time past."
And the slumbering apprentice never dared to tell the master. A noise.
It annoys me to look at this country

~

where some outcast people find a place at last and others wander
with an open and unplaceable heart in this most enforced of all wildernesses.

~

                                        . . . or of how we might
plead our case in the face of Sartre's observation
that this is a nation where those who care
are the damned of the earth

~

disposal so complete
is quite unbelievable
. . . the manner in which they dispense
with our world, i.e.,
how did we come to invade it, how
did we get
here, in their clutches, where are
we to go?

~

. . . how many waves
of hell and death and
dirt and shit
meaningless waves of hurt and punished lives shall America

be nothing but the story of

~

. . . o my people, where shall you find it, how, where, where shall you listen
when all is become billboards, when, all, even silence, is spray-gunned?

. . . .

when even you, when sound itself is neoned in?

~

. . . in a society like America energy if it is not moral is only

material. Which cannot be destroyed is never destroyed is only

left all over the place. *Junk.*

~

I don't want to know
wreckage, dreck and waste, but these are the materials
and so are the slow lift of the moon's belly
over wreckage, dreck, and waste, wild treefrogs calling in
another season, light and music still pouring over
our fissured, cracked terrain.

~

The cars run in a void of utensils
—the powerful tires—beyond
Happiness

Tough rubbery gear of invaders, of the descendents
Of invaders.

In the car, in Robert Penn Warren's "Going West,"

> With tire song lulling like love, gaze riding white ribbon, forward
> You plunge. Blur of burnt goldness
> Past eye-edge on each
> Side back-whirling, you arrow
> Into the heart of hypnosis.
>
> This is one way to write the history of America.

But this rapture of motor and open road is marked by a blunt carnage of "wing-burst," and all that is visible is

> The bloody explosion, right in my face,

On the windshield, the sun and
The whole land forward, forever,
All washed in blood, in feathers, in gut-scrawl.

Warren's bloody windshield, like Snyder's chronicle of "The Dead by the Side of the Road" and William Stafford's fallen deer, is a totem of alarm. "And by this we are carried into the incalculable," wrote George Oppen.

Strange to be here, strange for them also, insane
and criminal, who hasn't noticed that, strange to
be man, we have come rather far

We are at the beginning of a radical depopulation of the earth.

Oppen's warning is addressed not to the narcotized consciousness of the affluent American fairyland ("hygienic of / views not viable to this soil" where "The dust of intolerable social conditions packed like melting bombs floats the grease of the human condition"—or "Grimed tributaries to an ancient flow" in Hart Crane's line), but to those who know that the endless future world war is already well underway, and that this land is fueling—but ultimately fuel for—this war. ("One can be looted, burned, / bombed, etc., in company, / a Second World War sequel for real, / altogether, now and forever"; or Muriel Rukeyser: "American poetry has been part of a culture in conflict. . . . We are a people tending toward democracy at the level of hope; on another level, the economy of the nation, the empire of business within the republic, both include in their basic premise the concept of perpetual warfare" [*Life of Poetry*, 61]; "How much of it is still true with gene-pool smashed, / the end of knowing," John Clarke wonders about "a world of ritual but no more time"). "Total war / has been uninstructive"; but "the gathered gestures of historic particulars do not extricate from direction the concentrations of responsibility"; "We will produce no sane man again."

Vomito cogito

"We will produce no sane man again." "Can this *saying* and this *being unsaid* be assembled, can they be at the same time?"—this is Emmanuel Levinas's question—"whether one can at the same time know and free the known of the marks which thematization leaves on it by subordinating it to ontology. Everything shows itself at the price of this betrayal, even the unsayable" (*Otherwise Than Being,* 7). "This kind of speaking / doubles the unspeakable." This ontological subordination is rendered explicitly historical by liberation theologist Enrique Dussel. "Before the *ego cogito* there is an *ego conquiro,*" he says, echoing Martinican poet Aimé Césaire's "Vomito Negro."* In the peripheralized existence of the conquered, the bilious retchings of the Cogito affirm the centrality of the empire of Being. "Being is; beings are what are seen and controlled" (*Philosophy of Liberation,* 6).

> [M]odern European philosophy, even before the *ego cogito* but certainly from then on, situated all men and all cultures—and with them their women and children—within its own boundaries as manipulable tools, instruments. Ontology understood them as interpretable beings, as known ideas, as mediations or internal possibilities within the horizon of the comprehension of Being (3).

The *ego cogito* is canonized as an assertion of centers and metropoles, in the calculus of a metaphysics of Being, an ideological countenance structured into a knot of presence-knowledge-language-law and its subsidiary fleet of orbiting satellites, "nature" and "culture," "self," and "other." "Ontology," writes Dussel, "the thinking that expresses Being—the Being of the reigning and central system—is the ideology of ideologies, the foundation of the ideologies of the empires, of the center. Classical philosophy of all ages is the theoretical consummation of the practical oppression of peripheries" (5). This peremptory formulation forces a conclusion: global history is a *canontology.* Canontology—the canon or rule of Being—is artificial respiration, a life-support system: history as a prerogative of the West can be thought of as a comatose patient kept alive by a battery of hookups, an administrative milieu in which what is administered are prescriptive dosages through "state-of-the-art" apparatus linked to a vegetative function. History, as a canon, ensures that only certain people are beneficiaries of its life-support system. History is a mode of production, a technocracy that artificially sustains certain populations at the expense of other populations. But under the protocols of administrative rationality there is not even the ceremonial record of ritual sacrifice to remind the dominant community of the terms that underwrite its persistence.

* the white-toothed black flag of Vomito Negro
will be hoisted for the unlimited duration
of the brush fire of brotherhood

In the canontology of the *vomito negro,* Césaire finds that "my total is ever lengthened by unexpected mintings of baseness," "and our limbs vainly disjointed by the most refined tortures / and life even more impetuously jetting from this compost"—this compost being "Notebook of a Return to the Native Land."

> And this land screamed for centuries that we are bestial brutes; that the human pulse stops at the gates of the slave compound [portes de la négrerie]; that we are walking compost hideously promising tender cane and silky cotton and they would brand us with red-hot irons and we would sleep in our excrement and they would sell us on the town square and an ell of English cloth and salted meat from Ireland cost less than we did, and this land was calm, tranquil, repeating that the spirit of the Lord was in its acts.

> We the vomit of slave ships
> We the venery of the Calabars
> what? Plug up our ears?
> We, so drunk on jeers and inhaled fog that we rode the roll to death!
> Forgive us fraternal whirlwind!

~

Drunken start, drowned
Atlantean root, repeated
whisper. Namesake,
undersea
rift rearisen. Blocked,
butchered brother. *Baja*
mar.

. . . .

Flatted A. Long ah re-
peating after itself.
Ba. . .
Broken body. Bartered
parts.

"Whoever would not understand me would not understand any better the roaring of a tiger," Césaire declares. "But who misleads my voice? who grates / my voice?"—the voice of the alter-ego, the supervisory voice-over analyzed by Césaire's fellow Martinican Franz Fanon in *Black Skin, White Mask.* From this precarious margin of misconnections emanates Adrienne Rich's powerful question:

If your voice could crack in the wind hold its breath still as the rocks
what would it say to the daughter searching the tidelines for a bottled message
from the sunken slaveships?

The bottled message, in Nathaniel Mackey's diasporic traceries, resorts of necessity to anagrammatic redirection, the historic violence of *that* registered in an "Alphabet of Ahtt":*

anagrammatic
ythm, anagrammatic myth . . .
Autistic.
Spat a bitter truth. Maybe misled but
if so so be it. Palimpsestic
stagger,
anagrammatic
scat.

Edward Dorn chronicles the palimpsestic stagger of westward migration slumping into spiritual ennui:

No one
has loved the west I came into, this is not
a Shulamite maiden, nor does anyone care to whisper
this far into our ear, the allegory does not exist, the marriage
will not come who would marry Simplot or Anaconda
I warn you world of good intention the birth of Mohammed
will be fought in this neck of the cut-off world
and moved on, any new blood will
turn to an unnumberable plasma
we could still walk into the banks
and demand the money, but the usual sadness
—we have been preceded, there is
nothing so lame and halt as lateness.

In the extremity of this condition the only response to the fact of "The North Atlantic Turbine," as Dorn calls it, is the thesis that "Only the Illegitimate are beautiful"—a variant on William Carlos Williams's Elsie, "expressing with broken // brain the truth about us." The Illegitimate are the disaffiliated, unassimilable

* Place names, too, require anagrammatic rearrangement: "To the outer / principalities of Onem we were / brought, bought, / sold / on blocks, auctioned / off."

populace (the Appalachian faces of Walker Evans and James Agee, the dustbowl migrants, the hollow-eyed immigrants of Ellis Island, the silicosis victims of Muriel Rukeyser's "Book of the Dead") that is a "minority" in the rhetoric of the good life, but in America too often a "minority" in a different, pejorative, usage—the convalescent human wreckage of minoritarian afterthought, tended by the nurse who "blows with her every skill on the spirit's embers still burning by their own laws in the bed of death."

Rolled a
joint with gunpowder
inside, struck a match,
whispered, "This is
what history does."
Said, "Above sits
atop its Below, each
undoing the other
even though they
embrace."

The twentieth-century corollary of the *vomito cogito* of the Middle Passage is the holocaust, or "khurbn," the Yiddish term favored by Jerome Rothenberg since it has less connotation of ritual slaughter.

THOSE WHO ARE BEAUTIFUL & THOSE WHO ARE NOT
change places   to relive
a death by excrement

victims thrown into the pit & drowning
in their ordure
suffocating in the body's dross

this is extremity

"this is extremity   this place / . . . where the warm flux inside the corpse / changes to stone." The only recourse—which Rothenberg adopts in open defiance of Adorno's remark that after Auschwitz poetry was impossible:

"practice your scream" I said
(why did I say it?)
because it was his scream & wasn't my own
it hovered between us

~

Where shall the scream stick?
What shall it dent?
Won't the deafness be cracked?
Won't the molecules be loosened?

Are you listening? We need the scream to leave its mark . . .

In a grammar of "let" recalling Christopher Smart's madhouse poem *Jubilate Agno*—along with the propositional logic of the calculus (that vectorial afterimage of Nazi "experiments" on human subjects)—Rothenberg summons a profound sense of the utmost brutality as all too familiar, uncannily so.

Let a great pain come up into your legs (feel it moving like the earth moving beneath you)
Let the earth drop away inside your belly falling falling until you're left in space
Let his scream follow you across the millennia back to your table
Let a worm the size of a small coin come out of the table where you're sitting
Let it be covered with the red mucus falling from his nose (but only you will see it)
Let the holes in his body drop open let his excretions pour out across the room

~

Write this. We have burned all their villages

Write this. We have burned all the villages and the people in them

Write this. We have adopted their customs and their manner of dress

Write this. A word may be shaped like a bed, a basket or tears or an X

That origin which is act . . . that riddle which is awe

The final measure of the "Chiasma" lectures for the New Sciences of Man is the outcome of Olson's concern with materialized humanity, something like tin or coal to be tuned or used up or burned off. Rexroth saw this as "the pure form / Of the cutting edge of power— / Man reduced to an entelechy." For Olson, "man himself is the universe the materials and motions of which call for primary investigation, that he is the unknown—and no longer allowably unknown" ("Chiasma," 68). At midpoint of the century, which in 1953 Olson clearly felt astride, the dead heaped in the pathway,* in plain view, imposed the equation:

The dead in via
                    in vita nuova
                                        in the way

You shall lament who know they are as tender as the horse is.
You, do not you speak who know not.

        "I will die about April 1st . . ." going off
        "I weigh, I think, 80 lbs . . ." scratch
        "My name is NO RACE" address
        Buchenwald new Altamira cave
        With a nail they drew the object of the hunt.

There are two images here to ponder: the hunt and the sacrifice. Since the domestication of plants and animals (and urbanized humans), hunting has become one of the great unconsidered constants of human instinct, to the point that now, post 1945, we have doubts about the ultimate identity of the victim: man or animal? After citing Jane Harrison on the link between Greek drama and animal sacrifice, Olson says, "the dance was both mask and twin to the paintings under which they were performed, that the men who danced were costumed literally in the animal's features (again, the literal)" ("Chiasma," 54). We have, between the routinized genocide of Buchenwald, and the carefully prescribed assault on larger mammals on Altamira cave wall, a midpoint, neither dance nor image, but ritual: the Aztecs, when sacrificing prisoners, would cut and peel the skin of the victim's head away so carefully that it was fitted over the celebrant's head literally like a mask and worn for days until it stank.

From the mute bodies of exhumed bog people (victims by hanging) to the ceremonial transit in a death barge, D. H. Lawrence's "Ship of Death," "Bavarian Gentians," and the rest of his *Last Poems,* or Whitman's late "little tags and fringe-dots (maybe specks, stains)" and Dickinson's "Goblin—on the Bloom" (no. 646), there

* For Mackey, they are signs of "gnostic import, known, / it was ours to infer, by none if / not by / those who no longer spoke . . . / Inductees into a school of scramble" (Mackey's ellipses).

is a fitful alliance of writing with mortuary circumstance, at once commemoration and indictment, celebration and dispatch. There is a sense with the exhumed bodies of Egyptian kings—in vaults filled with trunks of books, the walls of the vaults covered with writing, the kings' bodies wrapped in discarded papyrus—that the bodies *are writing*—"Each word a / flash-pod correspondent / to an event / in the Great Beyond." The Bible opens with the universe created in or as a word and ends with the vision of a mortal god resurrected into the Word of his Book. The culmination of the Koran is orientation to the Ka'ba, a tomb. A tomb, vault, or sarcophagus is the receptacle of a treasure, immutable currency.

The dead that persist in books: this is what religious teachings commonly report and verify.* Earlier Egyptian and Mesopotamian scriptural and burial practices indicate that an entire library is required for the passage into death. Writing commemorates a relationship to death, a faith in the transmissibility of the dead psyche (or breath-soul) through association with the logos, that break in the flow that spurts, leaks, stains, ruptures into sediment. The dead are a library, a fulcrum of layers that unfold, unwrap, *untomb.* The interanimating negotiation of those apparently opposing principles, life and death, is made pliable to the mind in Lucretius's fecund concept of the *clinamen,* or unaccountable swerve of the atoms plummeting through the void. The swerve affords contact between them, and contact is magnified into concupiscent mortality, momentary cleavage and coagulation. The swerving atom endows a turbulent pocket, a cove or shelter of generation. These pockets are pleats of the manifold, the creases through which nature increases (the *pli* in complication, explication, application) in clump and clot. Clinamen: tiniest aperture opening on animation.†

It may be through Heraclitus, conspicuously, that we can trace the origin of *psyche* as the conceptual animation of a subhuman continuity through this rumored, difficult domain of the imponderably small. Heraclitus is unique among his contemporaries in taking psyche to be something other than a synonym for any of the other general "soul words" (*thumos, menos, etor, ker, kradin, noos, phrenes*). Among Heraclitus's esoteric resources were the visionary topographies of Persia and India,‡

* In matters of religion there are always dissenting views:
"Books" "books ruined us" "Scrolls & tablets" "created time," "created"
"keeping track" "Distanced us from the" "perpetuation" "of our
beautiful" "beginning moment . . ." "only moment" "Created death" "created
death . . ."

† For more on the *clinamen,* see Rasula and McCaffery, eds., *Imagining Language,* 532–60.

‡ See M. L. West, *Early Greek Philosophy and the Orient,* chapter 6.

enabling him to speak of psyche in such a way as to imply "a connection between the soul as the physiological animator and the cosmic processes to which, in that capacity, it is plainly analogized" (Claus, 127). Heraclitus is one of the earliest to imagine what life is from the perspective that life is what *imagination* is—a reciprocal animation of soul and cosmos in the medium of logos: "you would not approach the limit of psyche, so deep is its logos" (fragment 45).

Cosmos is made of neither men nor gods, but is all fire (to which he bears primary fidelity, and a key Zoroastrian link), kindled in meter and quenched in meter (*metra,* measure [fragment 30]). For Heraclitus, psyche becomes the medium through which the metrics of logos in cosmos are regulated and maintained. In the surviving tattered relics of his statements and turns of phrase (and punch lines, to judge by some), we have a deep logos: that is, he used common words of his day with such force of differentiation that we read him even in fragments as momentous, convening a place of enlarged exchange, composted fully in the sense that entire parts have disappeared. Depth is a contingency of disappearance. Reconstruction of a "philosophy" from such scattered remains is an act that the science of paleozoology and the classics portend in a single motion. It is only in instances of the willful violation of these bits of verbal matter—humus, compost—by poets and other wreaders that they remain active *as particles:* Heraclitus's fragments constitute a fiery particulate combustion like a volcano spewing elemental chunks (the terms *psyche, logos, cosmos*) into the atmosphere. In all subsequent measure of who we are to the dead and who the dead are to us, the use of these words has been imperative.

Heraclitus and the atomist philosopher-poets of the sixth century B.C. lived at the end of a civilization longer than that which the Christian West can claim for itself. Their relation to the mutation of lore and text in religious dogma, shrines and oracles, mysteries and myths may have encouraged an awareness that human perception registers with certain evident restrictions: we see something too far away to make out, hear something too faintly to know the words, touch too small a surface to know what we touch. By such analogies analytic thought was first imagined; by intuitions developed in the mutable world, on the principle (everywhere abundantly illustrated) that all organic matter cycles through compost, some could imagine these words that were by no means abstractions (or generalizations), but attempts at indicating specifics beyond the capacity of the isolate human perceptual apparatus to verify. They imagined all to be composed of atoms; they imagined the earth was round; they imagined words so deep nobody could ascertain their limits, and breath-potency so persistent it could survive the mortal body as logos or psyche—but only in a cosmos, a place where such minute imponderable contingencies could register as continuities (where truth must dazzle gradually, as Dickinson puts it [no. 1129]). This is—enlarged to a universal frame—the library, where all is stored consequentially, even if buried or as yet folded away from our attentions, dystopically rendered by Borges as a "feverish Library whose chance volumes are constantly in danger of changing into others and affirm, negate and confuse everything like a delirious divinity" (*Labyrinths,* 57). To read has always meant to unfold, to experience in the passage from sense to mind the implicit gesture with which a flower or leaf responds to the sun, implicated in its shining. As mortality is bound in the life ready to flow from a wound, so the psyche is ready to flow forth in sympathy (sym-patheia, fellow feeling), toward the cosmos, which is all we know of that which flows ("Everything flows" in Heraclitus's declaration [fragment 20]), and all we know also of psyche. From Heraclitus's composting intelligence, we carry the legacy of the library as a residuum of leaking souls.

> It is quite remarkable that Heraclitus applies to the ψυχή the journey metaphor by which the *daimon* of a Pythagorean would seek knowledge beyond that of ordinary men. One wonders whether there is not in this a reply to all such shamanistic pretensions. The journey that matters to Heraclitus is not the journey of the ψυχή but *within* the ψυχή, in the sense that one must try to understand the Logos by which the ψυχή in the self imitates the behavior of fire in general (Claus, 137).

To others the psyche wandered, but Heraclitus attends to a wandering in psyche, which opens the crypt, in a sense, to read the script, the "colossal cipher" Emerson insists on as the basic literacy of the new American poet. His (Shakespearian) mirror carried through the streets by the great artist pertains retrospectively as far back as the Paleolithic, in the caves of which we find a silhouetted horizon of animal life, a mirror of mortality humans conducted their own mortal epiphanies in the reflection of (a mirror of analogy, not resemblance). To reflect is to see reflections of mind in matter, to behold a cascade of elements in cosmos, "as if our condition now is / hugely umbilical" and perception itself enduring a confinement, a pregnancy seeking its issue in an enlarged view of the matter at hand. The mortal struggles of twentieth-century terrors are now giving birth to whatever unpredictable mode of being it is that follows the human—an era consummately named by Yeats's premonition of the "savage god" and Pound's lament for that wasteland "where the dead walked / and the living were made of cardboard."

The post-human—the posthumous Homo Sapien—passes from cosmos to chaos. But chaos has always been with us, intrinsic to cosmos if not to cosmology (words about the world). The subterranean transmissions of composting poetry have been compacted in the compost library, where biodegradable thinking occurs, where we can conceivably speak of an "ecology of consciousness" in which *psyche wandering* is in touch with human boundaries, noting the logos that forestalls the corruption of cosmos by chaos. Chaos, now, may be nothing other than business "as usual" in assuming reflection to be simply that which glitters.* But for the proportionate intelligence, seeking ratio or the metrical ingenuity of events, "Wisdom is whole: the knowledge of how things are plotted in their courses by all other things" (Heraclitus, Davenport translation, 31). The Indo-European root of chaos (and of chasm) is *ghi,* meaning "open wide." When Duncan writes of "opening the field," following Olson's propositions of composition by field in a continuum of open forms, chaos is the opening. The aperture and its fathom.

The archaic and the old lore

In *Gnomonology*—a primer of poetics and practical wisdom—Howard McCord speaks of the need "to SHAPE expression beyond the bleating self." "You would know the whole?" he asks, and amidst his bibliocentric cartography urges a path "Through the force of love, by the heart's blind eye, in the swiftness of glimpsed forms, in lightness, in balance." McCord's references range widely, including

* One poet who has made a conspicuous shift from verse formalism to a more open field practice—Jorie Graham—speaks of the need to incorporate chaos as an ethical stance. "No genuine form occurs without the honest presence of chaos (however potentially) in the work," she writes, reflecting on her growing awareness that "poems, by the implications of their formal characteristics, were providing a metaphysical view of the world which might be a terrible illusion, one which might, moreover, be permitting us to not take certain kinds of actions because we feel ultimately, as a species, *safe,* compelled me to try to break that illusion as often as I could. Mostly to make myself feel how often I *wanted* to restore that illusion." At issue, then, "is the distinction between suffering and understanding, and how we want to merge them in the act of writing a poem. We want to be able to suffer the poem so that the actions that we take in the act of writing are true actions"—because "poems are enactments, ritualistic enactments—fractal enactments—in language, of historical motions. And in the *process* of them, you experience your accountability" (Gardner, 227, 220, 226, 221).

works like Ron Linton's *Terracide,* the plant lore of Oakes Ames and Edgar Anderson, Yi-Fu Tuan's *The Hydrologic Cycle and the Wisdom of God,* Adolf Portmann's *Animal Forms and Patterns,* and a richly synthesized compilation of similar resources. Many of the coordinates continue to compel tactics of poetic attention, including Spencer Brown on "the membrane, the border" (in *Laws of Form*), René Thom's probing into catastrophe theory (*Topological Models in Biology*), Marcel Griaule's Dogon cosmology (*Conversations with Ogotemmêli*), Henry Corbin's *Avicenna and the Visionary Recital,* biologist C. H. Waddington's concept of the chreod (meaning "pathway of change"), and Michel Foucault's (then just published) *The Order of Things.* Vital evidence of a poetic eclecticism, and native savvy of the compost library.

Charles Olson provoked such cartographic study guides with "Bibliography on America for Ed Dorn." Elsewhere he proposes seven "hinges of civilization to be put back on the door" (*Additional Prose,* 25–26). These include the valuation of "a more primal consequent art & life than that which followed" to consist of the full Semitic prebiblical lore, an accounting of the roots of fifth-century Athens back in its earlier Asiatic connections (recognizing Heraclitus, Pythagoras, Buddha, and Confucius as contemporaries), and several other "hinges."* Another in this milieu of bibliographic provocations is Gerrit Lansing's manifesto "The Burden of Set" with its resounding declaration: "It remains to be seen what cannot be permitted" (92). The function of the trickster, that intrepid avatar of the impermissible, "is to add disorder to order and so make a whole, to render possible, within the fixed bounds of what is permitted, an experience of what is not permitted" (Radin,

* Robert Kelly, who in the early sixties had organized his magazine *Matter* around the Olsonian principle of poets as researchers on the primal, proposes some "Labrys" (or double-headed axes) as twelve "matters": (1) Mare Nostrum, (2) Central Asia, (3) The place itself, (4) The uses of earth, (5) Sound, (6) Traditionary sciences, (7) Techniques of Enstasy, (8) Techniques of Ecstasy, (9) Shape, (10) Story, (11) Time & (or as) dimension, and (12) The Nation. Kelly elsewhere provides an "Experimental Program for Dream Research" in *Io* 8 (1971): 299–301. The "Labrys" are from *In Time.* Repositories and forums of the old lore and the exploration of the archaic (all dating from the 1960s to 1970s) include Robert Kelly's *Matter,* Richard Grossinger's *Io,* David Meltzer's *Tree,* Jerome Rothenberg and Dennis Tedlock's *Alcheringa,* and Rothenberg's *New Wilderness Letter.* "I look for new forms and possibilities," Rothenberg writes, "but also for ways of presenting in my own language the oldest possibilities of poetry going back to the primitive & archaic cultures" (*Poems for the Game of Silence,* 121). Outlining "Intersections & Analogies" of primitive and modern, he cites such approaches to the poem as performance score; intermedia; corporeality; concrete and pictorial poetries; noncausal logic as in surrealism, dream, and deep image; and a visionary continuum from shamanism to dada performance (*Pre-Faces,* 73–74, originally *Technicians of the Sacred*).

185). "We are in a rough time, the most difficult transition age of all, a real Interchange of Tinctures, where a kind of personal life is being exchanged for a kind of 'universal.'" "To each man, for use, what he has is given, & if he hasn't, well, it's being taken away from him, & pretty fast" (Lansing, "Burden of Set," 90). Lansing also proposes certain labyrinthine labors as "beginnings, opening of the figures of Time that compose the structure of our necessity, how by poetry we investigate the needs" (87). The prophecy is exacting: poetry is investigation into "the structure of our necessity."*

The proprioceptive and ecological necessities impinging on the creative act—the psyche acting in the poem on cosmos through logos—are vital to Olson's legacy. His characteristic swagger was mostly a register of his *absorption* in the materials. Robert Duncan was more adept at making his claims understood as provisional. Turning away from heroic posturing is, as he puts it, a "phantasmagoria," invariably "mythological vision and folklorish phantasy," a bewildering interplay of chaos and cosmos, clown and king (*Truth and Life*, 38). This philosophical wedding, *hieros gamos*, which was taken by Freud and Jung to be the confrontation of psyche itself with the modern world, as if mind itself were atavistic, obscenely outdated (and with the increased offloading of computational tasks to random access memory devices, enfleshed psyche does begin to seem an anachronism). To activate this archaic capacity of mind or soul is to pathologize, as James Hillman calls it, or to be generative in Olson's term. Myth, in other words, is profane. Simply to

* This is not theory (speculation: reflection), but a gnostic determination of what will work. Such an approach marks key documents of a poetics-in-process: from *Call Me Ishmael* to *A Special View of History* and the many notes and essays by Olson collected in *Human Universe* and *Additional Prose;* Robert Duncan's *Truth and Life of Myth* and the copious *H.D. Book;* Louis Zukofsky's *Bottom: On Shakespeare* and the essays in *Prepositions;* Jerome Rothenberg's *Pre-Faces;* Robert Kelly's *In Time;* Michael McClure's *Meat Science Essays;* Gary Snyder's *Earth House Hold, The Old Ways,* and numerous other essay collections; Robert Creeley's *Collected Essays;* Edward Dorn's *Views;* Howard McCord's *Gnomonology;* Jack Spicer's Vancouver Lectures; Robin Blaser's *The Stadium of the Mirror* (and as yet uncollected prose), as well as the pieces by these and other poets included by Donald Allen and Warren Tallman in *Poetics of the New American Poetry.* Recent supplements include *Vow to Poetry* by Anne Waldman, Susan Howe's *The Birth-mark* and John Clarke's *From Feathers to Iron* (and, for that matter, *In the Analogy,* a book of several hundred sonnets, each including up to six epigraphs: one of the more vigorously composting moments in the Olsonian legacy). These are all documents of a poetics attentive to the poem as mutho-logistical, of psyche's logos, and cosmographic. This investigative propensity has been continued, with some different emphases, in such works as Ron Silliman's *The New Sentence,* Barrett Watten's *Total Syntax,* Charles Bernstein's *Content's Dream* and *A Poetics, Paradise and Method* by Bruce Andrews, *The Language of Inquiry* by Lyn Hejinian, and *The Public World/Syntactically Impermanence* by Leslie Scalapino.

tell tales of the gods is hubristic, misbehaving before the temple (pro-fanum). So Duncan regards the poet as involuntary mime of the marvelous, whose profanities (as in Bottom's dream) stumble upon the sacred. Ineptitude signifies that another order is at hand. When we try to imagine the archaic we know neither what we're looking for nor what we're seeing. The old lore is at once a body of testimony and an invitation to risk.

The stakes in myth are always high—that is, risks are not recuperable to the apologetic posturing of "development" routinized by history. It is a mistake to link myth with belief, says Roberto Calasso; rather, "we enter the mythical when we enter the realm of risk, and myth is the enchantment we generate in ourselves in such moments. More than a belief, it is a magical bond that tightens around us. It is a spell the soul casts on itself" (*Marriage of Cadmus and Harmony,* 278). As Duncan attests, "The depths emerge in a kind of dream informed by the familiar tale. It is important here that the myth be first so familiar, so much no-more-than an old story, that the poet is at home with what is most perilous" (*Truth and Life,* 27). The peril must be harbored by the familiar, so as to engage the possible. "So when we look at a little bit of American Indian folklore, myth, read a tale, we're catching just the tip of an iceberg of forty or fifty thousand years of human experience, on this continent, in this place" (Snyder, *Old Ways,* 80). This is from an essay on the trickster in which Gary Snyder can be seen working, like Olson and James Hillman, toward depotentiating the image of the hero: "so the trickster image is basic; it has to do in part with that turning away from heroes" (85), and putting Adrienne Rich's question to the tally of human cost:

> . . . male dominion, gangrape, lynching, pogrom
> the Mohawk wraiths in their tracts of leafless birch
>
> watching: will we do better?

Clayton Eshleman, watching a documentary on the Nazi concentration camps, ventures his credo "There is no proposal the imagination cannot assimilate / But it is only through Pleistocene mercy that we're still here."

Another of Snyder's imperatives is that we at least know we're glimpsing thirty or forty thousand years' experience. The only way of examining such material is by sniffing it out, through intuition, empathy, superstition. Reconstructing a history, unless it attains psychological animation, is not enough. History is inconsequential data unless animated by the old story sense of psyche (a protagonist) working on creation (cosmos) with some tool (logos). To recover the old lore as evidence of a prior logos is insufficient; one's own psyche mingles involuntarily with psyches elsewhere or in other times. Story—logos—stirs and disturbs psyche. We can now recognize the singularity attributed by Duncan to poetry's involuntarism and clownish trifling with sacred matter: this is elemental stirring, primary animation of cosmos by deliberately tampering with boundaries, loosening psychic materials by mouth, myth, muthologistics. This brings us to the relation between the old lore and the archaic I want to underscore: the old lore is logos tatters from the compost library; the archaic is the cosmos as we—our psyches so disposed—can conceive it, notably the broader "40,000 year view" the old lore invites.*

"The *psychosis* or principle of the soul-life," writes Duncan, "is its belonging to the reality of what we know to be true to our story-sense. In the light of the mythological, events and persons can seem true or false to the true story of who I am" (*Truth and Life*, 8). James Hillman: "It is not life that matters, but soul and how life is used to care for soul" (*Re-Visioning Psychology*, 175). William James: "the world that each of us feels most intimately at home with is that of beings with histories that play into our history" (*Pluralistic Universe*, 652). Psyche is always the "true" story—being true to its own story-sense—yet such truth is thought discrepant from historical truth. But even *history* lies outside the actual experience of psyche in a human lifetime. Myth is psychology—reenacting history in the imaginal palette of psychic issue: "To inherit or to evolve is to enter mythic existence" (Duncan, *Truth and Life*, 59).

Think of wings pushing through shoulders.
Think of drinking the compass to become a map.
Think of rain pouring from an eave
with no cloud above, a wet alphabet trembling
inside the spine.   Or to escape through the letter O
                    to be naked inside the curve of an S.

~

The past is not a husk   yet change goes on

~

oak powers renewing the mythopoeia

* The forty-thousand-year view refers to the human record. The planetary scale Snyder addresses in *Mountains and Rivers Without End* enlarges the scope: "Us critters hanging out together / something like three billion years." For a handy overview of the truly long-range view, see *The Eternal Frontier* by Tim Flannery.

Indian skin

"The past is not a husk": it persists not only in our stories, but *in* and *as* us. We are the genetic monstrance of deep time, living demonstrations of what the past forged. "The human mind is the result of a long series of interactions with other animals," writes ethologist Paul Shepard (*The Others,* 15), foremost of which, in terms of biomorphic resonance, was the hunt. In the provocatively archaic prospect of *The Tender Carnivore and the Sacred Game,* Shepard speculates that the lapse of hunting (or "cynegetic") culture was a catastrophe from which our species may not recover:

> The virtual collapse of hunting and gathering, the central activity of the ancient culture, would surely have affected the very heart of human existence. The great mystery of domestication is therefore not so much how men achieved control of plants and animals; but how human consciousness was reorganized when the cynegetic life was shattered—that is, the mental, social, and ecological complex based on hunting. All major human characteristics—size, metabolism, sexual and reproductive behavior, intuition, intelligence—had come into existence and were oriented to the hunting life. (7)

What is at stake, then, in speculation about the archaic is nothing less than metabolism, intuition, tactful solidarity with animal life: an inheritance more deeply implicated in physiology than those "lifestyle" options fortified by the biopimping menus of *fin de millennium* culture. But our genetic makeup imposes limitations. "The ecology of Paleolithic hunters," Shepard writes, "particularly the sparse population and stable environment, may have allowed the specialization of human intelligence to a degree that is intolerable in dense populations and an unstable environment" (227). As a species we have precipitated environmental changes more rapidly than natural adaptation can keep pace with. But where such changes are often ascribed to technology, Shepard cautions that "the main features of the ten-thousand year span of civilization are war and environmental crisis. Technology, as such, can hardly be held accountable for this. Man was already technological—a toolmaker—when he emerged as a species, and was so for two million years before the disasters of history began" (40). The difference is not in the tool, but in the mind that wields it. Shepard poses the distinction between hunting/gathering and agricultural sedentarity as one involving a shift from participation to manipulation ("Post-Historic Primitivism," 62). Carl Sauer similarly discriminates between yield and loot (*Land and Life*, 154). American ecological thinkers have been increasingly alarmed by the manipulative cash-crop orientation of agribusiness, as if natural cycles could be induced to conform to the rhythm of inflated expectations. In 1924 Aldo Leopold lamented "this headlong stampede for speed and ciphers," "the tragic absurdity of trying to whip the March of Empire into a gallop" (*The River*, 127).

As Lewis Mumford saw it amidst the carnage of World War II, "Western civilization became mechanically unified and socially disintegrated" (*Values for Survival*, 190). Twenty years later, from the vantage of Lyndon B. Johnson's "great society," Mumford's prognosis of civilized "development" was equally devastating. The supposed rationalization of technology, he found, often concealed pockets of irrationality: "immense gains in valuable knowledge and usable productivity were canceled out by equally great increases in ostentatious waste, paranoid hostility, insensate destructiveness, hideous random extermination" (*Lewis Mumford Reader*, 314). In a longer view, as Mumford noted in *The City in History*, the global pattern of civilization can be charted as a transit from polis to necropolis, "living urban core" became a "city of the dead" (53). City and history converge in the necropolis, a site disclosing the perspectival arrest of history as such. "History is not a neutral documentation of things that happened but an active, psychological force that separates humankind from the rest of nature because of its disregard for the deep connections to the past," Shepard wrote. Given the inadequacies of the historical sense, Shepard affirms "the prehistorical unconscious" in a final leap of faith (*Coming Home*, 14–15, 17).

With Shepard, poets like Clayton Eshleman and Gary Snyder regard the last ten thousand years as anomalous. In *Hades in Manganese*, Eshleman writes:

> By beginning to look at paleolithic cave art from the viewpoint of simultaneous psychic organization and disintegration, I hope to be extending our sense of "gods" and imaginative activity way beyond the Greeks, so that human roots may be seen as growing in a context that does not preclude the animal from a sense of the human . . . the crisis behind the making of what we call art as involved with the hominid separating the animal out of himself. (19)

"Therioexpulsion" is the term Eshleman coins for this separation. The ancient cosmological lore of hunter-gatherers accompanied the animals in their exodus. The poetics of open field/open form poetry is much engaged with the old lore as a legacy affording access to the remote past. The lore ranges from Greece and the Ancient Near East through native cultures around the planet, those "technicians of the sacred" in Jerome Rothenberg's sense. The biological awareness of human species-life animated by the compost library is a crucial link between dormant animal tact and the metabolism of intelligence as it flourishes in writing. Marking the extremity of therioexpulsion and its human cost is the image of Bibles bound in Indian skin in the University of Texas Humanities Research Library (Davenport, *Geography of the Imagination,* 355), in which biology and library blend in a single irreparable atrocity. But it attests to what is at stake in distinguishing the old lore from any putative historical record (particularly those records invested in valorizing History as the master narrative of imperial destiny). The moral charge is evident: to read is simply to scan words on a page, whereas wreading is feeling the texture of the skin on the binding of the book as it is held together by a spine.

The natives of the Americas—a rich culturally diverse array ranging from nomads to sedentary cultivators—were sloughed off into that capacious category of the "people without history" (which, for Europeans, could mean even the Chinese). By this same rhetorical subterfuge they were then inserted *into* history, into that scripture-soaked catalogue the civilized predators took pride in: "big masculine history / on tap." To be without history (in terms of the Texas icon above) is to be skinned for the binding of a prophetic canon, the Bible, its scripture used to sanction atrocities in the name of History.* This apocalyptic resource perpetuates in turn a "nature" left increasingly out of the equation, as vanishing animal species are commemorated in the names of cars (Cougar and Impala)—although the alienation is now so advanced that animals no longer connote automotive glamour, supplanted by formulaic names like Neon, Altima, Celica.† "In the Indian culture," Muriel Rukeyser writes, "the songs had religious presence. We have the spectacle of a culture which values its poetry driven into captivity and repression by a power-culture which sets no store on this art" (*Life of Poetry,* 91)—a plight memorably realized in *The Professor's House,* Willa Cather's fictionalized account of the excavation of Mesa Verde. "The capacity for invasion alive in the

* In Enrique Dussel's choice formulation, "the Indians were victimized in the name of an innocent victim and for the sake of universal rights" (*Invention of the Americas,* 50).

† Such drifting exoskeletal markers constitute an apocalyptic grid in Don DeLillo's novel *White Noise* (Mylex, Dacron, Orlon, Lycra Spandex, Dristan, Clorets, Panasonic, Tegrin, Denorex, not to mention the sources of common acronyms like Random Access Memory, Acquired Immune Deficiency Syndrome, and Mutual Assured Destruction). The protagonist experiences "a moment of splendid transcendence" when he overhears his daughter talking in her sleep: "She was only repeating some TV voice. Toyota Corolla, Toyota Celica, Toyota Cressida. Supranational names, computer-generated, more or less universally pronounceable. Part of every child's brain noise" (155).

human heart is the openness to an otherness that cuts both ways. Our inspiration is also our peril, a risk of inflation whose would-be rise can take us down into hell" (Mackey, "From Gassire's Lute," 211). The lost world is unrecoverable, and this entails the difficult realization of the alchemical nigredo: the fertilizing dark of the white whale's plummet in *Moby-Dick,* or the dissolution of entire cultures—extinction implicated in the larger creative adventure.

Darkness is another kind of light,
and stones are sweet as air to breathe.
The Anasazi, the old people, knew.
In the depths of canyons
for a thousand years, they unlocked
the rocks themselves and slipped
inside like bones fit into skin.

~

what history itself is longing for to demonstrate, not with names and not with dates, but these, our inter-interventions

~

for solitude and grieving are also instruments of vision

. . . .

shall we not shout and stomp to tell deep grief, and wild fandango celebrate the being able to, to be at all

On the extremest verge

Culture is said to live, while its makers die. The unsettling terms of this respiratory system have a long history, in which themes of truth and beauty (all you know and all you need to know, the Grecian urn tells humbled John Keats) emerge as consolations in the face of unyielding laws of organic life. In the Western world this has fostered a psychological legacy of perennial inadequacy: surrounded on all sides by "classics," we're overburdened not only with the malady of belatedness, but with the constant beguilements of consumerism. The apparatus of cultural life increasingly stands between the organism and the broad prospect of an integrated existence in the cosmos. In the culture cocoon, the central facts of the biodegradable energy web are concealed, compromised, or simply forgotten. "The tools we have invented for communicating our ideas and carrying information have actually impaired our memories" (Shepard, *Coming Home,* 6). To be civilized, then, means being dispossessed of all the discriminations and instincts of an animal birthright.

Our legacy of psychological dispossession attests to the fact that we inhabit a culture we can't keep up with; our adaptive resources, prosthetically shared out in the artifactual realm, are subject to misalignment and asynchronous alliances. Having generously extended our cybernetic capacities to the servo-mechanisms of daily life, the culture now appears to be outthinking us. Endocolonization, the "boarding of metabolic vehicles" in the regimes of techno-acceleration—as Paul Virilio describes it in *Speed and Politics*—is accompanied by an aesthetic transfiguration. "We have gone from the esthetics of appearance, stable forms, to the esthetics of disappearance, unstable forms" (Virilio and Lotringer, 84). Not only are we ineptly engaged with *psyche,* we can't even operate all the equipment, which is constantly changing out from under us by market-driven obsolescence. The dilemma is not unique to us of the late twentieth century. Tribes, cities, states, and entire civilizations have invariably reached that point at which problems are not matched by any collective resolve to address them. Weston LaBarre chronicles numerous instances in *The Ghost Dance,* amounting to a surrogate history of maladaptive cultures. Edward Hyams's *Soil and Civilization* recounts a similar story. Hyams offers a simple but valuable index:

> the artists and poets of the *balanced* phase of any civilization have a profound feeling for the grain of life. Poetry which runs against this grain, and is a product of the failure of the poet's community to retain their faculty of tact as members of life, may still be profoundly impressive: but so may any clever, bitter act of perversity and destruction (11).

American literature, as if to illustrate Hyams's thesis, offers two exemplary cases: Poe and Whitman. For Poe, the thought of death is such a delectable stimulation that his work is preordained to macabre hallucinations. For Whitman, on the other hand, death is the supreme organic event, the measure of all creaturely striving. No one would argue that Whitman's work embodies anything less than a "profound feeling for the grain of life"—making him, in Hyams's terms, a poet of the balanced phase. Whitman was indisputably intent on reminding his fellows of their "faculty of tact as members of life." But in the wake of the Civil War his poetic focus became increasingly compliant with that booster spirit that made C. L. R.

James compare Whitman's rhetoric to toothpaste and deodorant ads (*C. L. R. James Reader,* 206).

Whitman's vast inclusive organic vision, as it happened, was a democracy few were prepared to embrace, inciting lifelong racial and sexual mingling. Ezra Pound later came to see himself (in the mask of Mauberley) as a man out of key with his time, and Whitman's vision of 1855–60 was no less out of key with his. The adventure and scale of his America was, however, equal to the unmanageable proportions of the nation. And Whitman could no more sustain such a vision by himself than America as a nation could retain its revolutionary character after the war of independence. The nation of Whitman's youth was in flux, teeming with opportunity and risk. (Melville's *The Confidence Man* marks that volatile frontier as well as any other document.) Whitman's response in *Leaves of Grass* was commensurate with American exhilarations. He felt himself, rightly, the poet of the emergent condition. When the Civil War broke out, he assumed that to be there at all was to be the poet of the great debacle; and that he was. But the war, like all modern wars, was a sleight of hand concealing power plays beneath the state of emergency, and when the war was over the nation was no longer the same nation. While the jeremiad "Democratic Vistas" laments this degeneration of original prospects, Whitman the poet seems curiously oblivious to his own diagnosis.

By 1871 Whitman is chanting the song of imperialism, in step with the nation, but not with the persona of the poems. He sees the completion of the transcontinental railroad as "The road between Europe and Asia," but he fails to take account of the human cost—no mention of the tens of thousands of Chinese laborers who suffered the worst blizzard conditions in the Rockies, some freezing to death with picks in hand to meet the company schedules—a Whitmanian image if he'd used it. But maybe "public domain" is best: "Some poetry is in the public domain from birth," Muriel Rukeyser reflected in *The Life of Poetry,* citing the legacy lost to that domain by the inattentions and abuses of history: "the miner's songs of the past, the songs of the Chinese workmen on the western railways, the poems of the Nisei camps, the lost songs of the slave underground" (102). Whitman enjoins his soul to see a divine purpose in technological finality—"the earth to be spann'd, connected by network, / The races, neighbors, to marry and be given in marriage"—but again, not a word of the Chinese workers, forbidden contact with white women and not allowed to bring wives of their own. In 1860 Whitman had been the voice the polity could never absorb, visionary of American vistas forever antithetical to the greed of a nation on the brink of becoming a world power. But on and on he wrote, persuading himself he was merely repeating and embellishing the great themes of his former chants, leaving a big book of poems, most of which would be safely absorbed into the republic's new façade of the reconstruction years and their ambitious aftermath, the Asian market and Pacific expansion.

Whitman's copious contributions to the weeklies and dailies he edited and wrote for are deeply infused by the standard rhetoric of his time. Despite his affirmation of solidarity with contemporary life, it is intriguing to think of *Leaves of Grass* as a fantasy on the order of *The Earthly Paradise* by William Morris. Edwin Fussell perceptively designates 1855 as the point at which "Whitman was the West, i.e. the frontier between the American self and its imaginative New World" (*Frontier,* 412). As that frontier was pushed back in the postwar years, Whitman's habitat increasingly resembled Disney's Adventureland. The character of the American frontier was radically and definitively altered to one of exploitation rather than discovery and settlement at the precise moment of Whitman's euphoric sanitization. In old age Whitman avoided the malignant specifics of American history—specifics for which he had patiently amassed his vocabulary of inventory—and the later voice dims noticeably to that of the good conscience offering Boy Scout prescriptions (at the very end, in fact, Whitman hoped for success with a bowdlerization of his own book, to be called *Leaves of Grass, Junior*).

Looking back from the present abundance of American poetry, we can see in the multivolume *Testimony* by Charles Reznikoff and the road-show dystopics of *The Fall of America* by Allen Ginsberg, if not the Whitmanian rendering, at least the quantity of horrifying detail accompanying American imperialism. One installment of *Testimony* documents the years 1891 (the date of Whitman's death) to 1900. The different sections are comparable in length to the sections in Whitman's sequence poems, and Reznikoff displays much of Whitman's stamina (if not his personable gusto). The first two sections document teams of horses being driven out on weak ice to their death in the water below; the third a mule train hit by a locomotive. The book goes on to chronicle—in as toneless and unassuming a language as any American poet has written—thievery, rape, mutilation, murder, and sundry acts of astonishing viciousness. Driven by curiosity, a boy looks into a laundry only to be confronted with a woman saying, "You will look in here, will you!" as she throws a bowl of lye into his face.

> His mother came to the laundry
> and shouted, "Why did you do that to my poor little boy?"
> And the wife of the laundryman answered: "Yes, I done it,
> and will do it again if I have a chance.

I will make them keep away from my door!"

The boy's eyes ulcerated,
burst and sloughed away,
and the lids grew together on what was left of the eyeballs.

To read all of *Testimony* is unnerving; and it's no surprise that it comes from a man who also wrote a book-length verse chronicle, *Holocaust.* Reznikoff is not the poet Whitman failed to become, but he is an indication of Whitman's complacency as the nation assumed its modern dominance. No wonder Jack Spicer reproaches the bard: "you whose fine mouth has sucked the cock of the heart of the country for fifty years. You did not ever understand cruelty."

In the 1855 preface to *Leaves of Grass,* Whitman spoke of the poet as "the pioneer who 'leaves room ahead of himself,' . . . He places himself where the future becomes present . . . he glows a moment on the extremest verge." For a time he perched on that verge alert to every extremity, cognizant of a "dark obverse" to fledgling nationalism (Sauer, 147). But the most extreme verge Whitman could celebrate, as the century drew to its close, was the World's Fair, that comfortable descendent of the English peep-show spectacle of exotic Orient and faraway places of empire. The strongest section of the 1871 "Song of the Exposition" is its litany of a vanished world of European legend (lines 22–59), followed by a prescient transumption of American destiny in the person of the housewife, "install'd amid the kitchen ware!" The opening of the poem envisions the national task as "Not to repel or destroy so much as accept, fuse, rehabilitate, / To obey as well as command, to follow more than to lead." To accept, fuse, rehabilitate—these are the terms with which Thomas Jefferson sought to apply his racial philanthropy to the American natives; and Whitman's "to follow more than to lead" describes an arc in American politics scarcely completed yet. Whitman's final abdication from the actual history at hand is as much his legacy to American poetry as his earlier strident vision of the young prewar nation. His great five-year beginning was his "moment on the extremest verge"; as that moment receded, he uncannily took on the artificial glow of Edison's new invention, the electric filament bulb. "Song of the Exposition" hails the nation for its industry ("thy rapid patents") and its leviathan attainment of "wide geographies, manifold, different, distant, / Rounded by thee in one—one common orbic language, / One common indivisible destiny for All" which Whitman could hardly foresee becoming an omnivorous conformity. Looking back at the new buildings of 1871, we can hardly comprehend Whitman's acclaim of "Earth's modern wonder, history's seven outstripping, / High rising tier on tier with glass and iron façades, / Gladdening the sun and sky." The Treasury Building in Washington, D.C., gladdening sun and sky? Whitman's increasing use in later years of the antiquarian "thee" (forfeiting his arduous struggle to shed himself earlier of such poetic affectations) completes his mummification as resident national poet in the pornotopia of American kitsch culture, that bulwark of hyperbolic anachronism. Whitman even sings the sarcophagal stones into place: "this and these, America, shall be *your* pyramids and obelisks."

What distinguishes an early poem like "Our Old Feuillage" from the later "Song of the Exposition"—both poems undertake a kinescope version of the "continent of Democracy"—is the centrality of one Walt Whitman, vulnerable, mortal, polysexual watcher: the man who stands apart yet who is "the joiner, he sees how they join." In "Our Old Feuillage" he is not yet the self-effacing chronicler and neutral enthusiast of an emerging society of the spectacle. Whitman presents himself in the modern manner of the home-movie voice-over: "Southward there, I screaming, with wings slow flapping, with the myriads of gulls wintering along the coasts of Florida," but this image suggests a unison with his animal counterpart (as his lament merges with the mockingbird on the beach in "As I Ebb'd"), a union based on the scream. Later in the poem, in its only clear instance of aggression, he returns as the endangered animal: "In Kanadian forests the moose, large as an ox, corner'd by hunters, rising desperately on his hind-feet, and plunging with this fore-feet, the hoofs as sharp as knives—and I, plunging at the hunters, corner'd and desperate, / In the Mannahatta, streets, piers." The empathetic vulnerability of such scenes has its license from the threshold, the margin, the edge or verge of opposing spaces and types, a rim where sediment accumulates traces of a furtive passage. As Susan Howe speculates, "Maybe margins shelter the inapprehensible Imaginary of poetry" (*The Birth-mark,* 29).

. . . A
darkness there
like tar,
like bits of
drift at ocean's
edge. A slow

retreat of
waters beaten
back upon
themselves.

An undertow
of whir im-
mersed in
words.

The rim, the sediment

In its first fire Whitman's verse was magnificently tropic, a crisp, biodegradable composition of the States (not yet "United" but cosmically chaotic) into a demonized poetic topos; a body of work that might have as its most fitting epigraph not the overconfident "Song of the Open Road" singled out by D. H. Lawrence, but "This Compost." Of the major poems, only "I Sing the Body Electric," "Song of Myself," and "The Sleepers" precede it. The grand collection of shorter gems and "sparkles from the wheel" in the 1892 edition of *Leaves of Grass* are beach stones that roar and scrape under the immense tidal pressure of some two dozen poems written by 1860.*

The poise of Whitman's vitality was derived from that fluid terror of Being that courses unhindered through animal life.

> Now I am terrified at the Earth, it is that calm and patient,
> It grows such sweet things out of such corruptions,
> It turns harmless and stainless on its axis, with such endless successions of diseas'd corpses,
> It distills such exquisite winds out of such infused fetor,
> It renews with such unwitting looks its prodigal, annual, sumptuous crops,
> It gives such divine materials to men, and accepts such leavings from them at last.

Whitman the poet falls in love with the sweetness of such corruption, celebrating its fatal appeal in "Out of the Cradle Endlessly Rocking":

* In addition to those listed above, I would single out "A Woman Waits for Me," "Spontaneous Me," "On the Beach at Night Alone," "Song of the Open Road," "Crossing Brooklyn Ferry," "Song of the Answerer," "Starting from Paumanok," "To the Garden of the World," "From Pent-up Aching Rivers," "Our Old Feuillage," "Out of the Cradle Endlessly Rocking," and "As I Ebb'd with the Ocean of Life."

Whereto answering, the sea,
Delaying not, hurrying not,
Whisper'd me through the night, and very plainly before daybreak,
Lisp'd to me the low and delicious word death,
And again death, death, death, death,
Hissing melodious neither like the bird nor like my arous'd child's heart,
But edging near as privately for me rustling at my feet,
Creeping thence steadily up to my ears and laving me softly all over,
Death, death, death, death, death.

This is on no account the consolation provided by Keats's nightingale, "half in love with easeful death," but an implacably alien yet intimate insistence. The repetition of the word "death" establishes by rhythmic habitation an enlarged premonition. This word, this "strong and delicious word," "the word up from the waves," "the key" of a "thousand responsive songs at random," resounds in the mockingbird's lament for its lost mate. The mockingbird, embraced by Whitman as "my dusky demon and brother," is an erotic presence commensurate with the sexual testament of the poems "Spontaneous Me" and "A Woman Waits for Me." The keynote in these poems is unambiguously the "husky pantings through clinch'd teeth" (of "Not Heaving from my Ribb'd Breast Only"), and here the physical source of Whitman's lifelong emission of poetic lines as "Beautiful dripping fragments" is confirmed. The taste for death develops as a sexual exultation.

Love-thoughts, love-juice, love-odor, love-yielding, love-climbers, and the climbing sap,
Arms and hands of love, lips of love, phallic thumb of love, breasts of love, bellies press'd and glued together with love . . .

Whitman's own sexual identity is consistently that of the "limpid liquid within the young man," and it's here if anywhere that the demonic character of his romance with corruption has a truly pioneer quality. Whitman's sexual body is the dark spot on his verse, which no America short of his fantastic vistas of interracial and multisexual mingling will ever consentingly include.* The sea's whispered word

* The "homosocial" text evident in Whitman's verse has attracted much commentary, explicitly sanctioning the supposition of the poet's homosexuality. But the preoccupation with rendering Whitman gay begins to sound as prudentially fixated on its own terms as the former tendency to claim him as a heterosexual hero. The axis of distinction deserves to be differently drawn, possibly even in the terms advanced by his friends, who distinguished

from its "liquid rims and wet sands" is death, as "I too but signify at the utmost a little wash'd-up drift," "a trail of drift and debris," a coital detritus (echoed later in Rexroth's lines "The waves of the sea fall through / Our each others indomitable / As peristalsis").

> Me and mine, loose windrows, little corpses,
> Froth, snowy white, and bubbles,
> (See, from my dead lips the ooze exuding at last,
> See the prismatic colors glistening and rolling) . . .

"Song of the Open Road" concludes with Whitman's injunction to take to the road and "Let the paper remain on the desk unwritten." So the poem he's just composed to forge his commitment is made to unwrite itself. This is the fatal Whitmanian gesture: the writing unwrites itself, effacing the poet before the Republic. Whitman becomes a one-time pioneer, gradually surrounded by communities pledged to another form of commerce than that to which he committed himself in "This Compost" and "Out of the Cradle." His alliance with bodily joys was the resource of a telling vulnerability; and as long as the sense of sexual exposure was both the shame and the most exalted avowal in his work, Whitman's sensitivity to persecution and subjugation persisted, giving the poems over in emphatic comradeship to the survivor and the outcast.

Whitman's poems situate the tropics for later American poetry as simultaneously a scene of unwriting and a view of the body's compositional heat. The mockingbird's dirge is a lament for a lost sexual partner, and this harrowing cry combining sex and death is Whitman's surest mode, his bass drone. In the poem the bird's song arouses the poet out of the lad. The scene of composition is the ocean marge, its volume of sound far surpassing the isolated voice. As sensual passion and metaphysical argument, the ocean is irrepressible. Its tides write lines on the body of exposed land: "Held by this electric self out of the pride of which I utter poems, / [I] was seiz'd by the spirit that trails in the lines underfoot"—lines that are equally lines of the poems.

---

the sexual dimension of *Leaves of Grass* from " 'the anonymous lascivious trash spawned in holes and sold in corners' "—a dimension Whitman pioneered in order " 'to rescue from the keeping of blackguards and debauchees, to which it has been abandoned . . . the great element of amativeness or sexuality, with all its acts and organs' " (Reynolds, *Walt Whitman's America,* 206).

On the beach, that strip of land between "all the water and all the land of the globe," the lines underfoot are the imprint of the tide, just as the ocean of life ebbing in Whitman's body is a reflection of geophysical song lines that become lines of the poem. In poetry, topographic space is coextensive with a typographic dimension. This has been amplified by Olson's insistence on taking "SPACE to be the central fact to man born in America" (*Call Me Ishmael,* 11). Whitman's lines drawn on sand by the ocean are the first facts of his geophysical identification of the labor of the poem with the ocean as ultimate compost, organically "Hissing melodious" its chant of "death, death, death, death."

Systems of energy are being proposed here in something so apparently simple as the setting of the poem. The various means of transcription—the writing of the waves on the beach, the ocean of life surging in the poet's "I" and the styles of the poem or chant—are simultaneous but not identical. As the refrain comes "Hissing melodious, neither like the bird nor like my arous'd child's heart," there is a harmony or polyphony of the three voices: the sea, the bird, and the child-poet. Their vocal union is achieved only on "The rim, the sediment that stands for all." Here on the rim the "arous'd child" curiously becomes displaced by the poet, who never ceases to proclaim himself the (sexually) aroused man. The terms of the vision continue to split and multiply. Not only is the aroused wonder of the boy fused with the sexual arousal of the adult, but within the man a sexual split occurs by which he identifies sex itself as polytropic.

With "Song of Myself," Whitman had ineradicably written his story as the plot of the nation, unalterably written sex and death into the plan ("Copulation is no more rank to me than death is") and thereby made the national epic a compendium of "forbidden voices / Voices of sexes and lusts, voices veil'd and I remove the veil." And from "Song of Myself" the scene of vision—the *rim* on which the vocal and sexual unions sing part-song with the Union of the States—is a kind of no man's land where litter drifts up in the sea spume. The scene reappears (deformed) a century later in Oppen:

> The sea and a crescent strip of beach
> Show between the service station and a deserted shack
>
> A creek drains thru the beach
> Forming a ditch
> There is a discarded super-market cart in the ditch
> That beach is the edge of a nation

This, remember, under Whitman's tutelage, was to have been the scene of transfiguring *vision:*

> Fascinated, my eyes reverting from the south, dropt, to follow those slender windrows,
> Chaff, straw, splinters of wood, weeds, and the sea-gluten,
> Scum, scales from shining rocks, leaves of salt-lettuce, left by the tide,
> Miles walking, the sound of breaking waves the other side of me,
> Paumanok there and then as I thought the old thought of likenesses,
> These you presented to me you fish-shaped island,
> As I wended the shores I know,
> As I walk'd with that electric self seeking types.

But now, "A cold wind chills the beach. / The long lines of it grow longer," Stevens writes (echoed by Michael Palmer: "The lines through these words / form other, still longer lines"), seeking with Whitman the "spirit that trails in the lines underfoot"; like John Ashbery, convinced that the beach is "The sum of all that will ever be deciphered / On this side of that vast drop of water" (anticipating his convex mirror by globalizing the ocean into a single sphere); or for A. R. Ammons, the locale "where not a single single thing endures, / the overall reassures" in "limited orders, / the separate particles." For Ammons in the seashore amble of "Corsons Inlet," "I allow myself eddies of meaning: / . . . but Overall is beyond me: is the sum of these events / I cannot draw, the ledger I cannot keep, the accounting / beyond the account." The effort, taken in concluding resolve, is "to fasten into order enlarging grasps of disorder, widening / scope." In Ammons's affirmation of

> an order held
> in constant change: a congregation
> rich with entropy: nevertheless, separable, noticeable
> as one event,
> not chaos

it is as if Whitman's own lines were becoming the beach sediment where Olson notes the opulence of ocean sludge en route to the De-Hy to be processed into cat food. And like Olson, Ammons secures the order of his poems on a fund of disorder permeating the occasion and charging it with energy out of entropy:

> the possibility of rule as the sum of rulelessness:

the "field" of action
with moving, incalculable center

"I've often said that a poem in becoming generates the laws of its / own becoming," Ammons remarks in "Essay on Poetics," rendering composition by field accessible in his homespun way. Ammons's qualification of the organic model is relevant to the "extremest verge" of Whitman's poetics. As he notes, the growing plant executes a preordained genetic code, whereas

> . . . real change occurs along the chromosomes, a risky business
> apparently based on accidence, chance, unforeseeable distortion:
> the proportion of harmful to potentially favorable mutations is
>
> something like 50,000 to 1: how marvelous that the possibility of
> favorable change is a flimsy margin in overwhelming, statistically,
> destruction and ruin: that is the way nature pours it on . . .

"What does not change / is the will to change," Olson declared in "The Kingfishers." In *Sphere* Ammons concurs: "we want to change without changing / out of change." "We change to keep all else the same" (James Koller). And Muriel Rukeyser: "The only danger is in not going far enough. The usable truth here deals with change" (*Life of Poetry,* 201). One does not "change the world"—a futile repetition of the Prometheus complex—but change the mind that conceives, and accedes to, that composition of the real we acknowledge as a world. Succinctly, Ronald Johnson advises young poets, "Your task is to change the world by word alone" ("From Hurrah for Euphony," 31). A daunting prolegomenon.

"The usable truth here deals with change"; and this entails corresponding injunctions. For Clayton Eshleman: "Watch out for unity as you age, / it's in cahoots with reduction." This reflection arises on another beach ("I'm a little boy in my glandbox / sifting mommy purr, / the simmerunderoar spreads / a virus under tone") where, yet again, a poet confronts his calling.

Mallarmé's throw still tumbling in the air,

poetry as shipwreck,   oceanic page,
"a throw of the dice"   the gamble of alchemical research
"will never abolish chance"   no way
   to predetermine reception—

Unless a work of art is its own shipwreck
a master is proposed outside the maelstrom

Poets of the composting imagination remain on that rim, still seeking, like Whitman, *types* (and Olson would later extend this literally to the typewriter, then trace it back to the Greek word *typos* to suggest the groove on the page that is the material residue of the blow of the type).* These are archetypes in the true sense of *arche*—they are "blows from an original," as it were. Remember that *psyche* as a verb (ψυχειη) means "to blow" (Onians, 120), and this blowing or motive force that leaves *types* on parchment or sandy beach is an original force, a psycho-typography. So one of the more persistent stories in American poetry *is* this persistence. There may be a fallacy in the notion of "getting back to the basics," but there is no mistaking the blow of the original. As long as bodies persist, sex and death imprint us with types of the *arche*, blows of polysexual sediment commanding *psyche*. The word *Whitman* remains one of those archetypal blows, as all the psyche there is of him now (as if this were the instruction) is in type. Dickinson also offers her remains, not in type (though it has come to that) but in the antitype of script, her fascicles reading like poetic ligatures of a provisional camaraderie she was in search of, private monstrance of some Brook Farm in psyche. Her work reaches an apogee of reversals† in which, abjuring publication (as untoward auction of the soul), she gains personal access to an unimaginably larger "public"—nothing short of an exfoliating cosmos where " 'No' is the wildest word we consign to Language" (*Selected Letters*, 246)—in which there could be no "Privacy / From Nature's sentinels," in which "Creation seemed a mighty Crack — / To make me visible —" (no. 891).

* Sadly, this haptic resource is no longer evident in books produced by photographic methods, the universal standard of publication since the 1960s.

† We go no further with the Dust
Than to the Earthen Door —
And then the Panels are reversed —
And we behold — no more. (Dickinson, no. 920)

Necropoetics

The seashore is a summons:

These things I would record:
        the drift of sand
at the edge of the sea's eternal roar
where my dry hands impetuous for sound
        unlock from keys
inventions from inventions of the world's music

The face of the shore is under ceaseless erasure by overinscription, awash with spirit traffic in sublunary plenitude, composing in tidal rhythms "runes upon the sand / from sea-spume." These traces are nudges and winks from the dead. "They are dead. That is they do not answer. What is this busyness of theirs they do not answer to our calls?" They are nurses of a dismembering undertow, the oceanic vegetal threat Zukofsky feels in "green kelp waves arms, dips / tons my only eyes fear."

Poets since Whitman have gone to the shore to watch the great trails of writing, entrails of earthscript; to be themselves reduced to spectres and revenants *within* that typology. In this "Zwischenraum," or betweenland (to use Rilke's word), "death also / can still propose the old labors" in the sundering of worlds and realms.

white white white   like
        a boundary in death advancing
that is our life,   that's love,
        line upon line
breaking in radiance, so soft-   so dim-
        ly glaring, dominating

        . . . as if half the universe
(neither sky nor earth, without
        horizon)   were forever

breaking into being another half,
        obscurity   flaring into a surf
upon an answering obscurity.

This between-space of ocean rim is the singular gap—like the inside of Heidegger's jug whose emptiness is sustenance (*Poetry, Language, Thought,* 172–73)—the workable ground of tropical poetics. "Like the pieces of a totally unfinished jigsaw puzzle my grandmother left in the bedroom when she died in the living room," this is the space of life, the uncompleted, which in itself composes purposes of living—"As if my grandmother had chewed on her jigsaw puzzle before she died. / Not as a gesture of contempt for the scattered nature of reality. Not because the pieces would not fit in time. But because this would be the only way to cause an alliance between the dead and the living."

Necropoetics is a pledge enacted between the dead and the living. In contrast to the Melville scholars ridiculed by Olson ("you must excuse us if we scratch each other's backs with a dead man's hand"), necropoetics thrives in the tropical heat of the apprehension that

> The realized
> is dung of the ground that feeds us, rots
> falls apart
> into the false,
> displaying wounds of the pure
> urge, mounds
> mulch for covetous burrowing thought.

Thought itself, like an animal snout, roots passages, sniffing its way in to that constant circumference, that spatial and temporal surround of the "realized," mulched in encircling Okeanos.

Affirming Whitman's reminder in "This Compost" that the earth is an immense reservoir of pestilence, Duncan's temporal extension in "Nor Is the Past Pure" realizes a mortuary perimeter. The fantastic anomaly of culture is that the living are exiles or outsiders, the most isolate of all minorities. The small community of the living extends to the past only by trafficking with the dead, whose mounds are "mulch for covetous burrowing thought." The ground of the dead constitutes the outer limits of the local; and the space of habitation is like a cistern, its hollowness resoundingly provocative. "We have broken through into the meaning of the tomb," writes Ashbery near the opening of *Three Poems,* where "To formulate oneself around this hollow, empty sphere" is the immediate challenge. "Our life is an apprenticeship to the truth, that around every circle another can be drawn," as Emerson puts it in "Circles." In the familiar model of a tossed pebble spreading rings in a pool, the proliferation of circles encompassing other circles benumbs observation. It is a singular narcotic, this manifest realization in stunning symmetry and simplicity, testifying that as we lapse out of ourselves a more vigorous providence scoops up the remainder in a different exaltation—"spelling light for hymn to day recast around loved sound phantom / petal vocable apparent rose stride forward bulky from the tomb."

> To have the whole outline in mind yet not notice the individual changes as they occur, and then one day it dawns on you that you are the change, so naturally you could have seen it coming.
>
> ~
>
> For it is the inert effort of each thought, having formed itself into a circular wave of circumstance . . . to heap itself on that ridge, and to solidify and hem in the life. But if the soul is quick and strong, it bursts over that boundary on all sides, and expands another orbit on the great deep, which also runs up into a high wave, with attempt again to stop and to bind. But the heart refuses to be imprisoned; in its first and narrowest pulses, it already tends outward with a vast force, and to immense and innumerable expansions. ("Circles")

For Duncan, these are "intimations of the secret Mover. / Which we are not permitted without corruption."

> It is only the midden heap, Beauty: shards,
>   scraps of leftover food, rottings,
>   the Dump
> where we read history, larvae of all dead things,
>   mixd seeds, waste, off-castings, despised
>   treasure, vegetable putrifactions
>   : from this adultery committed,
>
> the plant that provides, Corn
>   that at Eleusis Kore brought
> out of Hell, health manifest.

We live in health by the wealth of Hades's house. But when Death dons modern garb, as in Olson's sighting in "Cole's Island," it's in the lugubrious aspect of the property owner and "sportsman." The natty plaid of the necropolitan real estate developer constellates the modern image of "eternal repose"—funereal effigies of

Forest Lawn mocked in the spectre of Mr. Joyboy, ace mortuary cosmetician in *The Loved One.**

The upshot is
(and this the books did not tell us) the race
does not advance, it is only
better preserved

Now all lie
as Miss Harlow

as Sunday supplement mammoths
in ice, as there used to be
waxworks

as ugly as Jericho's
First Citizens, kept there

as skulls, the pink semblance

painted back on

The dead become cosmetic laminations of *nature mort* in a secular age. But the conditions of composition, as of decomposition, are graphic (like the exhumed woman in Snyder's poem "Under the Hills Near the Morava River," with "Diadem of fox teeth round her brow" and "Burnt reindeer-pelvis bone bits / in her mouth"), and it is only as graffiti that writing survives its sediment and stands clear on the rim connecting different times and people, living and dead. In its mortal testimony as graffiti, writing is clutter and debris; trace, husk, scar, sign, particle, element: *bodily remains.*

Duncan's title *The Opening of the Field* declares not just a clearing of space for dancing and benign frolic, but an opening downward, opening the crypt, expounding the glyph of putrefaction. Duncan's book is a manifesto for trafficking with the dead. Not only does the "Structure of Rime" series propose a set of instructions for handling the raw particles of the composted field, but the efficacy of a composting practice is declared throughout in such poems as "Evocation," "Nor Is the Past Pure," "A Poem of Despondencies," "A Storm of White," "Out of the

* Evelyn Waugh's novel was made into an unforgettably lugubrious film in 1965 by Tony Richardson, with a script by Terry Southern and Christopher Isherwood.

Black," "Bone Dance," "Under Ground," and "Food for Fire, Food for Thought." Olson's *The Distances* likewise moves in that vicinity. "The Kingfishers" opens the book, more effective a manifesto than the famous "Projective Verse" essay could possibly be. But nearly every poem in *The Distances* hinges on death or the dead, though certain pieces strike conclusions of a renewable poetics out of that proximity: "In Cold Hell, In Thicket," "The Death of Europe," "As the Dead Prey Upon Us," and "Variations Done for Gerald Van De Wiele." Jack Spicer's *Heads of the Town* completes this triptych of 1960, with its Orphic descent into the underworld to liberate the pronouns, in the process depositing a "Textbook of Poetry" that remains profoundly radical in its disintegrative propensity. Spicer's proximity to the particles of an authentically composted language, taken with the examples of Olson and Duncan, works at the limits of post-Whitmanian necropoetics. Spicer follows Orpheus into a final descent. The emblem of this permission is ancient—as in the *memento mori* or death's head iconography of the visual arts: the oracular skull commanding the trade routes of local traffic, incarnate in the living as ephemeral episodes, constituting a passage of life and death out of holes in texts, vowels like sockets, consonants of bones, meaning as moaned.

> A deer skull, the nasal passages
> like rolled parchment, the forehead
> riddled with geometry (bones
>   are old books and stone liturgies,
>   hidden as the shores of Egypt . . .)
>
> ~
>
> a sheepskull forehead with its horn prongs
> sitting on a boulder—
> an offer of the flower of a
> million years of nibbling forbs
>
> to the emptiness of intelligence

Muses' archetext

Here (hear) is a concord of inaugurations:

And then went down to the ship,

~

Off-shore, by islands hidden in the blood

~

A
 round of fiddles playing Bach

These are the beginnings of poems that mark the boundaries of their authors' lives. (*The Cantos* and *The Maximus Poems* were never definitively completed, while Zukofsky died a few years after finishing *"A."*) Inspiration verges on expiration. This is precisely the nature of the duplicity of the Muses, whose gifts of song or honeyed words are always initiatory detours, beginnings, and "a beginning shows us how much language, with its perpetual memories of silence, can do to summon fiction and reality to an equal space in the mind. In this space certain fiction and certain reality come together as identity. Yet we can never be certain what part of identity is true, what part fictional" (Said, 373). The founding myth of Hesiod's encounter with the Muses on Mount Helikon has proven enormously consequential for poetry. The Muses tell him that "we know how to say many lies similar (or identical) to true things, but if we want, we know how to sing the truth" (*Theogony,* book l, lines 26–28). It is not for Hesiod to determine whether the discourse, the *logos,* bestowed by the Muses is true, or a lie masquerading as truth. In the Muses' visit to the poet, the abridgement of sense *is* their inspiration, and the sense that they might make is possibly nonsense. In *Hesiod and the Language of Poetry,* Pietro Pucci comments on the predicament: "Not all song, even that produced by the Muses, is true; nevertheless, sung in the voice of the Muses, it always appears as truth. This disheartening message leaves the poet alone, facing the precariousness of the *logos*" (12). The poet is never to know whether he has been given a true or false discourse. In turn, readers "can never be certain what part of identity is true, what part fictional."

Poems—as distinct from poets—have always known that the Muses bestow *words,* not truth, that the "truth" of the Muses is available only in the sense that "I put down words, and these words desire other words" (Noël, 7). The opening of *"A"* 15, a morphemic transcription of particles desiring other particles, is in an English cohabiting the sound of Job: 38 in Hebrew.

> He neigh ha lie low h'who y'he gall mood
> So roar cruel hire
> Lo to achieve an eye leer rot off
> Mass th'lo low o loam echo
> How deal me many coeval yammer
> Naked on face of white rock—sea.
> *Then* I said: Liveforever my nest
> Is arable hymn
> Shore she root to water
> Dew anew to branch.

It is as if the condition of the schizophrenic prevailed in which "All words become physical and affect the body immediately" (Deleuze, "Schizophrenic and Language," 287). These too-tangible words become lumps of an excrementitious husk taunting the "body without organs" (Humpty Dumpty scorns Alice because her *organ*ized body is punctuated with differentiation—ducts, holes, passages). Deleuze defines the poetic as whatever reflects that which makes language possible, and "Whatever makes language possible is that which separates sounds from bodies, organizes them into propositions, and thus makes them available to assume an expressive function. Without this surface that distinguishes itself from the depths of bodies, without this line that separates things from propositions, sounds would become separable from bodies, becoming simple physical qualities contiguous with them, and propositions would become impossible" (284–85). Alice, in her underground adventure, attaches herself to "sliding along in such a way that depth is reduced to nothing but the reverse side of the surface" (280). The inscrutable obverse need not be *deep.* Like Saussure's model of language as a piece of paper, with the concept on one side and the expression on the other, to cut one is to cut the other (*Course in General Linguistics* 1: 4); or like the rabbit/duck diagram in psychology, in which even prior awareness of the encoded images will not help you see them both at once; in the flicker of difference a world of "différance" is inaugurated—a world like that attested to by the Hassidim, who remark of Heaven that it's just like this world, only a little bit different. Through its propensity to tropism, poetry takes both sides, adopts contrasting perspectives; it suffers the damage of each position. It undergoes this suffering as *typos,* blow or impression, literally the mark of the letter as impressed by pen or type, which makes it a text and composes its surface. The poem stains, scars, dismembers, and disperses itself, not through the punctuation that organizes and dispenses prose meanings, but through the highlighted "music" of the verse, the line breaks, and more recently the actual scatter of words across the surface of the page. Might it be possible to conceive of the dots on Mallarmé's inscrutable dice as punctuation marks *hazarded* on a surface that might be a body after all?—as if, in Kelly's lines, "Art is to show other people / what you cant see yourself" (playing "ars" on the hind part). The purpose of surface "is precisely that of organizing and displaying elements that have come from the depths" (Deleuze, "Schizophrenic and Language," 293). If the reader can be said to understand a text, she *sets its type.* The writer would be on the obverse, *standing under the text.* Olson even speculated that "you wrote as though you were *underneath* the letters" (*Mutbologos* 2: 34)—sticking a head up out of earth, calling to Athena (as in *Maximus* 2: 160)—an image he derived from the typesetter's position of being literally on the underside, facing the bottoms of the letters being set in place in the coign.

The peculiar skill of any art is in making all that is available of itself be surface; even its depths (like the picaresque profundities of *Moby-Dick*) are disclosed only as surface events. This puts writer and reader on more or less equal footing, because although each has a different approach to the text, once the text is in place the surface it makes available is haunted or shadowed by an obverse, the obvious perversity by which it affords glimpses of eaches and anys where every and all appear to lurk. Both sides are never visible at once, although a fundamental tropical urge is to make both sides available in such rapid succession that, like a coin trick, a continuity of the alternating surfaces blends into one demonic animated texture that is posed as identity and surplus indistinguishably; and with this trick, the axis of combination (metonymy) blends into the axis of substitution (metaphor), yielding a New World every time.

Among available modes of discourse, poetry is unique in favoring utopia as transient occasion, not universal city. Poems effectively consume all the energy they generate, and "Every time the poem is read, it disintegrates" (Fussell, *Lucifer in Harness,* 65). At the same time, its disappearance is not a loss of meaning, but a recovery of its obscurity, its underside. The paradox of poems *is* paradise, or being around on the other side of light and law—like the bog Barbara Hurd celebrates in *Stirring the Mud,* "the glistening, soaked, uncertain ground of reverie" (37)—satisfying sense with nonsense, thing with word, context with text, all by each, as if William James's suspicion held, that "*reality MAY exist in distributive form, in the shape not of an all but of a set of eaches, just as it seems to be*" (*Pluralistic Universe,* 688).

The distributed sets of eaches might be said to achieve a constellation in the astronomical sense; but on the human level, there is an accompanying estrangement provoking Olson's declaration, "Isolated person in Gloucester, Massachusetts, I, Maximus, address you / you islands."

> . . . The hand holds no chalk
> And each part of the whole falls off
> And cannot know it knew, except
> Here and there, in cold pockets
> Of remembrance, whispers out of time.

To read poetry is to suffer a continual lapse of meaning into being, message into event. A digestive sensation—even excremental. As the fable of the Muses suggests, poetry displaces or disables the author's putative authority. Yet poetry is inaugurated with Hesiod's willingness to persist as if the words they breathed in his ear were the truth ("just as it seems to be"). He is willing to absorb the naïveté of that confidence into his discourse, and say things that in any other context would appear preposterous. He sings a song of gods, mouthing their myths, while the modern poet appropriates the myth (or mouth) of consciousness (the *episteme* that has replaced myth and been institutionalized as psychology) and, as in Wordsworth's *Prelude,* would make consciousness as such commensurate with mythic awareness. The confounding challenge: "the initiate is expected to remain sober at the feast of thought, even though the language will begin to dance" (Krell, 73).

Because of its tropological associations, poetry can be conceived as a turning back in time, and its resources (riddle and charm [cf. Welsh, *Roots of Lyric*]) can make it seem atavistic. But to turn is not always to return: Hesiod proceeds with the confidence that the Muses' gift will disclose to him not only past and present, but future. The irreducible plurality of the texture of poems is partially an attempt to occupy all three temporalities at once. In a cunning inversion of the archaeological paradigm, where one delves into the earth to divine the past, Emerson suggests that "poetry was all written before time was, and whenever we are so finely organized that we can penetrate into that region where the air is music, we hear those primal warblings and attempt to write them down, but we lose ever and anon a word or a verse and substitute something of our own, and thus miswrite the poem." The "primal warblings" are denominations of the same fund from which Muses arise. A peculiar dividend of Emerson's account is that the poet is able to distort the "colossal cipher" of primal language; so his proposed defense against this willful individuation is a libidinous oracular thaw of fossilized nectar, the "ravishment of the intellect by coming nearer to the fact":

> . . . until at last rage draw out of thee that *dream power* which every night shows thee is thine own, a power transcending all limit and privacy, and by virtue of which a man is the conductor of the whole river of electricity. Nothing walks, or creeps, or grows, or exists, which must not in turn arise and walk before him as exponent of his meaning. Comes he to that power, his genius is no longer exhaustible. All the creatures by pairs and by tribes pour into his mind as into a Noah's ark, to come forth again to people a new world. This is like the stock of air for our respiration or for the combustion of our fireplace: not a measure of gallons, but the entire atmosphere if wanted. ("The Poet")

An entire atmosphere, transcending all limit and privacy as Emerson forecast: this is what makes *"A"* and *The Maximus Poems* a circumference within which recent poetry internalizes the local, enacts its location, sustaining evidence of the outermost in syntax rather than reflection (the old sublime), trope as grammar unbound. The great labor of these two texts inheres in smudges, mistakes admitted, reflections in which thought (reflection) is subject to the subject's (reader's) breath fogging the glass—condensation that clears, revealing a bounty of lucent interiority to which Robin Blaser returns (shard after shard) in "Image-Nations."

the voice is *recognizable*
as fragments
of a greater language,
a live and changing
face

~

the language, older and other
than we are
prehistoric, sacred
geography
turns in the wind
uprooted

~

but language is other than ourselves,
older, moves by itself,   and my
heart in it is only an event-

series   a discontinuity rather than
the author's unity

In antiquity, Psyche appeared in myths as a person, with a predicament, not as an animating principle. The commonplace usage of the word *psyche* was as "breath-soul," from *psuchein,* "to blow." Psyche was associated with procreation and with the head (from which semen was thought to derive), but not with consciousness as such—hence its association with sneezing, the involuntary expression of something (psyche) in the head ("ecstatic / contorting / of the / soul"). In the living, psyche appeared to cooperate with *thumos,* blood-spirit. At death, *thumos* disintegrates, while *psyche* flies to Hades as an *eidolon,* or image (a symbol as it came to mean). As such, "the *psyche* is memory or intelligence dormant, and can under proper circumstances be recalled by grief, love, magic, or poetry" (Vermeule, 41).

The inspired voice of the Muse is *breathed into* Hesiod on Helikon: "The breath communicates a voice almost without sound, an incorporeal whisper. Such an image accounts for both the soundless nature of inspiration and the necessity of controlling poetic language so that it adds itself to things (or the referent) without intruding with its own body and sound" (Pucci, 28). Hesiod's poem is a song of memory and oblivion, which links its legacy with two sources of inspiration: first, the articulation of memory as Mnemosyne, essential for poetry or any system of graphic transcription; and second, the obliteration of memory in Hades, past the river of forgetting, Lethe. (Remember Zukofsky: "To begin a song: / If you cannot recall, / Forget.") In fact, the Greek word for truth, *alethea,* suggests that truth is that which has not yet been taken over the river of oblivion to the land of the dead, the "stupid dead." Small wonder, then, the duplicity of poets, whose strength is as much a foraging among necropolitan ancestry as it is a simple mirroring of *presentable* (appropriate) poetic objects.

"The gift of the Muses should enable the poet to recover a lost privilege, divine memory, and truth: yet it is unsolicited and uncontrollable; it can lead to truth or the worst fallacy; it establishes the origin of poetry in a territory that lies beyond the control of man" (Pucci, 3). The truth of poetry, like a sneeze, is involuntary. The link between poetry and truth is fortuitous and unintended. The Muses' whispers and the Sirens' songs ripple the surface and disturb the depth with sediment and surplus. The fable of the Muses emphasizes dispossession, *alieniloquiam,* or speaking otherwise; and the poet, lending tongue to an othered speech, resumes creation in the very instant of being confounded: "here is the table / Who knows the word for it."

B says, The real table does not exist
I sang my name and turned into a skeleton

. . . .

I sang my name but it sounded strange
I sang the trace then

without a sound,
then erased it

It is as if "through its drafts —conduits— the / poem unnames you as it goes." Sobin's "Dark Drafts" (in *Breath's Burials*), like Mackey's "Songs of the Andoumboulou" (or songs of the first drafts of humankind) and DuPlessis's *Drafts*, engage the world from this groundless prospect of naming as unnaming, where *draft* is both a preparatory version and source of deep chill: "a draft, a stroke, a kind of fear."

An intake
of breath by which birth might be proposed
of something said to've been known
as meaning made with a mouth filled
with air. The soul sucked in by something
said
as thru a crack in the door though the
doors dissolve.

"Unknownness did your sense of touch re-trace my own nothingness?" wonders Susan Howe. "Is a poetics of intervening absence an oxymoron?" (*The Birth-mark*, 27). Facing such a prospect, psychology can offer no *content.* Nor is myth content, but the mu- or mouth-theatre where envoys of visionary circumference appear and disappear, inspiring expirations on whatever margin language itself provides as muthologistical grounding, "the blur, the erasure that is the magic ground in which an image may appear" (Duncan, "Two Chapters from *H.D.*," 90). These images, or messages, are mouths mulching and musing, evidence also of a potent animal intelligence swarming in every text.

In antiquity myth was a repository of this swarming mulch, this publicly dissolving intelligence reformulating human agency in divine tableaux. *The Maximus Poems* are a series of interjections, written on whatever surfaces were available (margins of books, scraps of tickets and napkins, windowframes and walls of Olson's flat). They are transactions of poiesis seeping back into mythos. An Olson poem wants to feel itself scored in mind like a residue of fire, or like life-forms making the long migration from *bios* to fossil. They are musings, and it is to musings that the Muses attend, and a music begins.

> the Muse
> is the 'fate' of the poem
> its 'allotment,' ahead of time   the face of it
> at the end   seen
> at the beginning

Olson coined the word "archetext" as that which transcends an apparent condition, rendering the text itself transparent to the primary power it imagines (*Muthologos* 1: 58). Myth: not a content of the poem (myth, as is the case with wisdom, "is solely a quality of the moment of time in which there might happen to be wisdoms" [*Human Universe,* 71]), but the envoy of its visionary circumference. And within the domain that circumference establishes, both interior and exterior cosmos allow configurations of their powers and persons, agencies of compost inspiring expiration, envisioning the dispensation of particular adherences: for instance, "mythology is not reference / it is *inner inherence*" (*Charles Olson in Connecticut,* 21). Things hold together like the clutch of organs in the bodily cavity, proprioceptively poised. Given with this condition—the abounding bond of mortals—is *sophrosyne,* "the skill of mortality" (Arrowsmith, in Shepard, "Post-Historic Primitivism," 81).

A skin of mouths

To be inspired is to be inducted into danger, so the poet wonders:

> How can I leave you be in me—
>   myths to leap inside of—
> psyche's appetite, soul's mouth
>   bound to rock
>   with monster

"I attempt the discontinuities of poetry," writes Duncan. "To interrupt all sure course of my inspiration." Is inspiration to be understood as a kind of predation? This might illuminate the furor ignited by *The Waste Land* in 1922. It was hardly as genteel an affair as it now sounds; a "living literature" of classic titles was being cannibalized for its nutrients, skull soup, and much of it was being flushed through

Eliot's poem as a kind of sewage, until at the end only three Sanskrit words remained, an atavistic remainder. A bestial affair.

Around my life
an animal paces
alternate
in the shadows of leaves,
a beast whose skin
seems all of mouths.

The issue of poetry is a placental hunger, a craving wonder harboring a question: "what, anyway / was that sticky infusion, that rank flavor of blood, that poetry, by which I lived?" "I, too, have eaten / the meals of the dark shore."

The predatory heritage is at times evident in the carnivore's heavy breath, the animal pacing in the respiration of the text. Or it can be as simple as the paternal gaze, the maternal determination:

My Father . . . his
crowned eye, his horny beak,
  his lingering cry.

And from the thought of him I go
out of all human shape into that pain,
that crows-skin wizard likeness
ravaging man most is,
  having a hand in the claw's work,
the outraging talon
  scraping the hare's bone.

~

I would be a falcon and go free.
I tread her wrist and wear the hood,
talking to myself, and would draw blood.

"[A]nd so the stain uniquely gives consent." The language thrives with animal vitality that may be sustained by, but finally outpaces, pleasure in analogy.* In

* In *Beasts of the Modern Imagination,* Margot Norris considers "writers whose works constitute animal gestures or acts of fatality," artists "who create *as* the animal . . . with their animality speaking" (1). In this "biocentric" lineage an organic vitality prevails over ideas and systems. Norris singles out Darwin, Nietzsche, Kafka, Lawrence, and Max Ernst; but

the demonizing suction of language, where texture gushes, where meaning drains away into whimper and gasp, the poem becomes a shadowland where spectres of fright and gratification arise: "The owls shiver down into the secrets of an earth / I began to see when I lookt into the hole I feard"—in which the recessed owls are sentinels of "the brooding of owl-thought, counselings / . . . ever mute and alive, hidden in all things." Owls are vowels in another intimation by Duncan:

> The vowels are physical
> corridors of the imagination
> emitting passionately
> breaths of flame. In a poem
> the vowels appear like
> the flutterings of an owl
> caught in a web and give
> aweful intimations of
> eternal life.

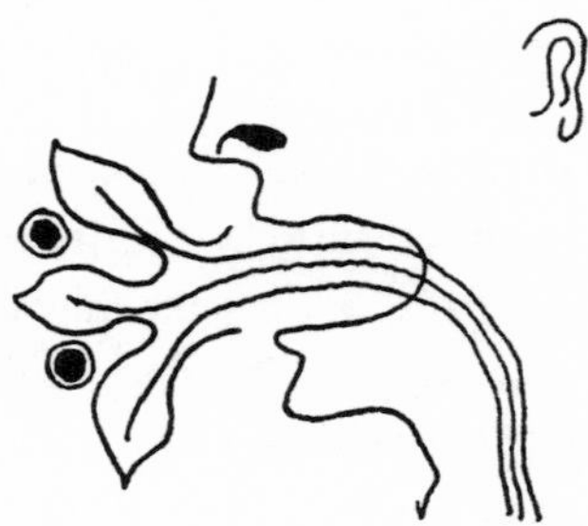

Robert Duncan's pledge to enlivening predation in "My Mother Would Be a Falconress," like Robinson Jeffers's savage alliance with hawks and other predators, is given an alleviating twist in Michael McClure's *Ghost Tantras,* where the *meat science* of the body (routinely glorified by McClure) assumes glottal tremors, vocal stigmata amounting to an *inhumanism* truly exceeding anything Jeffers considered.

> . . . we are strange and deep
> unknown creatures of unspoken melodies:
> GRAYHAYYOWW REEEEEER WEEE GRAHH.
> —OOOH NAYY TAYOWW WEEEEEB, OOOH
> THAH. OOOOOH GRAHHH RAYHOOAYORR
> RAHHR ROOOOOW MAH TAY OHWNEY TEEERZ.

---

her European matrix takes on another resonance when brought into the compass of the composting perspective outlined here. Recapitulating her argument, Norris observes that "anthropocentric theories 'behave' progressively and impressively, like cultural humans, while biocentric theories 'act' regressively, like beasts" (237). The Olsonian insistence on *act* places him within the orbit of bestial reflexivity, as does his concern with marking territorial imperatives in history. The biocentric/projectivist stance adheres always to the embodied agent, the exigent drive that in the end defers any progressivism to its own implacable autopoeisis. The most determined and meticulous biocentric poets since Olson are Michael McClure and Clayton Eshleman.

These animal roars are not even texts, but ritual incitements to mammal wrath. The whole body, performing them, becomes a suction event, a heave of circulatory rhythms; the arterial walls swell, the brain reverts to reptilian dart-eyed predatory awareness, uncannily calm amidst the moans and growls.

Every poem has an alter ego, an animal body as secret sharer of its respiratory distress and its sexual exultation. The panic-euphoric doppelgänger is made explicit in John Ashbery's "Litany," which in its double columns openly shadows the act of reading with its spectral companion (like the apparition in *The Waste Land*—"always another one walking beside you"). The shadow in "Litany" takes place both *alongside* and *as* the text. The parallel columns of verse confound the simple act of reading because each column is haunted by its adjacent twin, unreadable if only for the moment the eyes are already focused on the other column.* The poem stalks itself; its doubling is sinister. "Litany" is a poem working off the hypnotism of the inbreathed, the inscribed encrypted instruction of the text as it arises from both *in*spiration and *ex*piration.

> It goes without saying that
> To have it make sense you
> Would have to belong to all who are asleep
> Making no sense . . .

A different predator hounds Olson in the late *Maximus Poems*. The animal succulence of devotional address is menacing, demanding its share.

> Space and Time the saliva
> in the mouth

* Sixty-five pages long, at midpoint "Litany" includes a dramatic cessation of the left-hand column for nearly two pages (30–31). This gap offers clear enticement for the reader to invest in the other uninterrupted column, to switch loyalties, as it were. Yet even there a haunting occurs: as the left column returns, the right opens the motif of a "Silver Age, which [is] ours" (31), which is subsequently echoed by the other column's " 'Beautiful Lady' " who "Arrives to announce the Brass Age" (33). The polyphonic potential created by adjacent columns, in other words, begins to exponentially exceed the scope of the Joycean leitmotif, transferring it to another dimension. Instead of calling it abstraction, it makes more sense to refer to Ashbery's cross-, inter-, and intratextual torques as distraction (to draw or set apart, subject to centrifugal force; rather than abstraction, getting away from). In general, Ashbery does not allow the reader to "get the point," to glimpse a message, or assign intent—not, at any rate, without being uncomfortably reminded that these are the trappings of a melodramatic set piece.

your own living hand amputated living on
in the mouth

of the Dog

The Dog here is the perimeter of human habitation: (1) as *bios* the dog is the outer circumference of the personal habitus; (2) as *logos* the dog takes a hand, which writes, into his mouth, which does not speak since it's animal: writing is "animal" in its substitution of grapheme for phoneme, writing as biomorphic marking; and (3) as *mythos* the dog belongs to another order of actions and only intersects with the poem and the personal life as an obliquity. There is a bit of vampirism, too, in Keats's "living hand," *mano a mano* with Olson's in the spook of Dogtown. To pass across the perimeter, to trespass the circumference of bios-logos-mythos, is to be penetrated by a *circumferation:* to feel its bite, the circumference of its threat.

the dirty filthy whining ultimate thing

entered,
when none present knew

entered as the dog,
slept in the night

tore the bloody cloak then
literally tore the flesh

of the conjoined
love I was

a dog who had
bitten into

her body
as it was joined

to mine,
naturally

. . . .
the demon
the canine

head piercing
right through the letter carrier

trousers and into the
bone, the teeth of Fenris

craves and locks
directly

into
the flesh, there isn't

any room
except for

pieces, holes
are left

The darkness soaks through the holes. The holes might have been eyes. (The ashes might have been pleasures: "through this hole / at the bottom of the cavern / of death, the imagination / escapes intact.")

I heard words
and words full

of holes
aching. Speech
is a mouth.

"Here the holes in the sieve of your mind open wider. Chunks of forgotten matter drift in. You follow a trail of remains. You get lost, disoriented, hunted. You notice your skin, how the pores themselves can open and close like millions of tiny fish mouths" (Hurd, 142). The hole keeps pouring and aching as long as the language flows. Antonin Artaud picked at his psychic scabs to keep the pus in flow. In *History* Robert Lowell embalmed the pus and sealed each scab as public ornament or mimic monument. The New England jeremiads commemorated in *Lord Weary's Castle* were the elixir in his blood, at once arousing "the jack-hammer jabs" of his cadences and leaving him ruefully surveying his past: "Poets die adolescents, their beat embalms them," Lowell wrote in "Fishnet": "genius hums the auditorium dead." Model poet for his generation, Lowell knew himself to be prey as well:

. . . I heard
The birds inside me, and I knew the Third

Person possessed me, for I was the bird
Of Paradise, the parrot whose absurd
Garblings are glory.

Lowell understood better than anyone the perils of adulation and eminence in a culture confusing aesthetics with commerce. Armand Schwerner, like Olson, finds a predator in the quotidian: "the enemy surrounds us. Words lose their substance, are coopted by mimetic IBM ads, depress; the attitude of distrust toward words spreads to objects. We need a new language, one that we cannot speak, may not be able to speak, unseizable, proliferating like elementary particles in physics: no end to it" (*The Tablets* 136). In fact, his last *Tablets* portend such inscrutable proliferation:

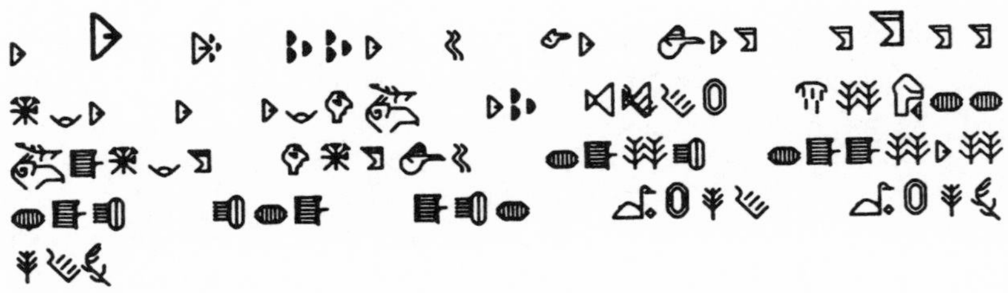

Each word is a boundary where the speech-breath upends into conductive herms of letters. An entire narrative hinges on the indiscretions of particles; holes *in* words and words in holes—fracture of an ancient shamanistic lore in Empedocles's parables of transmigration. "All things have intelligence, and a share of thought" is his guiding principle (56). "Press these things into / the pit of your stomach," he recommends in one fragment; and in another, "sift these words through the guts of your being" (55, 33).* "And you will bring back from Hades a dead man's strength" (56). Language is the animal that returns, *recurs.*

I lie without sleeping, remembering
the ripped body
of hen, the warmth of hen flesh
frightening my hand,

* Blaser rehearses Empedocles's cycle in "Image-Nation" no. 9: "I was once another man's heart / an eagle, a wolf cloud, smoke, / splash / *psychron* (cold, refreshing / *anapsychsai* (to be refreshed from evil // we have eaten ourselves luxurious and / careless."

all her desires,
all her deathsmells,
blooming again in the starlight. And then the wait—

not long, I grant, but all my life—
for the small, soft
thud of her return among the stones.

Can it ever be true—
all bodies, one body, one light
made of everyone's darkness together?

The vessel

In scenes of inspiration, as in cases of shamanistic transport, language descends from a higher power to brutalize the human vessel who suffers it knowingly, gnawingly. To assent to this condition is to follow Robert Kelly in believing that "Language is the only genetics," or to follow Robert Duncan's faith in the somatic pantheon of biochemistry guiding the composition of the poem; or, with Jack Spicer, call it dictation from the Martians. Taken together, these and other testimonies insist on the capacity of the language in its most subconscious particularity as nourishing and enabling, while conceding that unilateral "meaning" may be retarded and balked. Why "enlarge" your mind, asks Ishmael: "subtilize it" (*Moby-Dick,* chap. 74).

The dearth of paraphrasable meaning is acutely evident in Zukofsky's *"A,"* a work that proceeds almost without "thinking" but which everywhere incarnates a fund of sapience. It proposes, in fact, a poetics of condensation and density within which any overarching thematic or philosophical assertions clearly occupy positions of limited relevance. Like the Watts Tower of Simon Rodia or the Palais Ideal of Facteur Cheval—acknowledged models for Ronald Johnson's *Ark* (along with *"A"* itself)—*"A"* is a bricolaged monument that is propositional in its means, in the intricacy with which part weds part: this is why it is finally a book of the family, the household, and the secret of why it is also (like *Finnegans Wake*) conspicuously public (as family life is, as skin, as words). An aggregate cumulonimbus of genetic determination.

To work on a poem spanning fifty years (Pound, Zukofsky) or for several decades (Olson, Johnson) demands not so much stamina as a persistent faith in obscurity, working underground, in the dark, subscribing to indeterminacy as the conditional atmosphere. Negative capability (Keats's famous term adopted as *ars poetica* by Olson): "when man is capable of being in uncertainties, mysteries, doubts, without any irritable reaching after fact and reason" (*Special View of History,* 32)—where the key terms are *capable of being* and *without irritable reaching,* for fact and reason remain salutary options, and doubts and uncertainties are not being affirmed as desirable but as inevitable. Keats's is a vision of good nature. With slight adjustment, it might be taken as an alchemical dictum.

> Alchemy is the science of becoming aware of the whole project in which we are being engaged. Alchemy is the science of being used. Alchemy is the science of use. Its name probably means *the art of the black,* & alludes in all likelihood not to the black soil of Egypt but to the black blankness of the unknown brain, the "silent areas" in which the Operator, bent night & day over his fire, eventually kindles a Voice, one that guides him in the science of penetration, science of final separations. (Kelly, *Alchemist to Mercury,* 82)

To suppose with Lacan that the unconscious is like language is to see in that "black blankness of the unknown brain" an overcharged surface, like Freud's mystic writing pad, a tablet that keeps adding new impressions without erasing the old, becoming a palimpsest of unreadable, impenetrable density.

Olson's animation of Gravelly Hill plays on the boundaries of temporal strata (such as glacial and interglacial), incorporating them into a minutely registered proprioceptive geosophy, hatching personhood from the core of density:

> Gravelly hill was 'the source and end (or boundary' of
> D'town on the way that leads from the town to Smallmans
> now Dwelling house, the Lower
> Road gravelly, how the hill was, not the modern usableness
> of any thing but leaving it as an adverb as though the Earth herself
> was active, she had her own characteristics, she could
> stick her head up out of the earth at a spot
> and say, to Athena I'm stuck here, all I can show
> is my head but please, do something about
> this person I am putting up out of the ground into your hands.

For the condition of the poetry is not enclosed in a book, but knitted into your skin; it folds your wrinkles into its holography; it makes reading a compact with writing, becoming wreading. It is the juncture of two worlds, the simultaneous identification of yourself and your text as a language so immediately present to consciousness as to be unconscious, as close and intimate as the tactility of your inner arm or thigh.

the Greeks
                    made much of *chros,* face of the body's
joining with the world, membrane of the self
at the brink of the gap, where the chaos of all
not integumented with
                                        the world of order we feel
from inside out
                        begins. Skin.

Dermal appetite; parchment of skin; where "craving" and "carving" exchange phonemes in a murmur of particularities.

In the synactic compactness of *"A"* 22 the location is plainly *language indiscriminable from earth:*

. . . Laminated marl—fret changes
only himself, to prove peach
blooms, cherry blossoms, dogwood: seen
seeded flower; unaltered flowerless marriage
of spore. Races endure more
slowly than languages unconsciously sounding
skills as of bees in
a hive, animal passions range
human, alike their affections individual:
if created Once (*a thought*)
or thought of consecutively fossiliferous
marl saved froghopper, ladybird, glowworm,
red admiral, mingling in dredged
lake mud, anachronous stone, horn,
bone, jade, an armlet's brass
wire, flax plaited, not woven,
carbonized apple, raspberry, blackberry seed,
wild plum drupe, reindeer antler
nowhere, remains of a larger
hunting dog, a forest pony,

a burnt brick, and round
small bodies—fossils of the
white chalk—might have been
strung together as beads, the
bond that united them unbroken.
The departed celestial radiated alive
under earth rest will not
return above to hunger, sustained
by mayapple root, their children
unmolested fleeted by glowworms before
stars course ocean flicker continents.

Excavation of a Neolithic settlement; compost library: the mystery of terrestrial space "strung together as beads, the / bond that united them unbroken," all the elements in this vast involuntary configuration concurring that surface then is "not / Superficial but a visible core"—where "bright life needles every clod." It becomes possible to read layers of earth as multitemporal surfacing, as Olson comes to it in "Maximus, From Dogtown—II":

earth is interesting:
ice is interesting
stone is interesting

flowers are
Carbon
Carbon is
Carboniferous
Pennsylvania

Age
under
Dogtown
the stone

the watered
rock Carbon
flowers, rills

~

tropical forests hardened to coal

and the making of mountains:

the wedge of sediments pressed and up-
lifted
crumpled squeezed wrinkled
raised and eroded
overturned
and overthrust over the planes of fracture

~

. . . I became aware
That beneath me, beneath the gravel
And the hurrying ants, and the loam
And the subsoil, lay the glacial drift,
The Miocene jungles, the reptiles
Of the Jurassic, the cuttlefish
Of the Devonian, Cambrian
Worms, and the mysteries of the gneiss;
Their histories folded, docketed
In darkness; and deeper still the hot
Black core of iron, and once again
The inscrutable archaic rocks,
And the long geologic ladder,
And the living soil and the strange trees,
And the tangled bodies of lovers
Under the strange stars.

~

the faithfulness I can imagine would be a weed
flowering in tar, a blue energy piercing
the massed atoms of a bedrock disbelief.*

The issue of such wreading, then, is persistence in negative capability, dark burrowing while sending up fresh shoots (as in the alchemical engraving of the buried king's legs sprouting as a tree), in this subterranean density of copenetrating lan-

* I would add to Rich's placement here her homage to Olson in naming *The Will to Change* (1968) after Olson's line from "The Kingfishers"—Rich's epigraph as well as title—"what does not change / is the will to change."

guage and earth that is nonetheless *all surface,* a biodegradable strata of attention in which

> the tree, the cup, the star, the bird
> in all the rich garden of what we would cultivate in ourselves
> *moan*   and strive to utter what they are
> up.

The tropological discovery of language as material has enabled this dynamic recognition of thought *as matter* to emerge in the work of Zukofsky, Duncan, Spicer, and others. Ashbery's "Self Portrait in a Convex Mirror" is a poem concerned with precisely this issue of a soluble surface in which "more keeps getting included / Without adding to the sum," yet within which nothing appears that doesn't immediately enter the distribution of parts in time. Ashbery's strict attention to the cognitive relativity of objects in a field (particularly in *Three Poems*) complements Olson's geophysical thematic. "I cannot explain the action of leveling," Ashbery writes, "Why it should all boil down to one / Uniform substance, a magma of interiors." Olson:

> the greater the water you add
> the greater the decomposition
> so long as the agent is protein
> the carbon of four is the corners
>
> in stately motion to sing in high bitch voice the fables
> of wood and stone and man and woman loved.

A giddiness, a weightless suspension attends this call of the sirens, who might well be voices from a legendary place under Ocean where everything comes apart. In Duncan's "Adam's Way," Mrs. Maybe tells Adam:

> You were fluid then, a network of soul,
>   spread for miles about,
> breaking and remaking itself in waves.
> God and Nature broke and remade themselves in you.
>
> All this fluid Being was calld Atlantis . . .

What Kelly calls "The gods / broken into the pieces that are us," Zukofsky is astonished to recognize as familiar neighbors: "why that was you that / is how you weather division." Or Duncan, considering the "Place Rumord to Have Been

Sodom," allows that it "might have been. / Certainly these ashes might have been pleasures." Sodom; Atlantis; Olson's Dogtown in the hills above Gloucester; Pound's Templar holdout, Montsegur—"wind space and rain space"—all are places reflecting that insatiable drive of poetry (as Paul Valéry said of philosophy) to transform everything we know into what we would like to know. Another French poet, Francis Ponge, said "the function of poetry . . . is to nourish the spirit of man by giving him the cosmos to suckle. We have only to lower our standard of dominating nature and raise our standard of participating in it in order to make the reconciliation take place" (*Voice of Things,* 109). Confronting such an imposing order, Ponge seeks "a poetry through which the world so invades the spirit of man that he becomes almost speechless, and later reinvents language"—something like the art envisioned by Emily Dickinson (no. 1247):

> To pile like Thunder to its close
> Then crumble grand away
> While Everything created hid
> This — would be Poetry —
>
> Or Love — the two coeval come —
> We both and neither prove —
> Experience either and consume —
> For None see God and live —.

So "truth" (like any reified percept) is only a function of what might become of it, the detour or possible moment of nontruth as in a trope—the aspiration of Stevens's "Sleight-of-Hand Man" who seeks "the life / That is fluent in even the wintriest bronze," the grim yet benevolent imagination "which in the midst of summer stops // To imagine winter." And what could it imagine but that unwobbling, empty pivot, "The Snow Man," as the poem vaults out on its comely surmise:

> For the listener, who listens in the snow,
> And, nothing himself, beholds
> Nothing that is not there and the nothing that is.

With these lines the poem closes in on that vessel (bearing in mind the alchemical vessel) that is the object of Heidegger's scrutiny in "The Thing," in which he maintains that the jug does not contain its liquid; rather, "The emptiness, the void, is what does the vessel's holding. The empty space, this nothing of the jug, is what the jug is as the holding vessel. . . . The vessel's thingness does not lie at all in the material of which it consists, but in the void that holds" (*Poetry, Language, Thought,* 169); "in the shattering of the cup He / keeps the cup," Duncan writes.

The work of snowman, jug, or poem is not to exist *as* that material phenomenon, but to bring to focus the space and to enlarge the sapience through which pass transient forms with their combustible magnifications. The blank aperture the language itself holds in trust is exemplified by the shifters (deictic terms like pronouns and prepositions—you and this, she and there and now—the meaning of which is always context specific), the clearing into which articulate combinations of material reform and trope themselves back to unboundedness. "[W]rist high unwearying bent, cosmos / fingers order trope to trope," Zukofsky writes in *"A"* 22, "AN ERA / ANYTIME / OF YEAR"—a text of which it can be said less that Zukofsky writes than that "Zukofsky" *is composed* of such particularities as "a," "an," "&," "and," and "the," which generate history, language, and *whomans* (Don Byrd's delectable neologism shuffling woman and man into that monstrous hybrid, an interrogative noun [*Great Dimestore Centennial,* 98]), trope on trope.

The work of poetry is less to entertain images than to pass human order through the mulching of language. Not a *naturalism,* but a means of keeping in touch with the principle of natural depletion; to hold—in whatever clearing can be achieved in verbal space—that confluence of public and private ends, so that "end" may be taken in both its "proper" sense of *goal* and its "tropic" sense as *ground,* compost, *costume* where "The Cosmos / begins at the end of yourself":

> The wickedness
> for man is that he is only self begotten only begotten son of
> himself monogenetic creature circumferated by the limit of himself
> circumambulating in the Dogtown meadow with the chance not to struggle
> with the bull but on the air to smell and follow the perfume of the rotting
> fish: as you bear to the left circumambulating the black stone the *niger*
> of the fish, if that's what is at the center of the pasture drunk
> in the night or in splendor in matador's costume in the Sunday light of
> afternoon whatever smell the fish the degradation under control produces
> one hundred percent protein or nature is busy eating it up The Cosmos
> begins at the end of yourself It includes you It wavers and retires it
> advances and disappears it gathers as the flies do on the pile of smoked
> fish it evaporates into the air . . .

~

Jack Clarke's 'we are under image'
rythmos (form's movement) to walk into 'the
primordial always exists' face to face always outside
ourselves the astonishment is
that *it is kosmos*
playing out with one man entheos
they are
the *flowing boundary* taking birth *taking leave*
at the point of the heart a continual
division of halves

The name of such halving is sharing. It is a work of symbolism, of sundered pieces rejoined; the law of push and pull, or Emersonian "compensation," in which "An inevitable dualism bisects nature, so that each thing is a half, and suggests another thing to make it whole"; and in which "Every excess causes a defect; every defect an excess" ("Compensation"). Of course for Emerson the defect belongs to the arcana of good fortune, also known as "nature": "Nature sends no creature, no man into the world without adding a small excess of his proper quality . . . a slight generosity, a drop too much" ("Nature"). In "Compensation" this is the principle by which "The value of the universe contrives to throw itself into every point." The points are like numeric dots on dice, and "The dice of God are always loaded": "What we call retribution is the universal necessity by which the whole appears wherever a part appears."

Nigredo

To every ascension there is a corresponding descent, involving passage over a threshold or through a gate.

All things move toward
the light
except those
that freely work down
to oceans' black depths
In us an impulse tests
the unknown

~

> I passed through the lens of darkness
> as through a furrow, and the dead
> gathered to meet me.

A herm is a pile of commemorative stones left for Hermes, the Bringer, guide of soul from world to world (soul as message, Hermes the messenger), from vessel to vessel, moment to moment to endowment. Under Hermes's sponsorship, dice, bones, sticks, and quills begin to speak, forming a living body of graffiti, a graphic crypt of signs. The herm evoked in every roll of the dice enumerates the name of the throw. As if throw were thaw.

> The descent to a level plain with scattered small hills before the river—there is a mound we climb in the moonlight to look for the mountains of the plains, never visible by day—and the chill that comes then is the shake of an oracle, the cast of an augury, small haruspices cut in the air—there, the small stone picked up without thinking is everything, the unattended stray memories, everything, in the throw of the vision, the catch of us in the vision.

Earth ventriloquism. Penetrating, suffusing, hypnotic. A narcosis of tropical conductivity, blending the living with the dead. Lure of a gregarious polysemia. It is a hermetic propensity of psyche to compact all space and distance into exertions of the local:

> strong like a puddle's ice
> the bios
> of nature in this
> park of eternal
> events is a sidewalk
> to slide on, this
> terminal moraine.

The scale of *that* puddle—"150,000 years ago to the t"—is the timeform of continental drift, sea voyage of a world under composition, tectonic plates malleable as "a puddle's ice." Continental immensities *gesturing* through tectonic mass, volcanic and glacial heave.

> Continents of water and of earth,
> Gaia! Time's mother too
> must wear guises,
> hop on one leg

and hide her head in a hut,
dance with the rest among the maskt guys.

~

The war of Africa against Eurasia
has just begun again. Gondwana

~

There is only
the one continent, the one sea—

moving in rifts, churning, enjambing,
drifting feature from feature.

The work obeys a process. The worker is dissolved at the crown of creation. A tropic summit; a crypt. "In the mind, the bone pile grows." And on this "sarcophagus of we know not whom, / each figure, impending, become a sign," each sign a seed *(sema),* each seed a *soma* (some body), is forced through hermetic (sealed) passages by the heat of the process. The fire smokes until the whole mass is illegible chiaroscuro. Black sun. Nigredo.

tomorrow rustles in yesterday's corpse.

Light the death lamps, see the shadows condense!

~

Not lost battles or even defeated people
But blackness alive with itself
At the sides of our fires.
At home with us
And a monstrous anti-grail none of those knights could have met or invented
As real as tomorrow.
Not the threat of death. They could have conquered that. Not even bad magic.
It is a simple hole running from one thing to another.

~

downward,
to darkness,
to chill
and darkness

—its sybilline letters in the form of bones, blackened against the cooled ash-white of the page. A composite portrait, a monstrous calligraphy disassembling and reassembling itself hypnotically before its maker as it goes along. Aroused to plangency, semenslippery quick, the exoteric is propelled out of reach.

> The dreams pursue us over the snow. I wanted the country beyond the garden, over the garden wall. The wall was *orgasm,* to give it a common name, soft red brick always in sunlight, some of the bricks black with age & with an intrinsic moisture that slipped down the rough channels of the brick
>
> . . . .
>
> Past the skin & over the wall
> to the shape I have seen stretched out
> solider than darkness
> before I lost my purchase on the wet brick.

In Ammons's corresponding vision of

> . . . the whole mystery, the lush squeeze, the centering
> and prolongation
> . . . .
> if one can get far enough this way imagination
> and flesh strive together in shocking splendors, one can
> forget that sensibility is sometimes dissociated and come.

Carnal rotation in the erotic compressor blanks out the dissociated "split man" of modernity who is momentarily baptized again as an animal, in the flicker of sexual grace, where

> supraliminal language-field is body-field
> is feeling
> and feeding:
> . . . .
> so I am always finding in feeling
> locating in shifting
> the terms that compose me
> the rhetorical cinnabar lode
> whose clavicle's wavicle's key.

No wonder a ritual drama marks the occasion. Irby's "Offertory" condenses layers of mineral wealth into a theme-schist of hypnogogic masturbation and geophagy:

> to call up the dead from dreams
> and break the heart's stone
> whose cock is it? not just my own.

"Expression" takes on a difference in the sensorium; "but along the edge of the wall, later a new stain." The leakage is heraldry with semiotic implication—a *pli* or pleat in meaning,

> yolk openings in the hand
> back into which the bird had fled

—in the easy slippage of the dreamwork alchemy these messengers are alternately owl, duck, and finally

> crows on Tufts Hill
> silver by night
> turned black again by day.

These are the crows of the completed opus (the egg on the steps between Irby and his brother*), nigredo of the upspringing vigor in compost. "Offertory" ends on an image of the oracular surplus of the earth:

> and now there will be a footstep uncovering a rock in the mud, and in the line of sight will appear a quartzite boulder brought down by the glacier, carved with the rotations of the star, leading inward, Northeast—and from the foot lifted to the one remaining ancient spruce, the air is folded in on itself, capturing the moisture, shimmering, opening a pool through which the hands reach, yolk-stained.

Hands and even whole heads may emerge from the rubble's froth

> . . . where,
> From huddle of trash, dried droppings, and eggshell, lifts
> The unfeathered pitiless weakness of necks that scarcely uphold
> The pink corolla of beak-gape, the blind yearning lifeward.

Warren's hatchlings resonate with Olson's kingfishers, out of whose "dripping, fetid mass" comes a brighter excrement, disclosing (as in "The Lordly and Isolate Satyrs") the other half of the beach, unsuspected.

*James E. Irby, editor and translator of Borges's *Labyrinths,* the New Directions compilation issued (in its enlarged edition) in 1964, the same year brother Ken published his first book, *The Roadrunner.*

The Visitors—Resters—who, by being there,
made manifest what we had not known—that the beach fronted wholly
to the sea—have only done that, completed the beach.
The difference is
we are more on it. The beauty of the white of the sun's light, the
blue the water is, and the sky, the movement on the painted lands-
cape, the boy-town the scene was, is now pierced with angels and
with fire. And winter's ice shall be as brilliant in its time as
life truly is, as Nature is only the offerer, and it is we
who look to see what the beauty is.

The contrary side—the verso of the whole globe—comes into play. "In any case the whole sea was now a hemisphere, / and our eyes like half a fly's, we saw twice as much." These Visitors ("Resters" in contrast to the agitated revenants in "As the Dead Prey Upon Us") are the sleeping dead, the hungry dead, and as the Greeks most feared, the *stupid dead,* unknowing in death's narcosis; unable to retain the *sophrosyne* of their own identities (headstones were to remind the dead, not the living, of their names)—but, for all that,

gnostic reminder of
world-rut, remnant, revenant,
whirled, unraveling, whir . . .

World, word, whirred: these necropolitan visitors are vessels, part of the alembic.

Hail them solely that they have the seeds in their mouth, they
are drunk, you cannot do without a drunkenness, seeds can't,
they must be soaked in the contents of the pot, they must be all one mass.
But you who live cannot know what else the seeds must be. Hail
and beware the earth, where the dead come from. Life
is not of the earth. The dead are of the earth. Hail and beware
the earth, where the pot is buried.

Greet the dead in the dead man's time. He is drunk of the pot.
He speaks like spring does. He will deceive you. You are meant
to be deceived. You must observe the drunkenness. You are not to
drink. But you must hear, and see. You must beware.

From Saturn to Demeter

From emptiness or blank, a scene arises; there is always a scene, a presentiment of knowing, the viewer's gnosis in the prehensile grasp of the elements. But prior to the scene there is a mood, a predisposition, whether expectation or aversion. The mood is black bile; whatever its temperamental coloring, it does dark work, work in the dark. The black bile "obliges thought to penetrate and explore the center of its objects, because the black bile is itself akin to the center of the earth" (Ficino, in Klibansky, Panofsky, and Saxl, 259). Each object is fruit, a fleshy covering over the treasure of the pit or pith, the myth or meat of it. Saturnian bile is Ficino's name for the sovereign esoteric genius of melancholy: "by withdrawal from earthly things, by leisure, solitude, constancy, esoteric theology and philosophy, by superstition, magic, agriculture, and grief, we come under the influence of Saturn" (261).* The Hermetic function of Saturn is division, making many out of one, these from that. But in astrology and in the humours there are baleful associations: paralysis, fixation, obsession—countertrends to the more positive features, motion, flexibility, and vivacity. So melancholy is a mood of dark breaks, segues of blue notes and duende.

The scene, then:

Boulders blunted like an old bear's teeth break up from the headland;
  below them
All the soil is thick with shells, the tide-rock feasts of a dead people.
Here the granite flanks are scarred with ancient fire, the ghosts of the tribe
Crouch in the nights beside the ghost of a fire, they try to remember the
  sunlight,
Light has died out of their skies

—light has died out of their *skins*, I'm prone to read. "Apology for Bad Dreams" names a mood of despondence and dread. The Saturnian gloom that rekindles

* Ficino's strange medley bears some resemblance to the zany catalog of Borges quoted by Foucault: "Animals are divided into: (a) belonging to the Emperor, (b) embalmed, (c) tame, (d) sucking pigs, (e) sirens, (f) fabulous, (g) stray dogs, (h) included in the present classification, (i) frenzied, (j) innumerable, (k) drawn with a very fine camelhair brush, (l) *et cetera,* (m) having just broken the water pitcher, (n) that from a long way off look like flies" (*Order of Things,* xv). The original passage can be found in "John Wilkins' Analytical Language" (Borges, *Selected Non-Fictions,* 231).

by virtue of sheer intensity a black explicitness. It is a masculine severity Jeffers practices, in which breakdown extends to the whole tissue of human affairs in a communal narcosis of grief.

> He brays humanity in a mortar to bring the savor
> From the bruised root: a man having bad dreams, who invents victims, is only
> the ape of that God.
> He washes it out with tears and many waters, calcines it with fire in the red
> crucible,
> Deforms it, makes it horrible to itself: the spirit flies out and stands naked, he
> sees the spirit,
> He takes it in the naked ecstasy; it breaks in his hand, the atom is broken, the
> power that massed it
> Cries to the power that moves the stars, "I have come home to myself,
> behold me.
> I bruised myself in the flint mortar and burnt me
> In the red shell, I tortured myself, I flew forth,
> Stood naked of myself and broke me in fragments,
> And here am I moving the stars that are me."

Only at the end does Jeffers come to any abatement of rage, let alone tranquil acceptance. He is the Saturnian seismologist of harsh times gleaned from the rugged visage of ocean and sky, rocky shores and headlands—the cruelty sometimes generalized (a symptom of melancholia) as the given condition of things.

A conceptual and temperamental alternative to Saturn is Demeter, the corn goddess. Hers is an instruction about black descent as germination. Her perspective construes division differently than Saturnian collapse. In the voice of Mina Loy, writing as one of "The Dead":

> We have flowed out of ourselves
> Beginning on the outside
> That shrivable skin
> Where you leave off
>
> Of infinite elastic
> Walking the ceiling
> Our eyelashes polish stars.

"We splinter into Wholes," Loy goes on to specify. "Our tissue is of that which escapes you / Birth-Breaths and orgasms . . . / The unsurpassable openness of the circle." And in "Parturition" the circle assumes a new dimension:

> I am the center
> Of a circle of pain
> Exceeding its boundaries in every direction.

In this parturition Loy finds that an "open window is full of a voice"; and in that voice she finds a backward-spiraling nebula of other voices, animal noises, and a continuum of birthing-matter with the "Stir of incipient life / Precipitating into me / The contents of the universe."

> There is a climax in sensibility
> When pain surpassing itself
> Becomes Exotic
> And the ego succeeds in unifying the positive and negative poles of sensation
> Uniting the opposing and resisting forces
> In lascivious revelation
>
> Relaxation
> Negation of myself as a unit
>   Vacuum interlude
> I should have been emptied of life
> Giving life
> For consciousness in crises   races
> Through the subliminal deposits of evolutionary processes
>
> ~
>
> The was—is—ever—shall—be
> Of cosmic reproductivity
> . . . .
> Rises from the sub-conscious
> Impression of small animal carcass
> Covered with blue-bottles
> —Epicurean—
> And through the insects
> Waves that same undulation of living
> Death

Life
I am knowing
All about
        Unfolding

Milk light

The stars point to an articulate order surpassing language, evolving a realm in which

> *art is not construction, artifice, meticulous*
> *relationship to a space and a world existing*
> *outside   it is truly the 'inarticulate cry'*
> *as Hermes Trismegistus said, 'which seemed*
> *to be the sound of the light'*

~

These stars
are fragrant and I follow their scent.
I am their hunting hound,

predator of the marvelous.

In the region of the inarticulate cry, where all sensations reduce to blank dazzle, "Life is an ecstasy. Life is sweet as nitrous oxide," Emerson writes ("Illusions").* "Thus events grow on the same stem with persons; are sub-persons. The pleasure of life is according to the man that lives it. . . . Life is an ecstasy" ("Fate"). "We are extrusions, facets, auras, in vibratory flowing surge of infinite possibilities," McClure barks in unison with his animal cohorts in "Wolf Net" (*Scratching the Beat Surface*, 160). And "A ribosome in a liver cell in a salmon might relate to a field of

* William James has interesting things to say about nitrous oxide in *The Will to Believe* ("On Some Hegelisms"): "It is impossible to convey an idea of the torrential character of the identification of opposites as it streams through the mind in this experience," he writes (677). Noting that the propensity of gaseous intoxication was indubitably Hegelian, he offers as an example of the "most coherent and articulate sentence" he produced under the influence: "There are no differences but differences of degree between different degrees of difference and no difference" (678).

energies or a point within a quasar or a distant sun" (126). "Our experience of the universe is also the universe perceiving itself" (127)—the same bifold self/other inspection, the fertile sundering of a universe that has to slice itself in two to observe itself (according to Spencer Brown in *Laws of Form*).

In the wisdom of the ancients, the stars were mirroring provocateurs of human affairs. To look up was to gaze inward and see the milk of the stars become the maternal plangency of galaxy's *gála*—its milky blast, its nourishing forecast of fate's influx in animal blessing; the inimitable span and paradox of poetry that *"love is not made caressingly from pore to pore, but from pore to star"* (Lezama Lima, 175).

Sex on earth is rhymed angelic motion.

Outer space and inner space misnomers
when what is meant (nomen, numen)
is rhymed in megalith and microspore

. . . .

But the solar heart defines the blood

How far out you go
it is within.*

As, even for the infant in utero, "pressing a knee or elbow / along a slippery wall, sculpting / the world with each thrash"—even there in *that* sanctuary—"the stream of omphalos blood [is] humming all about you." In the plush grace of the womb, every heartbeat resounds, as "The sweet virile hair of thunder storms / Brushes over the swelling horizon."

Stars and storms are respirations:

before us   gods   goddesses at the ends of words

dead and alive   among apple trees in the old
orchard   the sky is first an inhalation,
then smaller and tinted, an exhalation —
and the words are not winds
but small movements, ruled
in a largeness that is not ourselves

~

*John Muir notes in a journal: "I only went out for a walk, and finally concluded to stay out till sundown, for going out, I found, was really going in" (Slovic, 351).

A transparent base

shuddering . . .
under and through the universe

rides the brows of the sounding whales

& swells in the thousand
cow-bells.

It undulates under each meadow
to thunder in the hills, the crow's call,

& the apple-falls.

I hear it always, in a huge & earthy fugue,
from inner ear, to farthest owls

~

The ringing in your ears

is the cricket in the stars.

The reckoning of selfhood in the span of planets and stars is not instantaneous, but a labor of time: "the distance between the star and its subject are complemented by the antiquity of the light which finally arrives" (Kuberski, 77). The legendary music of the spheres is the sound of that arrival, a gratified constellation attuned in audible delight, in musical realization.

Freedom. It isn't once, to walk out
under the Milky Way, feeling the rivers
of light, the fields of dark—
freedom is daily, prose-bound, routine
remembering. Putting together, inch by inch
the starry worlds. From all the lost collections.

The dance of the stars is real and consequent motion, directly engaging earthly affairs, "mold[ing] them to its sequences in a cosmic manifold in which past and future called to each other, deep calling to deep" (Grossinger, 56).

But the long-held glimpse of these heavenly measures lapsed, and medieval cosmology endowed sublunary existence with a purely receptive capacity: in the Christian worldview, ascension was a contingency of faith, not deed. The modern (post-Renaissance) cosmos is dualistic, folding the inside over against the outside like type and antitype, but endowing both with an unlimited power of expansion (as infinite universe and craving ego). Kant pitches his moral law on the fulcrum of the balance between "the starry heavens above" and the unique mortal soul.

> The [starry heavens above] begin from the place I occupy in the external world of sense, and enlarges my connection therein to an unbounded extent with worlds upon worlds and systems of systems, and moreover into limitless times of their periodic motion, its beginning and continuance. The second begins from my visible self, my personality, and exhibits me in a world which has true infinity, but which is traceable only by the understanding and with which I discern that I am not in a merely contingent but in a universal and necessary connection, as I am also thereby with all those visible worlds. (Kant, in Kuberski, 70–71)

What Kant understands as a force that "exhibits me in a world which has true infinity" is extensively described by Suhrawardi (the Ismaili Sufi) in terms of the *mundus imaginalis,* a "concrete spiritual universe," not a (Kantian) world of concepts or paradigms or universals.

> [T]he archetype of a species has nothing to do with the universals established in logic, but is the Angel of that species. Rational abstraction, at best, deals only with the "mortal remains" of an Angel; the world of archetype-Images, the autonomous world of visionary Figures and Forms, is on the plane of angelology. To see beings and things "in the northern light" is to see them "in the Earth of Hūrqalyā," that is, to see them in the light of the Angel; it is described as reaching the Emerald Rock, the heavenly pole, coming upon the world of the Angel. (Corbin, *Man of Light,* 6)

The encounter with the Angel instigates "the awakening of consciousness to the soul's condition as a stranger, and, in this emergence to itself, its meeting with him who shows it the way, its Guide, its *Noūs*" (Corbin, *Avicenna,* 23–24).

The gnostic precepts underlying this vision of cosmic estrangement are evident also in Corbin's attention to the concept of *ta'wīl,* in which the Guide leads the soul on a journey of homecoming, *turning* (troping) from exoteric to esoteric, and *returning* to its source in a "universe 'in which spirits are corporealized and bodies spiritualized'" (35). *Ta'wīl* also refers to a mode of textual exegesis Corbin takes pains to distinguish from allegoresis: "instead of seeking a secret *in* or *under* the text, we must regard the text itself as *the* secret" (33)—a principle worth bearing in mind while reading the poets of *This Compost.* The concept of *ta'wīl*—in both its cosmological and textual applications—was important to Olson (who thought it might provide "a basis for a physics of psyche at this revolutionary point in re-taking the cosmology of creation as fact, both in instant and in consequence" [*Additional Prose,* 71]); discussed at length by George Quasha and Charles Stein in conversation with Robert Kelly (probing the notion of the poem as *ta'wīl* of its first line, the exemplary instance for Kelly being Duncan's "Poem Beginning With a Line by Pindar" ["Ta'wīl or How to Read," 117]). Ta'wīl is also vital for Nathaniel Mackey in his ongoing multivolume "Songs of the Andoumboulou" and *"mu."* Mackey is explicit about his debt to Corbin: "The idea that essence is alienated rather than immediate and the linkage of gnostic estrangement, esoterism and poetics are among the things that stuck and stayed with me." "My adoption of the Andoumboulou as a figure for our present as well as past condition, the suggestion that the Andoumboulou are a rough draft of human being and that we're (still) that rough draft, is a gnostic one" (Naylor, 655, 656).

The gnostic yearning is to return to the pleroma, the fullness of Being. It's too easy to equate pleroma with a Golden Age or a Heavenly City. Corbin obliquely offers a useful discrimination when he says "*ta'wīl* causes the letter to *regress* to its true and original meaning" (*Avicenna,* 29). Mackey's work is intimately bound up with such regression, testing the legroom available to that "atavistic two-headed / beast, / one head we call Stride, the / other Obstruct."* The *muthos* mouthed in travail belabors a " 'mu' more related / to miss than to myth"—where, however, miss becomes gnostic mission. In its repudiation of materiality, gnosticism sees earth and body as symptoms of a cosmic degradation. But these are prejudicial terms; there is more at work in what was occult to begin with. Poets preoccupied with gnosticism—like Olson, Duncan, Kelly, Mackey, Gerrit Lansing, Brenda Hillman—have been drawn to its hidden dimensions. Another poet, Kenneth Rexroth, clarifies the nature of the appeal: as a heterodoxy, gnosticism was open to a bewildering diversity of resources and seems capable of assimilating

* In another rendering, *ta'wīl* is explicitly evoked in the space of this standstill:

ta'wīl said to've been sown
at the foot of a page,
flew
but for the weight of Ogun's
iron shoe, shod ghost we
imagined we rode, running
in place.

them all, coupling scientific knowledge with ancient ritual ("Primer of Gnosticism," ix); and it established the individual at the center of a cosmic drama. Ripe material for poets working in the compost library.* Rexroth adds another incentive: "Since the official Church was patriarchal and authoritarian, Gnosticism gave expression to those matriarchal and libertarian tendencies which are there, suppressed or not, in all societies" (xix). The psychodynamic absorption of social trauma, coupled with spiritual presentiment of cosmological redemption, is richly evident in *The Maximus Poems* and in Mackey's work in particular,† which certainly answer to Rexroth's claim that "[Gnostic] mythology is a symbolic portrayal, almost a deliberate one, of the forces which operate in the structuring and evolution of the human personality. It is, more than almost any other religious system, because it is of all others the most invented, the most 'made up,' an institutionalized panorama of what Jung has called the Collective Unconscious. The whole Gnostic heresy is a sort of socially therapeutic dream" (xix). At the heart of the dream is *therapeia,* or work to be done; pragmatic, restorative labor that might as well go by the name *ta'wīl.*

The therapeutic dream continued to erupt in sectarian form long after gnosticism subsided in the Mediterranean, and Ezra Pound commemorated the last of them, the Albigensians, integrated in the *Cantos* into a matrix of luminosity. Pound's illuminations are always light bound, oriented to that "room in Poitiers where one can stand / casting no shadow, / That is Sagetrieb, / that is tradition." The vegetation rites of *Rock-Drill* and *Thrones* petition the deep visage of the sky, asking what compensation is to be made for the capture and cultivation of photosynthetic compounds in the heavenly body of falling light. The stars *ensoul,* as Kuberski points out. " 'To look at' is a figure of speech which presupposes a discarded theory of optics which holds that our eyes emit rays of light toward

* Some Gnostic sects were deeply invested in these incentives to imaginal reverie. A Christian bishop complained of the Valentinians, "Every day one of them invents something new, and none of them is considered perfect unless he is productive this way" (Jonas, 179). As Hans Jonas indicates, such poetic fertility was germane to gnostic cosmology, which supposed the world to be the result of divine malfeasance; so the creative potential of individual gnosis was conceived on the grandest terms as "the inverse equivalent of the pre-cosmic universal event of divine *ignorance,* and in its redeeming effect of the same ontological order. The actualization of knowledge in the person is at the same time an act in the general ground of being" (176).

† See O'Leary's "Deep Trouble/Deep Treble" for an informative discussion of Mackey's gnosticism. It's also useful to note Mackey's heretical (gnostic) swerve from the traditional African American tendency to construe historical calamity in biblical terms.

perceived objects. To see the stars, to be looked at *by the stars,* is to be penetrated and illuminated by starlight" (*Persistence of Memory,* 63). To encounter light at all is to be consumed in its enigma, time,

> to see the world focused back at us
> like a wide flower:
> river, vascular lightning
> & leaf-vein.

The condition of this consumption is mortality. "After a long time of light, there began to be eyes, and light began looking with itself. At the exact moment of death the pupils open full width."

The floor of the upside down

Predation has its solar remainder:

> Only the sun
> in the morning
> covered him
> with flies
>
> Then only
> after the grubs
> had done him
> did the earth
> let her robe
> uncover and her part
> take him in

Robinson Jeffers documents a late encounter, "Vulture," in which the bird of prey sizes up the aged poet and savors him for another time. "I tell you solemnly / That I was sorry to have disappointed him. To be eaten by that beak and become part of him, to share those wings and those eyes— / What a sublime end of one's body, what an enskyment; what a life after death." And what else could this be but Hart Crane's visit with Melville's tomb,

The calyx of death's bounty giving back
A scattered chapter, livid hieroglyph,
The portent wound in corridors of shells.

Then in the circuit calm of one vast coil,
Its lashings charmed and malice reconciled,
Frosted eyes there were that lifted altars;
And silent answers crept across the stars.

The stars speckle the sea surface with the patterned stencil of an answering report, while the nautical depths perform another labor:

. . . anything
nature puts in the sea
comes up,

it is cornucopia
to see it
working up a sluggish
treadle,
from a ship's hold

to the truck
which takes it to the De-Hy
to be turned into catfood,
and fertilizer, for nature's
fields

~

afternoon Manatee of my mind? Rock picture
of a beast? Lausel woman, holding out a ladle? Actually
sluggish treadle up which nature
climbed Wet white body dried Old picture Andromeda
awash Norn nurse waitress.

The "great mother" is not a personage but a nest of deposited urges, a port of access to the underworld signaled by the herm, its stones like magnetic embers of a final *mappa mundi.* "Work the old images from the hoard, / *el trabajo en oro* that gives wealth semblance / and furnishes ground for the gods to flourish." *Masa confusa.*

The pageant, growing ever more curious, reaches
An ultimate turning point. Now everything is going to be
Not dark, but on the contrary, charged with so much light
It looks dark, because things are now packed so closely together.
We see it with our teeth.

Workers on the real guide the threads, sort the grains, bind the seams. Heraclitus is distantly signaled there where Olson sees him disappearing into the ability of humans to know themselves as their own *matter*—Heraclitus among the few who acknowledged as workers the sleeping and the dead ("Even sleeping men are doing the world's business and helping it along"—which answers in polyphony to another adage, "We assume a new being in death: we become protectors of the living and the dead" [Davenport translation, 22, 31]).

"Be the Oedipus of your life and the Sphinx of your tomb," a spirit-medium told Victor Hugo, indicating the dual creative labor of life ventured in poetry by day and by dreams in sleep.

All night long
I was a Eumolpidae
as I slept
putting things together
which had not previously
fit

The work of the dead and the sleeping is the work of discerning the bottom, the earth as ground of the upside down or inside out, as vowels and consonants are ambassadors of arrival and departure:

upside-down trees
and sky, shadowy, at the bottom
other step-stone
holes in the world.

Zukofsky derives his poetics in *"A"* 12 while mourning his dead father and marveling at language,

That closed and open sounds saw
Things,
See somehow everlastingly
Out of the eye of sky.

Poetics. With constancy.

My father died in the spring.
Half of a fence was built that summer.
For minutes as I drove nails in the lower stringer
The sunset upside down
Tops of trees, even an inverted hill,
Gauze.

~

Who bury the dead
must from the grave
establish a habit

~

for 'the

blossoms to
fall up'
for the

under round
of our
world had

TOP marked
hopefully for
a printer.

~

. . . Only when the Flower—only when the uproar
has driven the Soul
out of me, only then shall the God
strike
the three Towns. The three Towns
shall first
be born again. The Flower shall
grow down.
The mud of the
Bottom
is the floor
of the Upside Down.

as if the earth under our feet
were
an excrement of some sky.

The stars are hermetic implements, making explicit an implicate order.* "The eyes, clamped shut, squeeze to a star"—

those stars in beautiful cosmology
if no other reason to be than this—.

look up

Feeling oneself a "head full of stars," and "lost / as earth in such a / world," the balance of inner and outer, self and other, planetary content and astral provocation raises a challenging question: "how / can I expel these roomy stars?" Expelled, they constellate the sky; ingested, they crowd awareness and perception until figure and ground collapse into one unfigured groundlessness. But from that opening lapse or collapse the zero speaks and encompasses, revivifies in concentric constellation the ouroboros of the blood tides.

The immense stellar phenomenon
Of dawn focuses in the egret
And flows out, and focuses in me
And flows infinitely away
To touch the last galactic dust.

This is the prime reality—
Bird and man, the individual
Discriminate, the self evalued

* See David Bohm's sense of "the *implicate order* (from a Latin root meaning 'to enfold' or 'to fold inward'). In terms of the implicate order one may say that everything is enfolded into everything. This contrasts with the *explicate order* now dominant in physics in which things are *unfolded* in the sense that each thing lies only in its own particular region of space (and time) and outside the regions belonging to other things" (*Wholeness and the Implicate Order*, 177). Pertinent to the implicate order is the fold—*Le Pli* in the title of a book on Gottfried Leibniz by Gilles Deleuze—delectably deployed by Steve McCaffery as an approach to the work of Robin Blaser. "The great architectural fold is the labyrinth, whereas the ontolinguistic fold requires a plication of the subject into the predicate. The Self—itself—is not a Subject but a 'fold' of force. Souls are folds upon corporeal surfaces provoking dialogues, not syntheses. A new consciousness is a fold in the old and a dream a fold in waking life" ("Blaser's Deleuzean Folds," 374).

Actual, the operation
Of infinite, ordered potential.
Birds, sand grains, and souls bleed into being

~

The orders
are elaborate:
the strings are tuned.
Inside every image
another is visible.

In the lust of traces (the venatic paradigm of Carlo Ginzburg) we convulsively follow Hermes's precedent, piling signs around any gap, cut, space, lack, sacrifice, incision. Every stylus, in the track of its spinning groove, tropes its own motion. Daimonic fatality—Nietzsche's *amor fati*—has less to do with extinction or cessation than with the wild palpation, the syncope that heaves being from one point to another in a spasm of unbinding, a declaration of the discontinuous that any medium (music, art, dance, writing) adapts to its own form. So representation pulsates with its own libidinously declared fractures that simultaneously bind and separate.*

I looked up and saw
its form
through everything
—it is sewn
in all parts, under
and over

~

. . . no tomb
is solid,
not even
this hour
holds.

~

can it be said to have come forth from the tomb?

* "What is closed? What is open? What is a connective path? What is a tear? What are the continuous and the discontinuous? What is a threshold, a limit?" asks Michel Serres (*Hermes,* 44), soliciting guidance by way of Oedipus and the Sphinx. "Thus everything is repeated, enigma and knowledge, on the road to Thebes and the road to Delphi, catastrophe and passage, tear and connection" (47).

Or is the tomb
forever
so much
part of its story
it carries it with it
wherever it goes?

Zukofsky makes ear a bier and wonders whether this is abstract or concrete, *All* or *"A."*

When I am dead in the empty ear
you might ask . . .
. . . .
what if the song preserves us?
As *you* said stone sculpture's still and moves
and to intrigue us further the mobile moves
with its sustaining current the space is still:
which is less abstract solid or more sensed?

~

Tell us of excess.
What was the sign that limited?

The starry horizon

Every planet conforms to a celestial orbit in which the cosmic order repositions itself, one by one: a planet is a hunter of times.

This language is a horizon
terraced into a ladder that spins
into a blade of light, and drugs the darkness
with its brilliant stem.

Desire smiles in all directions at once.

In *The Spell of the Sensuous,* David Abram recounts a memorable experience. Stepping out of a hut in Bali built on stilts above rice paddies, he finds himself acutely disoriented, with "no ground in front of my feet, only the abyss of star-studded space falling away forever":

> I was no longer simply beneath the night sky, but also *above* it—the immediate impression was of weightlessness. I might have been able to reorient myself, to regain some sense of ground and gravity, were it not for a fact that confounded my senses entirely: between the constellations below and the constellations above drifted countless fireflies, their lights flickering like the stars, some drifting up to join the clusters of stars overhead, others, like graceful meteors, slipping down from above to join the constellations underfoot, and all these paths of light upward and downward were mirrored, as well, in the still surface of the paddies (4).

~

I went out on my cabin porch,
And looked up through the black forest
At the swaying islands of stars.
Suddenly I saw at my feet,
Spread on the floor of night, ingots
Of quivering phosphorescence,
And all about were scattered chips
Of pale cold light that was alive.

~

'the shape of heaven   is as confused
as the heart   when you place

your feet on your head,   you will
stand on the stars,'

these words whisper   as the sea folds
a thousand forms

~

The vast onion of the actual:

. . . .

History seeping from capsule
To capsule, from periphery
To center, and outward again . . .
The sparkling quanta of events,
The pulsing wave motion of value . . .

Among its other labors, the old lore facilitated imaginal *placement* as a coordination of mind and map, psychodynamics and geophysics posing together in astronomical apparel. In the account by Giorgio de Santillana and Hertha von Dechend in *Hamlet's Mill,* star lore of the pole as it guides the equinoctial routes around the four corners of the circulating earth is regionally encoded in myths around the world. C. G. Jung recognized this in his consideration of Naassene creed:

> The Original Man in his *latent state*—so we would interpret the term *axarakteristos*—is named *Aipolos* . . . because he is *aepolos,* the Pole that turns the cosmos round. This recalls the parallel ideas of the alchemists . . . about Mercurius, who is found at the North Pole. Similarly the Naassenes named Aipolos—in the language of the Odyssey—*Proteus* . . . "who owes allegiance to Poseidon and knows the sea in all its depths." (*Aion,* 216)

Through such burrowings in the compost library we begin to glimpse an ecological import in mythic lore, which makes a point of recalling and imagining a world of profundities exceeding comprehension. Gods are the humanized manifestation of the unknowable, even as their behavior makes sounds audible to humans like that "wise tomcat" who tells tales when climbing the equinoctial pole and sings songs when he slides down it.

> The Archanthropos is the Logos, whom the souls follow "twittering," as the bats follow Hermes in the *nekyia.* He leads them to Oceanus and—in the immortal words of Homer—to "the doors of Helios and the land of dreams." "He (Hermes) is Oceanus, the begetter of gods and men, ever ebbing and flowing, now forth, now back." Men are born from the ebb, and gods from the flow. (*Aion,* 209)

I read this passage as a charter of compost poetry, from Whitman's "As I Ebb'd with the Ocean of Life"—its "spirit that trails in the lines underfoot, / The rim, the sediment that stands for all the water and all the land of the globe"—to Pound's *nekyia,* his descent through sediments of text down to the tale as bedrock, Odysseus in the underworld; to Olson's Maximus as Archanthropos, whose eyes also look out to sea, "Off-shore, by islands hidden in the blood" (hearkening back to Whitman's "fish-shape Paumanok where I was born"). These are all figures who follow a logos in their poetry, twittering, to ocean as literal place and Okeanos as imaginal location.

Okeanos, R. B. Onians reports, "was believed to be a bond around the earth, apparently of serpent form even as Acheloos, the primal river or water, was conceived as a serpent with human head and horns. The procreative element in any body was the *psyche*, which appeared in the form of a serpent. *Okeanos* was . . . the primal *psyche* and thus might be conceived as a serpent in relation to procreative liquid. The conception of *Okeanos* has no basis in observation. It can now be explained as the imagined primal cosmic *psyche* or procreative power, liquid and serpent. The name appears to have been borrowed from the Semites (?Phoenicians) and to mean 'circling' " (*Origins of European Thought*, 248–49).* Amulets, bracelets, necklaces, tokens, and crowns are archaic symbols of this encompassing world, signs of submission to sublunar existence in a cosmos encircled by chaos, that serpentine perimeter of the incomprehensible, the unmanageable, the nonhuman. Against the harmonic ratios of an ideal "ichnography,"† psyche is a personal stain, a portable speck of chaos, a gleaming scale of the ouroboros.

There is something more that speaks in this image. If psyche is partial chaos, it is also partial ocean, in touch with procreation and the ecological circulation of elements. Psyche itself becomes the ocean of wisdom and tact spans the human world as the oceans of water span the globe. Greek lore provides images of this: Okeanos, Proteus, Kronos, Pan—all images of All, as Pan's name translates; figures of totality, serving individually as autonomous figures in the pantheon, and collectively as a heraldic display of psyche cosmetized or "made up." Could it be that the Greeks imagined themselves distinct from what they called the barbarians because they conceived an inner circumference to the surrounding chaos, a realm of human sapience that could absorb and pacify that chaos, or could at least be known (both as ocean and as old lore) as the only feasible transportation route through the life of a community *in time*—and that, in its essential nature, the species itself was not distinct from chaos but was its inner circumference, psyche tight against it as the satyr-play to the three tragedies it accompanied?

Plot as "first principle" for Aristotle was "arrangement of the incidents" but also the "soul of tragedy" (*Poetics*, VI); and, as Robin Blaser adds, the logos or

* "Every snake biting its tail becomes a circle, a circle which the Gnostics discover over and over again at all levels," writes Jacques Lacarriere, citing the cosmic level of the Leviathan "constituting the ring that divides the domain of darkness from the domain of light"; the terrestrial compass of Ocean encircling the globe; and the coils of the intestinal tract inside the body (*The Gnostics*, 81–82).

† In Platonic idealism, says Michel Serres, "This is how the miracle is accomplished: the transparency of volumes, the metaphorical naming of the realism of idealities. From the cave to the world outside, the scenography turns into an ichnography: the shadow of solids played on the plane of representation and defined them by boundaries and partitions; now light goes through them and banishes the interior shadow" (*Hermes*, 94–95).

discourse of emplotment means "running around arranging / things, ourselves among them."

action is, perhaps, the *magnitude*
of the body
the stain of form
turning among the
marriage clothes
the starry issue
the horizon
the beauty
and terror composed inextricably mingled
in an unfixed freedom

Beauty and terror define the "soul of tragedy." The Greeks built their tragedies on hubris, as heroes like Oedipus prove incapable of realizing the truth of their fates written in the stars. Through these tragedies we glean the cost of the Greco-Roman embrace of alphabetic literacy and the corresponding lapse of star and ocean lore, those archaically disseminated universal codes—the "strange hologram of archaic cosmology" documented in *Hamlet's Mill* (Santillana, 346). "Bits of it reach us in unusual, hesitant form," Santillana writes, "in the wisdom and sketches of Griaule's teacher Ogotemmeli, the blind centenarian sage. In the magic drawings of Lascaux, or in American Indian tales, one perceives a mysterious understanding between men and other living creatures which bespeaks relationships beyond our imagination, infinitely remote from our analytical capacity" (347). Confronting the loss of this great "Star Menagerie," we might envision our entire acknowledged civilization as nothing but a series of adolescent gang-related incidents. To heed Paul Shepard, the consequences of the neglect into which the adolescent threshold has passed may be unbounded (a return to chaos). As with the maintenance of any other delicate prototypes, both adolescence and the old lore are left to chance. Adolescence is the embodiment of enquiry, the flowering and culmination, the volatile eruption of the continuous questioning all childhood has been. Without the interrogative apotheosis of adolescence, a culture loses its questions. Nobody knows what to ask. We're hard put to know what to make of all the evidence lying around. Squinting into the past and seeing only burly carnivores with clubs is a profound lapse of imagination, a lapse institutionalized in the cartoon milieu of Hanna-Barbera's cuddly Flintstones. The Greeks as first last men tally with Americans as last first men to breed that monstrance, a civilization whose entire institutional propagation has been riddled with profound lapses of imagination.

Along with the ravaging of natural and human resources in America, there is a corresponding disregard for the American past. We have little dissemination of such basic contradictions to the inherited views as the Bat Creek, Tennessee, Hebrew coins of 100 A.D.; New England engravings in Roman Numerals indicating adherence to Sosigene's calendric reforms of 45 B.C; or traces of an ancient Libyan alphabet in the Virgin Islands. Where go for such news but to the poets?

The impatient dead go out announcing
their immersions, dots
and doublespiraling crescents
etched
eventually as far north as
Nova Scotia . . . *

~

Libyans and Egyptians entered the Mississippi from the Gulf

penetrated to Iowa, the Dakotas

and westward along the Arkansas and Cimarron Rivers, the
Oklahoma-Colorado border

. . . .

Celts in the rivermouths of New England, North Africans in the
heartland of the continent, centuries before Christ

~

So the Jews, we now
from Tennessee inscriptions
guess again the Indians the lost
ten tribes, may have run
that whole economy, the blood
line, equally black
say, under my fingernail
a crescent the fertility

* Nathaniel Mackey here follows Ivan van Sertima's work *They Came Before Columbus.* Discussing it in an interview, he adds "Of course, poetry has throughout the ages been a vehicle for imparting and keeping alive secret knowledge, secret information, secret wisdom" (Rowell, 707).

of that ancient money touch
become the thread
of absolutely unambiguous
felt Direction

so to the Mystery . . . *

In Kenneth Irby's poem, by sheer office of high school yearning Jesus steps off the train in Fort Scott, Kansas. History and cosmology overlap. One might come to know something about the Bar Kochba coins of Tennessee by folding them into imagination: "invagination," Olson would call it shortly before he died (punning desperately, it seems, on his failed liver as Lady Live Her, undergoing a gender reorientation in the process†). In the late *Maximus* Olson comes to a view arrived at independently by Santillana and von Dechend in *Hamlet's Mill:* that the mythic encoding of astrological lore records a catastrophe in the shift of the ecliptic and the crisis of a new pole star each astrological era. In its balanced phase, " 'earth' is the ideal plane going through the four points of the year, the equinoxes and the solstices" (*Hamlet's Mill,* 62). It's the same plane to which we make reference even now, as last first men, gone laterally out to the tip Indo-European migration routes have tended toward, America, where "Having come Far West, the musculature reflected another climate than Old World or Atlantean, a shifting around of the magnetic poles, widely rearranging the felt directional lines of force." These momentous excursions into the old lore come full tilt at the end of Irby's "Delius":

A band of seduction, about to fall off the continent
certainly *not* the East getting home
beyond Sacramento is the *essential* roughage of the Western edge unsettling a
magnetic intestinal pole track
bloodred in the sky as the Spider Woman of the North and South fades away,
sustained in the, *only* in the

* And by way of lore among poets: Irby here follows information from archaeologist-historian Cyrus Gordon, included by Olson in 1961 in "Bridge-work" in a list of "men worth anyone's study," along with Edward Hyams, Carl Sauer, linguists Sapir and Whorf, G. R. S. Mead, Aleister Crowley, Ernest Fenollosa, and others (*Additional Prose,* 24).

† Robert Duncan recalls that "As he was dying of terminal cancer that had come into his liver and was eating away each day, Olson was writing out, as if to unlock in a logographic magic the secret message or to break the code of that event, *'LIVE-HER.'* He is trying words, to find in the body of the language he loved and worked in and incarnated himself in, this event that was eating at him. He had to know it in words, what he knew in flesh" ("As an Introduction," 83).

what man has matured as a creature of, ice
the Climatology of Attention is not the Extension of Empire
an Elephant palm we might say, nursing its dying with a nuzzling trunk to
reach the stars
Deneb in the Swan over Bolinas the umbrella of an unquenchable reach
the drunken Strangers of the Earth stumbling into each other's arms falling off
the road to
find their way back to that barely remembered home

in the hills the Leader of the Wind holds up a painted hand
pecked like a petroglyph into the rock
the Entry Sign upon the fallen shelf
down the stream bed of all many-colored rocks
leading the Wind that holds Direction

"to find a new vocabulary"

the Moki feather cloak
"hovering on the verge"

"so we must look not at the mound underfoot, but at the starry horizon"

for "the soul knows itself, and would live its own life."

And what it would know as its own is not exempted from the farthest ravishment of astronomic fermentation:

Nebula, whirlpool, mist & cloud; knotted, asymmetrical branchings

formed like a labyrinth

—are form, even as a sphere, crystal
& flower.

'Patterns

are temporary boundaries' . . .

. . . .

And Orpheus, the metamorphosis

before us

of coral,
acanthus,

leopard's-paw, bird's-foot

. . . .

For 'where the figure is, the answer is.'

The frozen being

The mytho-astronomy of *Hamlet's Mill* advances the challenging concept of the sky as another kind of compost; "the sky was an exacting teacher and the order of the stars an ancient gnosis" (McCord, *Gnomonology*). In Kenneth Irby's view, "man matured as a creature of ice." We see at the end of his poem "Delius" a new crisis, need of a new vocabulary (to absorb the deglaciation? agricultural urbanization? pastoral nomadism? the passing of Virgo in 10,080 B.C. or Taurus in 1800 B.C.?) The sights are set not on the mound underfoot, but on that starry horizon the alchemist beholds in the famous engraving, as he plunges through the sublunar curtain of material generation to gape at the wide open universe.*

* This is the engraving used for the cover of Ronald Johnson's collection *Valley of the Many-Colored Grasses,* but since then overexposed on other book jackets, calendars, illustrations, and designs.

For Olson, also, the human is a creature of ice, albeit not glacial but figurative—a disorienting blankness forcing one to take bearings.

> Looking at a Nation herself untaken since before this Harbor
> of her Eastward Pointing Cape was tight in ice
> and measurements and lines were dropped through ice as far
> to the West of South as 207°, Ten Pound Island Ledge
>
> if I twist West I curl into the tightest Rose, if right
> into the Color of the East, and North and South are
> then the Sun's half-handling of the Earth. These aspects,
> annular-Eternal—the tightest Rose is the World, the Vision
> is the Face of God—in this aspect the Nation
> turns now to its Perfection. Its furthest or its highest
> Point, its Limit now reached, the Imagination of it
> here or anywhere men in duress or need in thought which taken
> is belief, go on the frozen being and do take the marks and bearings.

If it seems precarious to be standing on ice to take bearings, rather than on dry land, Robinson Jeffers had insisted on an even more severe precariousness:

> When the ancient wisdom is folded like a wine-stained cloth and laid up in
> darkness.
> And the old symbols forgotten, in the glory of that your hawk's dream
> Remember that the life of mankind is like the life of a man, a flutter from
> darkness to darkness
> Across the bright hair of a fire, so much of the ancient
> Knowledge will not be annulled.

For Jeffers, the old lore was burnished in the veins, genetically knitted into the chemical residuum that later compelled Robert Duncan to insist that even holocaust and conflagration do not erase the fabric of life's *matter.*

> The cosmos will not
>
> dissolve its orders at man's evil.
>
> "That which is corrupted is corrupted with reference to
> itself but not destroyed with reference to the universe;
>
> for it is either air or water"

Chemistry having its equations

beyond our range of inequation.

~

The tides are in our veins, we still mirror the stars, life is your child, but there is in me
Older and harder than life and more impartial, the eye that watched before there was an ocean.

That watched you fill your beds out of the condensation of thin vapor and watched you change them,
That saw you soft and violent wear your boundaries down, eat rock, shift places with the continents.

Mother, though my song's measure is like your surfbeat's ancient rhythm I never learned it of you.
Before there was any water there were tides of fire, both our tones flow from the older fountain.

Complementing Clayton Eshleman's theory of "therioexpulsion"—by which humans ejected their animal past—the industrial revolution launched another "boundary catastrophe," a *geoexpulsion* of the elements (preserved in traditional psychology in the humours) and reduction of all materiality to use-value. Consequently, allegiance to the planet, to the very notion of world or earth (let alone cosmos) strikes moderns as archaic, an ancient superstition.* Still, certain American poets persist in cultivating *the ancient superstition of the earth,* reckoning not only the intactness of a unique habitable planet but its place in a field of planets, as if there were

some part of us always
out beyond ourselves
knowing knowing knowing

Are we all in training for something we don't name?
to exact reparation for things
done long ago to us and to those who did not

* As of 1981 the cry was well underway, "to the stars to save ourselves." See Ben Bova, *The High Road* (Boston: Houghton Mifflin, 1981). That view is reaffirmed in Gregg Easterbrook, *A Moment on the Earth: The Coming Age of Environmental Optimism* (New York: Viking, 1995), 686–91.

survive what was done to them whom we ought to honor
with grief with fury with action
On a pure night on a night when pollution

seems absurdity when the undamaged planet seems to turn
like a bowl of crystal in black ether
they are the piece of us that lies out there
knowing knowing knowing.

Emanation

Any litany attests to marvels:

they look up at the sky they see
again the pink cloud move across the yellow cloud
again a pine cone bounce against the sun
again a diamond antler crack like sugar
again a new-born frog rise from the savage onions
again a flute melt to announce the light
again a blue eye peer from a headstone
again a dead bell speak without a tongue
again the animals shed their skins beside the furnace

"Take constant notice of the clarity of things," Empedocles advises (*Parmenides and Empedocles*, 32). Every act divides and multiplies. Heraclitus's proposal that nobody steps in the same river twice might be taken to mean that someone stepping into a river divides the river. The person multiplies, in turn, into one who knows the river as one, and another who knows the river as two.* As Edward Dorn writes of Creeley's "molecular consistency," "It assumes an address multiple to itself"

* Twenty men crossing a bridge,
Into a village,
Are twenty men crossing twenty bridges,
Into twenty villages,
Or one man
Crossing a single bridge into a village.

(*Views,* 121). Not multiple with respect to others (not schizotically refracted) but *multiple to itself,* finding an inherence (its inheritance) in change.

> . . . the limited body
> Can form in itself
> Only a certain number of images.
> If more are formed
> The images begin to be confused.
> If exceeded, they become entirely confused.
> The mind then imagines
> Without any distinction,
> under one attribute—
> A universal—
> *Man,* not
> The small differences,
> And predicates concerning an infinite number of individuals

In the tropics of American poetry, trope is the composting engine, a fundamental dislocation, forge or furnace of a different locus: the unpropertied space germane to language. Not the mysticism of another world, but another economy (another *oikos* or household) of language-in-production, words in emanation, not nation. A tropical poetry is an agency of partial bodies, effluvia, surplus meaning: partial to polysemy, many-seeding. Odysseus is called "polytropos," many-minded amidst the rhythmic undertow (and sonic undertone) of a nomadic and renegade intertextuality. He has been split, composted, divided like Heraclitus's river for twenty-five hundred years. Yet he recurs, graphemic cluster that he is. "Odysseus" now names a polytropic conductivity, a homing device outward bound, destined for such propositional recasting as "My bikini is worth yr/raft." All that the summoned name brings with it to the beach, the tideland strip, roars with the burst and gush of its "rot into intricacy":

> *What is*
> hisses like a serpent
> and writhes
>
> to shed its skin.

This writhing serpent is a wraith of writing shedding its length scale by scale, abiding by its heap (grain by grain). Psyche (who sees her "monster-husband . . .

Serpent Desire" as fair and comely) is "brought to her / insect instructor . . . must follow to the letter / freakish instructions. // In the story the ants help." "When the mind swings by a grass-blade / an ant's forefoot shall save you."

> It begins with the root of the tongue
> It begins with the root of the heart
> there is a spinal cord of wind
> singing & moaning in empty space

Memoranda and signatures

Order is relative.

> 'An apparent confusion if lived with long enough
> may become orderly'. Charles Ives
>
> . . . accumulating,
>
> a humus! (The upper strata—dry, newly-
> fallen leaves, twigs, lichen.
> Seeds from the size of the whispered dandelion, to
> acorns
> big as thumbs.

This passage (from Ronald Johnson's "The Different Musics") continues in a scrupulous documentation of layers of disintegration, to "the under-ooze & loose loam of slug & worm."

> . . . to find, out of the design,
> words may be pulled up
> like onions, a humus still
> clinging to them, sweet to the taste—
> nutty & fragrant.

One way that nuttiness and fragrance is plucked is in the hybrid medium of the anatomized citation (made even sweeter here in a palimpsest of Emerson on Goethe):

All things
are engaged in writing their history.*
The air is
full of sounds;
the sky, of tokens;
the ground is all memoranda & signatures
& every object
covered over with hints
which speak
to the intelligent.

This compost harbors another design, Johnson's aspiration "that poems / might be made as Harry Partch makes / music, his instruments / built by hand / —that we might determine our own / intervals between / objects, / as he constructs octaves." So Johnson fancies himself, like Thoreau,

. . . engrossed,

'between a microscopic & a telescopic
world',
attempting to read

the twigged, branchy writing

of frost, spider & galactic cluster.

Finding that "the event is the print of your form. It fits you like your skin" (Emerson, "Fate"), things rouse to consequence. Entities appear as transcarnate compassions. And companions—as the implicate order in the "Dizzy ravine" of "Mont Blanc" provokes Michael McClure's consideration that "These lines seem to be the energy of the universe expressing itself upon the complex organism of Shelley's body as if he were a typewriter of protein spirit" (*Scratching the Beat Surface,* 67). McClure's own spinally centered poems differ from Johnson's vertical symmetries mainly through the mammal exaltation of the former and the botanic exfoliations of the latter. "I wanted to write a poem that would come to life and

* history the dark crumble

of last year's compost
filtering softly through your living hand

be a living organism" (89). McClure understandably perceives the action painting of Pollock or Kline as "transcriptions of arm and brush that are statements, like pawprints of physical being. Wolfprints!" (137). Like McClure, Robert Duncan knows writing as a postural and gestural amplitude, incisively somatic. For the act of composition,

> My whole life
> needs to be here
> to come alive in this
> consideration.

~

> My life
>
> in the leaves and on water
> My mother and I
>   born
> in swale and swamp and sworn
> to water.

As Guy Davenport writes, explaining Shaker Mother Ann Lee's adage "every force evolves a form": "A work of art is a form that articulates forces, making them intelligible" (*Every Force,* ix)—as Lorine Niedecker's "rich friend / silt" commemorates. "And if truth come to our mind we suddenly expand to its dimensions, as if we grew to worlds" in our newfound solubility (Emerson, "Fate").

> . . . And what might have been,
> And what might be, fall equally
> Away with what is, and leave
> Only these ideograms
> Printed on the immortal
> Hydrocarbons of flesh and stone.

Rexroth's hydrocarbon glyphs are imprints a woman's hip shares with lignite ("Tiny red marks on your flanks / Like bites, where the redwood cones / Have pressed into your flesh. / You can find just the same marks / In the lignite in the cliff / Over our heads"). This is in "Lyell's Hypothesis Again," a visit to earth's memoranda in the transitory signatures of passion, in accord with Emerson's recommendation that "A man ought to compare advantageously with a river, an oak, or a mountain. He shall have not less the flow, the expansion, and the resistance of these" ("Fate").

And a kind of greening speech comes from those mouths

all but winged—each leaf
cleft & articulate.

~

Each leaf is an encyclopedia
Slowly reading itself, keeping
Inviolate the secret of its
Discrimination, falling slowly
Through the counter-glow of which it is a part.

The genealogy of glow and counter-glow is everywhere. "If I am overflowing with life," Thoreau discovers in a journal entry (May 10, 1853), "all nature will *fable,* and every natural phenomenon will be a myth." Everything signifies. Every signature applies. The sign *has* a nature.

So goes: first, *shape*
The creation—
A mist from the earth,
The whole face of the ground;
Then *rhythm*—
And breathed breath of life;
Then *style*—
That from the eye its function takes—
"Taste" we say—a living soul.
First, glyph; then syllabary,
Then letters. Ratio after
Eyes, tale in sound. First, dance. Then
Voice. First, body—to be seen and to pulse
Happening together.

No glyph or signifying scrap resists being immediately put into play by more commanding form. *"A"* and *Maximus* bend out convex, so each book anamorphically condenses a spot of insertion like a smokehole through which the reader fits, blackened by the passage as if through Paleolithic cave meanders ("the cave wall socket in which the current is called *animal*"); turned inside out to the world again—in woods, fields, clearings, thickets, or in "foliaceous heaps [that] lie along the bank like the slag of a furnace, showing that Nature is in 'full blast' within," revealing earth as "living poetry like the leaves of a tree" (Thoreau, "Spring,"

Walden)—following the path of things through forms, the park of eternal events, just this recent and local:

THEN I KNOW I AM NATURE, AS TOPOLOGY
UNROLLS ABOUT ME.
Forests turning
into books and rugs.
Things
are carbonized.
Cinders remain where life was/
but power remains
in the frame
of new shapes.

McClure's all-cap lines can be read as a sublimate of the text. "THE PREDATORS MAKE PATTERNS IN THE AIR"; "WE ARE STICK FIGURES CARVED ON CLIFFS OF STARS." Kinship with all that is affirms a "Selection of Heaven" in which "yours was the mouth of the wish the tongue of my speech sought."

It's in the nature of the sign to arouse a design (or impose one*), a design that signals the otherwise imperceptible difference inscribed in vast sidereal motions. Not all the traces can be read or comprehended, but all that are can be realized as trace, sediment, remnant, nature's signature.

John of the Oak was here:
these words, as letters,

hang in the air
over the mercurial eye

that maybe saw & always
answered as if it did.

The words pretend
to be painted on the wall.

* I wanted . . . a *Guneaform*—a woman's form—of writing
and thought, perhaps, Cuneiform it, so tactile that script, palpable
wedges pressed in wet clay: writing "at once," as a fresco

is painted. But in this book, in the pictographs
that underlie Cuneiform, there is only one sign for woman,
pudendum.

John. Everything pretends
to be just the place where we find it.

We find it sighing, we kiss it
singing, we call it Real

& measure with our newfangled minds
the distance from that glistering Real

to those heavenly twins our eyes,
& call that *the world.* That is,

the place where John was
when he wrote or said, *John was here.*

Such glimpses are not only signatures, but

monumenta. In nature are signatures
needing no verbal tradition.
oak leaf never plane leaf. John Heydon.
. . . .

as to hsin 心

In short, the cosmos continues.

Proprioception

The living word masks the crossroads where a mystery prevails, blending corporeal substance with inscrutable breath, apparent premonition of a spirit world corresponding, at the somatic level, with the equally inscrutable depths of the body.

> *How can a body be made from the word?*—language, a shivaree
> of transparence—jigsaw—glass immensity

Proprioception has to do with the cavity of the body, the body's cave, ward of dark matter, where there are not only functional organs but a phylogenetic inscriptive insistence: "the 'body' itself as, by movement of its own tissues, giving the data of, depth" (Olson, *Additional Prose,* 18). The proprioceptive is the body's cave, and the sense of human history finally attends to the social organization of what goes into, and comes out of, all the aggregate bodies and bodily cavities. Proprioception refers the dark of our own bodies to a ground of tropes (tropes are the babies of imaginal fecundity). Writing, yoga, music, medicine, and prostitution share proprioceptive overlap. All tell what can be turned into body, what turns are taken in bodies, what ends up in bodies, and what bodies themselves end up as in the end—the heart sent "boldly travelling, / on the heat of the dead & down" in Gary Snyder's poem "Toward Climax."

Proprio- as prefix underlies the sense of what is proper, appropriate. *Proprio* pertains to one's own, as does *idio* (idio -graphic, -pathic, -syncrasy, -lect). *Identity* is the differentiating principle we deploy to hitch a ride on that discourse. It appropriates without proprioception, however; identity is "other directed" in David Riesman's terms (like *persona* and personality). For Charles Olson thinking of absentee ownership encroaching on Gloucester fishing, or Pound fretting about usury interposing "interest" between lovers and other agents of natural production (e.g., Adam Smith's "invisible hand" of market forces), *polis* is always *propriously* configured. Pound's axe handle—adopted by Snyder as a book title—is a Neolithic signature of craft sensibility, but also a model of statecraft. To represent a constituency as one's own is (or should be, Pound and Olson felt) to nurture belonging—*member/ship*—as a political dimension that precedes any specific political alliance. From this perspective, "property" begins a long withdrawal from, and eventual abdication of, fellow feeling (particularly where the fellows are not human, and the humans are not owners).

Property without proprioceptive tact is a danger William Carlos Williams warns against in *Paterson,* linking writing to monumental malfeasance.

> It is dangerous to leave written that which is badly written. A chance word, upon paper, may destroy the world. Watch carefully, and erase, while the power is still yours, I say to myself, for all that is put down, once it escapes, may rot its way into a thousand minds, the corn become a black smut, and all libraries, of necessity, be burned to the ground as a consequence.

It's a tricky recommendation, of course, not only for its hyperbole, but because it risks overvaluing "plain speech"—darling of demagogues. What Williams is really advocating is an orientation to process, the dialectical fertilizing of moment by moment and part by part. By reprinting Olson's "Projective Verse" in his

Autobiography, Williams endorsed composition by field for a generation heedful of his own practical care for poetic ecology. And if Williams's authority in the 1950s seemed thoroughly eclipsed by Eliot's, in retrospect it's obvious that his preface to *Howl* and his acclaim of Olson were decisive events in the erosion of postwar neoclassicism. "Liberate the words" he had proclaimed in "The Great American Novel" (*Imaginations,* 166); but while many retained only a momentary enthusiasm for this dada provocation, for Williams it was an ever-renewing perspective.

Composition by field became enormously attractive in the 1960s because of its tacit affinity for organicism. The sensible adherence to physiological rather than metrical orders in composition was persuasive (and persuasively incarnated for many in the figure of Allen Ginsberg), but in the end it obscured other possibilities. Understandably, the logocentric oral obsessions of projective verse provided the target that energized the phenomenon of "language poetry," beginning with Bob Grenier's famous declaration "I HATE SPEECH."* It's too easy to hypostatize such statements; and it was not at all ironic that, in the Bay area, the solidarity of language poetry was achieved by means of a series of public talks. The ease with which the oral occasion passes into print and vice versa belie any easy opposition of speech and writing. One of the most singularly *vernacular* poetic enterprises to arise out of the "New American Poetry" context was Ron Silliman's renovation of poetic line into the prose order (as if prosody suggested prose) of "the new sentence." Silliman's early fractal compositions, modeled as their titles indicate on ritual occasions (*Ketjak* and *Tjanting*), take their own urban proprioceptive care with the mutter and matter of words, their iterability and their irritability too. The legacy of the Muses supposed the intonation (the music) of poetry to have always utterly arrived, without practice or forethought. Silliman's work not only restored practice and tuning to public view, it also dignified the *respiration* of perception itself. "This is how we came to resume writing, that we might free ourselves of literature." The proprioceptive impulse is squarely addressed: "Get mind to hand or add tongue to eye" he writes, seeing in reading and writing a single impulse, a cooperative labor on the model of the opposable thumb and its chorus line of

* The full-caps declaration was launched in a more nuanced context, of course. "It isn't the spoken any more than the written, now, that's the progression from Williams, what now I want, at least, is the word way back in the head that is the thought or feeling forming out of the 'vast' silence/noise of consciousness experiencing world *all the time,* as waking/dreaming, words occurring and *these are the words of the poems,* whether they, written or spoken or light the head in vision of the reality language wakes in dreams or anywhere, on the street in armor/clothes" ("On Speech," 496).

fingers, making it possible to use a pencil. Silliman's practice—and its pragmatic posture, pedestrian with notebook locating each day in a compositional fulcrum ("The act of jotting these marks on paper organizes the whole of my life")—is a respiration of urban mulch; bright thought innate to the *breath* of "writing" as much through the pores of the hand as the sacs of the lungs.

The sentences are workers, and the paragraphs are studios. Silliman's is a study in assembly relations. All the litter that goes into production is left lying intact (or in pieces, most instructively) on the floor of the studio amidst the more purposively delineated chunks. The strategy is to recycle used sentences, supporting the frequency (as in a radio waveband) of their effects. "These words jump around like fleas": "This is orange is a typical sentence" bobs up later on as "This is typical is an orange sentence." The detritus of recomposed statements embark on their own subterranean work, becoming dilations in the ideological zones of a culturally regulated ability to form sentences. These subterranean deposits are in turn taken up into larger compositional units (paragraphs), invigorating the space convened: studio, workplace, a studied address. The place is San Francisco; the "subjects" last no longer than their tenure in sentences as "objects." Because the writing is nearly always specific to some daily physical experience, the act of reading feeds the text into reader-substantiating patterns of cognition and recognition as the sentences are rewritten successively and generate further and broader patches of animal attentiveness. "Conversing lazily over espresso, saying hello to friends, watching pedestrians lean off-balance out into the street to see if the bus is visible amid the coming traffic, one is apt almost thoughtlessly to speak honestly to the most casual of strangers. Ingredients active. He punched his fist through the window, shouting he was Chairman Mao & had orgasms thru his feet." The labor proposed by such writing is that the reader wread herself into the chronicle, not as subject insinuated by a grammatical order (a deictic occupant), but as agent of the particularities of sight and sound, smell and touch, contemplation, intuition, anxiety, release—all abundantly available in the textual vehicle. Which is to say that the work is *made* to come to life in the reader's hands. "Reading rewrites this"; "Rewriting reads this"; "While you read this you continue thinking, composing your own poem as you go"; "This text might be a guide, but it is the route of your own mind we are, both of us, in this instance, act, committed to pursuing, following, tracing." Its urbanity is utopian: the *nowhere / now here* of readers and writers convening invisibly on the page, that rare public space where everyone can come together in an aggregate coincident with singularity.

Silliman's work begins to enact that difficult demand of William James for a reality conceived in distributive form, as a series of eaches. "It is surely a merit in a philosophy to make the very life we lead seem real and earnest. Pluralism, in exorcising the absolute, exorcises the great de-realizer of the only life we are at home in, and thus redeems the nature of reality from essential foreignness. Every end, reason, motive, object of desire or aversion, ground of sorrow or joy that we feel is in the world of finite multifariousness" (*Pluralistic Universe,* 652). The *eaches* prevail by their insistence, their superfluity.* "The amount of possible consciousness seems to be governed by no law analogous to that of the so-called conservation of energy in the material world" ("Human Immortality," 1125). His brother Henry agreed, attesting of consciousness that the "beautiful sign of its character [is] that the more and the more one asked of it the more and the more it appeared to give" ("Is There a Life After Death?" 609–10). In fact, its superfluity is exactly what renders consciousness credible *as* abundance: "This mere fact that so small a part of one's visionary and speculative and emotional activity has even a traceably indirect bearing on one's doings or purposes or particular desires contribute strangely to the luxury—which is the magnificent waste—of thought" (610). In William James's corresponding insight, "Had [man's] whole life not been a quest for the superfluous, he never would have established himself as inexpugnably as he has done in the necessary. . . . Prune down his extravagance, sober him, and you undo him" (*Will to Believe,* 555).

* It is the quiddity, the "eachness," of the animal being that compels respect. Margot Norris's outline of biocentric thought begins in the appreciation that such a thing is "an oxymoron, a conceptual paradox," for biocentric thinking claims " 'act' as life does. . . . The theories of the biocentric thinkers prove nothing, demand nothing, and thereby abolish their own role in the play of human desire. Since biocentric theorizing is an autotelic act, it aims to reverse the traditional philosophical enterprise of substituting thought for life. And because it teaches nothing, explains nothing, and creates effects only by the most indirect and accidental means, biocentric thought is gratuitous: an excess, a superfluity" (*Beasts of the Modern Imagination,* 238).

A grand supplement to the biocentric tradition—and complement as well to Silliman's large compositional projects—is *Lip Service* by Bruce Andrews, a 380-page poem on love and eros organized with reference to the heavenly bodies of the planets and Dante's *Paradiso.* Andrews describes *Lip Service* as "an associative, or drifting, lacework of thematic argument; polyphonies of utterance, shapes of talk, of streams of consciousness & preconsciousness; a drastic constructivism of syntax: with twists & turns, normative tilts & denotations, with interruptions *as* grammar; fluidities & tiny magnetizings of word-to-word relations, attractions, pushes & pulls; with acoustic echoes & lyricisms as bridgework over its dissimilarities or as contrasts & highlighting juxtaposition" (*Paradise & Method,* 253–54). This also suffices as a description of method in *This Compost.*

Vertigo

Epic and lyric are the extravagant symptoms of an adventure.

> . . . Dante in my dream
> went into Occitan
> in search of a sentence that would flow both ways

~

> There is a mill which grinds by itself, swings of itself, and scatters the dust a hundred versts away. And there is a golden pole on top of which is also the Nail of the North. And there is a very wise tomcat which climbs up and down this pole. When he climbs down, he sings songs; and when he climbs up, he tells tales. (Santillana and von Dechend, *Hamlet's Mill,* 96)

If epic is the vision of action and sequence—the polecat's labor in climbing up the Nail of the North—then sliding down is the vision of voice, running the text through (like a tape in reverse) for the sound of it alone, the suddenness of its descent, the splinter in the flesh the perspective of voice becomes, vocalizing graphic stings: that perplexing nudging and suckling of moisture and dryness in the palate. The nasal passages focused in breath explode in the bellows of the throat, contracting the whole body as it *impends* in this eruption into a yearning, moaning, meaning being or being meaning. Vocal pressures lurk in writing like a vertigo.

> Tape recorder—tape reason—is that *my* voice,
> It is a philosophical-acoustical question
> If anyone ever hears his own voice.

Such an acoustic conundrum posits self as an epiphenomenon of the text, gregariously extending identity to anyone lending a voice; as if the wreading body were itself a lens being focused and unfocused by the text—granular textures weighed on the tongue of the lines (the lens), releasing and licking each phoneme—dispersing and contracting, meaning meaning approaches, meaning meaning recedes. The respiration of the text depends on bodily conduits between voice and sign, writer and wreader. Sliding its voices down the golden pole of song, mouth and throat become genitals of mind.

Poetry is omnivorous in its sensuality: each word, each breath or sign, means in a premise of moans. Tropical poetry animates the body of speech. Favorably attracted by a text, we say it moves us: it is moving in the double sense courted by Gertrude Stein, so that "if it were possible that a movement were lively enough it would exist so completely that it would not be necessary to see it moving against anything to know that it is moving" (*Lectures in America*, 170). "This is what is meant by life," she adds. Language is full of gesture and posture, gestation and expectoration. To read certain poems is to be immersed in a palpability of the tongue and its accumulated sensations and intentions, and it's impossible for the sexual dimension of the tongue and the mouth not to be relevant to language and the flow of speech. "All essential production," Ruskin told the merchants of Manchester, "is for the mouth, and is finally measured by the mouth" (Heinzelman, 6). Language arises in the mouth and intersects there with complex biological cycles, just as the hand as a biological instrument of writing is a vector of manumissions.

Insisting that "truth" was symptomatic of specific bodies, Nietzsche wondered whether "philosophy has not been merely an interpretation of the body [but] a *misunderstanding of the body*" (*Gay Science*, 34–35). Nietzsche's physiological reanimation of the question of knowledge hinges on the somatic urgency of poetry, which is that each act of articulation, in writing or speaking, is an occasion of wisdom, the circumstantial composition of the real. Emerson's insistence that "the definition of *spiritual* should be, that which is its own evidence" becomes Charles Olson's "nothing is anything but itself, measured so," such that the openness of bodily intelligence as the actual agent of knowledge comes clear late in the final volume of *Maximus* as "This living hand, now warm, now capable / of earnest grasping"—which itself, having been formerly composed by Keats, is composted here by Olson and passed on in the text to our imaginal heat in this phrase or place doubly signified by the vanishing of several warm, living hands, whose only capable earnest grasping is the physical volume of the poem, in which the reader arrives as ventilation, in the manual gesture of opening the book.

The vertiginous vocal trace in the glyph—sign or text—precipitates the uncanny as *that which speaks in signs.*

A hundred years ago I made a book
and in that book I left a spot
and on that spot I placed a seme

with the mechanism of the larynx
around an inky center
leading backward-forward

By itself, the text is mute, even as it demonstrates mutation. A text is also (as textile) a screen or containing grid. Privileging tropes, the poet turns screen into filter, sifting rule into detour, breath into mark, until "The unnamable draws from us a world / of names."* Every trope, dedicated to multiplicity in its abridgement of distance, uncovers a "nest of worlds." "It is a site where language hangs / over itself vertiginous." "Metaphor [trope] is the moment of possible sense as a possibility of non-truth. It is the moment of detour in which truth can still be lost" (Derrida, "White Mythology," 42). The *sense* of the thing given in trope is both palpable and vanishing. To step into the tropic current is to apprehend the animation of poetry, which can outpace understanding to the extent that understanding is always already committed to mirroring (reflecting on) this excitement. At one extremity, sensation overwhelms lucidity. In tropological animation, where words announce themselves like animals pacing around the perimeter of thought, the text becomes a medium of affectionate dismemberment—as it does for Wallace Stevens, whose late work reveals a mind that has torn the world to pieces with austere benevolence.

> It is an illusion that we were ever alive,
> Lived in the houses of mothers, arranged ourselves
> By our own motions in a freedom of air.

Stevens's poetics of the act of mind finds that nothing will suffice; so he offers a vibratory tropology mediating between the world as *nothing* and its *other,* "the nothing that is," the formative vessel.

> I wonder, have I lived a skeleton's life,
> As a disbeliever in reality,
>
> A countryman of all the bones in the world?

~

> & where is wisdom
> but where the easy is made difficult
>
> carved in mind
> a root
> to clutch

* "In the poem he learns to turn and turn, and prose seems always a sentence long"; so Michael Palmer "would live against sentences." Clark Coolidge adds: "Prose is a sentence and verse a version."

against the quick
abolishing waters,

twenty years to see a tree is not a tree
& twenty more to say: it is a tree

Characters

The word "person" means mask, from Latin *persona.*

The problem of personality
Is the problem of the value
Of the world as a totality

The precarious balance between the personal and the public is amplified in a torrid zone. Crossing the desert in a stagecoach with a corpse called "I," a character named Everything in Edward Dorn's *Slinger* makes the pertinent observation

it's gonna be hot soon.
I only mean I never met I
but if he turns out to be put together
like most people I's gonna
come apart in the heat.
You see what I mean?

The boy has a point Slinger
it could get close fast in here

The solution to the problem is commensurate with a soluble continuum baptized by Emerson and Whitman. "Every man's condition is a solution in hieroglyphic to those inquiries he would put," says Emerson, introducing his first book, *Nature.* Twenty years later (1856), one of Emerson's most inspired readers wrote in his "Sun Down Poem," after observing his solarized reflection in the water below, preserving the moment *in vitro* in the poem: "I too had been struck from the float forever held in solution, / I too had receiv'd identity by my body." (This is more familiar as "Crossing Brooklyn Ferry": the change of title was the only major revision Whitman made.) "Let us build altars to the Blessed Unity which holds nature and souls in perfect solution, and compels every atom to serve an universal end," Emerson reiterated in "Fate."

These formulations of "solution" leach up into *Slinger,* in which the dead "I" solves for the other pilgrims a storage and detection problem (Everything's "private batch" of LSD—"Straight man. / 1000 percent, / nothin but molecules"—can be hidden in the corpse) that has metaphysical ramifications:

What then, if we make I
a receptacle of what
Everything has,
our gain will be twofold,
we will have the thing
we wish to keep
as the container of the solution
we wish to hold
a gauge in other words
in the form of man.
It is a derangement of considerable antiquity.

~

The choice is simply,
I will—as mind is a finger,
pointing, as wonder
a place to be.

Robert Creeley's *I will* turns in the groove of Charles Olson's *What does not change is the will to change.* The word "character" is from Indo-European *Gher I:* scratch and scrape; rub, smear, tinge; Greek *character* is a mark scratched on a stone, or branded on a felon. Character means cut, incision. A character is not a person but a groove. Finding the groove means finding the person is the measure. (In a late poem, Creeley writes of echoes "In which these painfully small / endings shreds of emptying / presence sheddings of seeming / person can at last be admitted.")

Here now *you* are—
by what means?
And who to know it?

"It assumes an address multiple to itself," wrote Dorn of these lines. He reads a "molecular consistency" in Creeley's poems ("This verse is 'big,' in other words, by virtue of the distances the rhetorical instruments can resolve and not at all in proportion to some incapacitating ratio of subject to object . . . the common mistake of modern practice is the miscalculation of that ratio" [*Views,* 119]), which in his own *Slinger* obtains not by distances resolved, but by compacting the space so that a stagecoach holds I, Everything, the circumambient Slinger, Lil, and the Stoned Horse (Levi-Strauss), as well as the ghostly entourage of all their implications. The characters, as in Louis Zukofsky's *Bottom,* assume an address multiple to themselves. In *Slinger* Dorn extends the practice to include characters who *are* immanently extensible beyond their "personal characteristics," whose conspicuously public personal names constitute the thinnest of borders between identity and the Infinite Circumference. "*Scatter be / my name,* something said."

"Life is eating us up. We shall be fables presently," said Emerson, reflecting on his essayistic predecessor Montaigne. One of Emerson's successors, William James, recites the doctrine with a twist of his own:

> Every bit of us at every moment is part and parcel of a wider self, it quivers along various radii like the wind-rose on a compass, and the actual in it is continuously one with possibles not yet in our present sight. And just as we are co-conscious with our own momentary margin, may not we ourselves form the margin of some more really central self in things which is co-conscious with the whole of us? (*Pluralistic Universe,* 762)

"You never know what name the periphery's going to start with," C. S. Giscombe writes, pursuing the apparition of his own name in British Columbia, where, in the nineteenth century, John Robert Giscome ("a negro miner," "a pioneer") left his name all over the map (a town, a portage, a canyon, and Giscome Rapids on the Fraser River). With no evidence of relation, the poet pursues his namesake in a racial odyssey—"the blood as if it too were out there telling"—yielding up a whole territory in place of a person. It proves to be "the same old story / endlessly leaping from river to river but just ahead of the words":

> the story's the same old edge through the new twists, almost
>
> intestinal from all maps of it, knotted—
>
> the edge in the voice, the little edge creeping
>
> . . . .
>
> the longest song bends away from the hodgepodge,
>
> takes shape from below & beyond: no telling
>
> how it appears, no word for the way blood arrives.

No word without whir as Mackey puns it, his *School of Udhra* spinning a constellation of commensurate identities:

> His they their
> we, their he
> his was but if
> need be one,
> self-
> extinguishing
> I, neither sham nor
> excuse yet an
> alibi, exited,
> out,
> else
> the only where
> he'd be.

Language obeyed

Rachel Blau DuPlessis remarks, "Like translations, poems / say the unsayable twice, once to another language." Where types propose a reification of sense (author into authority, logos into lexis), tropes propound an anarchy of sense and sensation, abridgment of book into conjugal detours, hot fertilities;

> the work of Art to set words
> jiving breaking into crises

—where, in Robert Duncan's practice, "the line / [is] a trial" and "each element a crisis of attention."* The tropes of a text tell tales of how things are turned into

* In a late essay, "He Stuttered," Gilles Deleuze also links line to trial, which marks the point at which one becomes a stranger in one's own tongue, a foreigner who makes language convulse—cry, stutter, mumble, whimper, gasp. In the performative mode "the stuttering no longer affects preexisting words, but, rather, itself ushers in the words that it affects" (23). Deleuze's work consistently favors the insouciant posture, the looseness and rapidity of the rhizome, always on the move. With Félix Guattari, Deleuze extends the fantasy to a very tropological America, consanguineous with *This Compost.* "There is a whole American 'map' in the West, where even the trees form rhizomes. America reversed the directions: it put its

words, events into beliefs, and how all are blackened, sealed in the furnace of reduction.

> The common air includes
> Events listening to their own tremors,
> Beings and no more than breath
>   between them,
> Histories, differences, walls,
> And the words which bind them no more than
> "So that," "and" . . .

As William James claims in *A Pluralistic Universe,* "the word 'or' names a genuine reality" (777–78).

> Of *and* Or *are snails, repeat vegetable lessons, roaring*
> *a new will that lifts its horn into the heart of Man.*

"Language obeyd flares tongues in obscure matter." These are the dicta of a poetics attentive to (and retentive of) crumplings of discourse into folds and redundancies, vulvic recesses and hollows, fluency become granular, textured. Verbalized, vocally strummed.

Language, framed by the rivalry of law and desire, feeds on its own dispersal into elementary functions and particles ("eye net *I* / quoin own me"*), liberated into an elegiac plenitude, a funereal measure plying identity into the coign holding the type in place. If "*The unconscious is totally unaware of persons as such*" (Deleuze and Guattari, *Anti-Oedipus,* 46), poetry is language becoming unconscious of itself, developing its own propinquity in what André Breton memorably called convulsive beauty.

Jack Spicer's poetics of disturbance is a lesson in the somnolent helplessness of the will when it lets itself to be animated by linguistic involuntarism in puns and slips of the tongue.

Orient in the West, as if it were precisely in America that the earth came full circle; its West is the edge of the East" (*A Thousand Plateaus,* 19)—Olson's "last first place"—and ouroboros.

* In *"A"* we have presentiments of language as heap; something like the Buddhist concept of *skandhas,* clusters of sense aggregates and their compound emanations. (The skandhas are: the aggregate of matter, the aggregate of feeling or sensation, the aggregate of perception, the aggregate of mental formulations, the aggregate of consciousness.) Zukofsky is able to practice a very tight, even elliptical, syntactic condensation because he moves over an intuitively familiar array, the poem's own "heaps" or aggregates.

For example
The poem does not know
Who you refers to.

Even in the thought of Being, "Our image shrinks to a morpheme, an -ing word. Death / Is an image of syllables." "For the blue wash of sound drawn back to its shores. A shell appears, is rolld under, comes up again the ash Hell shadows, melts and divides into *ash* and *shell* from which the grave black tides of hell recede." The ash and shell are siftings, instructions from the inner lava that language mumbles in our heads all the time, a subliminal vocality.

Hello and goodbye
in some languages are one word.
Each exits for the other. Why, then,
are not the living the dead?
See, you know me.

In the plutonian realm of Spicer's *The Heads of the Town Up to the Aether,* intentionality decomposes at any moment, exposing phonemes, morphemes, and graphemes working like grubs. In the poet's descent, there is a precarious affiliation of self with parts of speech ("The verb divides us evenly into two objects"); and to venture unequivocal speech in Hades is to risk the condition in which *you* or *I* might crack on the lips like an egg: "the touch breaks / who touches." In Spicer's underworld—in which the pronouns are emancipated into a composting ensemble—an "Ontological Proof Of The Existence of Rimbaud" makes it clear that a poet would not have to be "he" or "she" but "would have to be mmmmm, and nnnnn, and ooooo, and ppppp";

A design Thoreau saw in
the flowing thaw of bodies, leaves & lobes
of a hand, &
lichen of an ear.
'No wonder the earth expresses
itself outwardly in leaves

it so labors with
the idea inwardly: *lobe,* a word
especially applicable to
the liver & lungs & the *leaves* of fat,

externally,
a dry thin leaf, even

as the *f* & *v*
are a pressed & dried *b*.'

Ronald Johnson here literally takes Thoreau at his word, sampling a text ("Spring" in *Walden*) in which Thoreau in turn takes Nature at her letter; and as Thoreau himself has sponged off Charles Kraitsir. In *The Significance of the Alphabet* (1846), Kraitsir prepared the conceptual template from which Thoreau's global vision of lobes and labors derived.

> . . . *crp, glb, grp, grb, blk, glm, krp, klp,* are roots of *corpus, globe, grope, crop, block, bulk, bulge, grab, group, conglomerate,* and words of similar meanings. These roots are essentially the same. So an object or action, which expresses free outward motion, or that in thought, which is naturally symbolized by free outward motion, will need labials and the liquids, thus: *lb, lv, lp, lf, fr, fl, pl, pr,* are roots, (or different forms of a root,) which vegetate into the words *labia, live, lip, liber, love, laub, life, free, flow, blow, bear, fare, plane, flat, pluvia, flamma, fire.* If the object or thing moves from within its own being, which implies deep, internal, essential action, we have a gutteral and the liquid, thus *gl, ql, cl, gr, cr,* which are roots of *glide, globe, glare, glance, vogel, eagle, volucris, creo, gradior, cylinder, columna, columba, aquila, circle, &c.* (in Michael West, 268–69)

These texts by Kraitsir, Thoreau, and Johnson are conjoined, coupled like serpents, and for several lines it's as if they *overlap* word for word in undulant mutuality.

Louis and Celia Zukofsky's translation of Catullus performs a salutary enactment of this condition at the limit of semantic accessibility. In their copulation of rival tongues, the Zukofskys roll Latin phonemes over into English, shaping a material reserve that comes to *inform on* the incipient meaning at every point (as if to say were to concede: everything testifies, all is incriminated).

denique testis erit morti quoque reddita praeda,
cum teres excelso coacervatum aggere bustum
excipiet niveos percussae virginis artus.

Then ache cue test his air earth mortal booty ready to pride ah
coom earth's ash excels so combustible heap round barrow burns now
she is given as new white snow pierced corpse by him virgin odd truce.

Like the oral epic mode of recitation that assigns to Athena the epithet "grey eyed" as a handy metrical mannequin, syllables so transposed are fateful preparations, ontological graffiti—discerning the composition of one text in the decomposition of another.

> Song's fateful. Crime
> fulfills the law. *Oedipus* is a
> ravishing order in itself.
> His tearing out his eyes—
> a phrase, secretly prepared,
> that satisfies.

Clearly, as in the premonitions of old myths as well as new poetry, "language obeyd flares tongues in obscure matter."

Pestilence

Language is inconceivable without a granary of words, a "mill of particulars" in Robert Kelly's parable. But particularity can run amok without an informing pattern, a disposing matrix. The pestilential vision of parts overrunning the whole takes the form of bacterial invasion in Kenneth Rexroth's vision of the onset of World War II,

> Spreading over the world, lapping at the last
> Inviolate heights; mud streaked yellow
> With gas, slimy and blotched with crimson,
> Filled with broken bits of steel and flesh,
> Moving slowly with the blind motion
> Of lice, spreading inexorably
> As bacteria spread in tissues,
> Swirling with the precise rapacity of starved rats.

In the matrix of total war, ghostly avatars of the past begin to swarm around the pools of blood, like the clamoring shades in Hades aroused by Odysseus's sacrificial slaughters as he prepares his descent to the underworld. Clayton Eshleman's heraldic figures are calculated incubations hatched in intestinal sanctuaries of the poems like the embalmed relics of his own childhood dipped into the contemporary atrocities of El Salvador in "Tomb of Donald Duck." As the figures of elsewhere and otherwise arise, an atavistic insistence overtakes us, and out of such grotesquerie oozes the bracing perspective of an "Aurignacian Summation":

> " . . . you must now take into consideration
> the savage Excalibur working back and forth
> against the ratio of the living and the dead.
> In 2000 A.D. the living may outnumber the dead.
> When the life side of the balance, heavier,
> swings down, the death end, lighter, will lift
> not only this bridge but this rowboat
> that to you still appears to be 'down there,' 'obsolete,'
> under the glassine shadow of a weeping willow
> but which in a way even we are just starting to grasp
> may already be carrying us toward a Jacob ladderjacked heaven,
> inverted Niagara in which the water rushing up and away
> is the suction of astronomical design to return
> to Betelgeuse the energy with which we have pick-up-styxed Orion
> when our task, from the beginning, was to learn how to vomit fire."

Eshleman's Aurignacians, inspecting the late twentieth century from the most remote region of Hades, conceive the earth as a system dedicated entirely to burning itself up, finding in our time their most conclusive evidence of human dereliction.

> For what we cannot accomplish, what
> is denied to love,
> what we have lost in the anticipation—
> a descent follows,
> endless and indestructible .

~

> The ear
> catches rime like pangs of a disease from the air. Was it
> sign of a venereal infection raging in the blood? For poetry
> is a contagion . And Lust a lord
> who'll find the way to make words ake and take on
> heat and glow.
> There is a land and a time—Morgan le Fay's—
> marsh and river country, her smoky strand

in whose lewd files I too have passt . to
tell the beads of that story again.

This is a *topos* to which Robert Duncan returns in "The Regulators"—specifically "In Blood's Domaine," a chilling summation of pestilential intensities and catalog of malignancy and debasement.

And if I know not my wound it does not appear to suppurate? . . .
Link by link I can disown no link of this chain from my conscience.
. . . .
What Angel, what Gift of the Poem, has brought into my body
this sickness of living?

"Mind comes into this language as if into an Abyss"—the language of "viral fragments" in atomic weapons and biological metastases alike. Duncan's understanding moves in the realization that "There is no ecstasy of Beauty in which I will not remember Man's misery."

In Wallace Stevens's "enemies . . . whose whispers prickle the spirit" and Duncan's "not men but / heads and armors of the worm," an imaginal pestilence feeds off its own worst images become incarnate, alive in the actual world, insinuating itself into the will. So a full commitment to the body of imagination opens directly on the incredulous realization that imagination can do no worse than the banal perpetrations, the horrors and atrocities that exceed the bounds and test the fortitude of creative empathy. Aldo Leopold reckoned the cost of ecological literacy as that of "living alone in a world of wounds" (Meine, 165). Nathaniel Mackey even considers the danger that "one could so rhapsodically lick one's wounds as to acquire and promote a taste for woundedness" (Naylor interview, 661). Assessing "the / hollow coil of our own dark scribbles," Gustaf Sobin estimates "nothing's written, in effect, that's not underwritten: / no world, in effect, that's not—ultimately—underworld." A. R. Ammons laments, "all this garbage! all // these words: we may replace our mountains with / trash: leachments may be our creeks flowing // from the distilling bottoms of corruption."

That constant local bilge of atrocity, the everyday, requires an extra effort of imaginative sympathy just because it is so mundane. The routinization of evil under the Nazis is still too flamboyant an image. Edward Dorn marks the reckoning on a much less charged, but no less consequent, circumstance:

Posses led by a promising girl wielding a baton upon the street
A Sacagawea wearing a baseball cap, eating a Clark bar

. . . .

And always they smirk at starvation
And consider it dirty . . . a joke their daughters learn
From their new husbands.

One of those daughters, author of *Snapshots of a Daughter-in-Law,* roused by the Gulf War, proves

. . . bent on fathoming what it means to love my country.
The history of this earth and the bones within it?
Soils and cities, promises made and mocked, plowed contours of shame and hope?
Loyalties, symbols, murmurs extinguished and echoing?
Grids of states stretching westward, underground waters?
Minerals, traces, rumors I am made from, morsel, miniscule fibre, one woman
like and unlike so many, fooled as to her destiny, the scope of her task?

Charles Olson comes to regard the suburban sanitation of the world's dark heave as terminus, end-of-species:

Actually the stirrings now of man faced
                                        with a wall going
up—man is now his own production, he is
omnivorous, the only trouble with his situation is he eats
himself and since 1650 this
                                        infestation
of his own order has
jumping to
2,700 million and
    going to 6,200 on
    January 1st 2000 is

his—the People are now the science
of the Past—his
increment. Only he has no
thought left, nor money nor
mortalness. He is only valuable
to himself—ugh, a species
acquiring

distaste
for itself.

When, in other words, do our own covert cannibal exertions stand fully disclosed as the complicitous reserve on which our sense of bounty abounds?—"To unmean with moaning, / adamant, / gutteral gist inexhaustibly / ancestral to itself"? "*Tellus* old earth whose houses are perched like 'the language of the birds' / giants of genocide slice the shadows to species suicide." William Carlos Williams, combing the century's calamities for solace, finds it intact in this grim extremity,

recalling the Jew
in the pit
among his fellows
when the indifferent chap
with the machine gun
was spraying the heap .
he had not yet been hit
but smiled
comforting his companions .

De rerum natura: *epic's lyric absolute*

As Europe succumbs to conflagration in 1940, Kenneth Rexroth, on the California coast, finds himself writing

. . . this poem
Of the phoenix and the tortoise—
Of what survives and what perishes,
And how, of the fall of history
And waste of fact—on the crumbling
Edge of a ruined polity
That washes away in an ocean
Whose shores are all washing into death.

Even as the sea subsides "To a massive, uneasy torpor," the "Fragments of its inexhaustible / Life litter the shingle, sea hares, / Broken starfish." Rexroth imagines the corpse of a Japanese sailor "bumping / In a snarl of kelp in a tidepool";

And, out of his drained grey flesh, he
Watches me with open hard eyes
Like small indestructible animals—
Me—who stand here on the edge of death,
Seeking the continuity,
The germ plasm, of history,
The epic's lyric absolute.

The emblematic features of Rexroth's poem, the phoenix and the tortoise, are versions of history. In the dystopic vision the State is "the organization / Of the evil instincts of mankind"; "Its goal is the achievement / Of the completely atomic / Individual and the pure / Commodity relationship— / The windowless monad sustained / By Providence." In the perpetuum mobile of administered ecstasy, "The assumption of history / Is that the primary vehicle / Of social memory is the State," obscuring the broader perspective of a living cosmos,

The vast onion of the actual:
The universe, the galaxy,
the solar system, and the earth,
And life, and human life, and men's
Relationships, and men, and each man . . .
History seeping from capsule
To capsule, from periphery
To center, and outward again . . .
The sparkling quanta of events,
The pulsing wave motion of value . . . (Rexroth's ellipses)

Fronting calamity on the Pacific rim, Rexroth, like Jeffers a few years earlier, turns to Epicurean atomism to account for the unaccountable marvel of such pulsation.

Endurance, novelty, and simple
Occurrence—and here I am, a node
In a context of disasters,
Still struggling with the old question,
Often and elaborately begged.
The atoms of Lucretius still,
Falling, inexplicably swerve.

And the generation that purposed
To control history vanishes
In its own apotheosis
Of calamity, unable
To explain why anything
Should happen at all.

One more Spring, and after the bees go,
The soft moths stagger in the firelight;
And silent, vertiginous, sliding,
The great owls hunt low in the air;
And the dwarf owls speak at their burrows.
We walk under setting Orion,
Once more in the dim boom of the sea . . .

Rexroth, like Lucretius, finds that "the thing that falls away is myself." The fall is the unfolding—making explicit an implicated universe—of Democritus's shower of atoms, to which Lucretius adds *clinamen atomorum,* the "gentle bias," Coleridge calls it. The *clinamen* is the skip of the needle, the bump of the table that tumbles the card house, the incalculable diversion, detour (like Duchamp's "delay in glass"—its shattered accidence preserved), deviation like that which style brings to a text.

Wallace Stevens's style seems too consistently sonorous to suggest in itself a swerve, but as "gentle bias" it does seem so inclined. Stevens may not have been an enthusiast of Lucretius, but George Santayana's *Three Philosophical Poets* (1910) would have at least placed the Roman poet in the immediate proximity of Dante and Goethe for him, a supreme altitude for the Connecticut poet to contemplate as he approached his own tropic suasions in *Harmonium* and "The Comedian as the Letter C." It is Santayana who tellingly asks, "Are poets, at heart, in search of a philosophy? Or is philosophy, in the end, nothing but poetry?" (*Three Philosophical Poets,* 8). Stevens ponders "the pensive man" as a "Connoisseur of Chaos." Because "The squirming facts exceed the squamous mind," there is a dissymmetry, a split of the sort that produces those matching halves we know as symbols. But importantly for Stevens, the symbol is not in the conventional sense a thing standing for another thing, but a record of mutilation, fracture, multiplicity. The fear of the pensive man is that "one more truth" is just "one more / Element in the immense disorder of truths" ("a plentiful waste and / waste of plenty" in A. R. Ammons's definition of poetry). The Lucretian proposition with which the poem begins, however, evokes in the very symmetry so alluring to Stevens the necessary result:

A. A violent order is disorder; and
B. A great disorder is an order. These
Two things are one. (Pages of illustrations.)

Order and disorder are an interplay of perceptions. The important thing is the give, the play in the system and its motion of admonition.

There is an exquisite movement, like it were chaos,

but of a sweet proportion
& order:
the atoms, cells & parsley-ferns

of the universe.

~

prosper
O
cell

through there where the forest is thickest

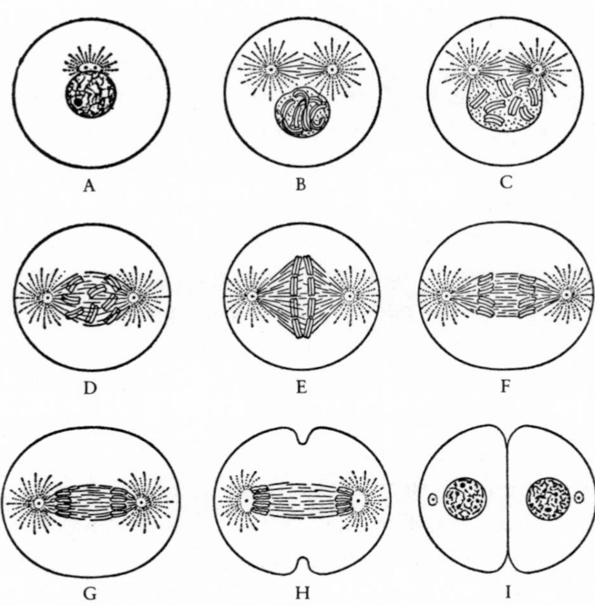

We find—"beckoned by pungencies"—that the air and even solid bodies "are nothing / but an immense swarm of / imperceptible / Animals"—

> Without dimension; where length, breadth,
> time, and place, are lost;
>
> Eternal
>
> embryon atoms
>
> as the sands
>
> warring winds, and poise
> adhere
>
> a moment:
>
> Chance governs all.

Peter O'Leary calls Ronald Johnson "the American Lucretius, writing a longer epic poem that really doesn't have a hero" ("Interview with Ronald Johnson," 45). In fact, the catalog of American poetry pledged to some version of *De Rerum natura* is copious and diverse. Newton Arvin offers the attractive parallel that Emerson was to Whitman what Epicurus was to Lucretius (*Whitman*, 90). The Lucretian epicureanism of Whitman seems a plausible source for the fully manifest *Leaves of Grass* of 1855, prior to which he wrote undistinguished verse in the idiom of his day. As immediate foreground, Whitman had in fact been patiently transcribing into his notebooks (seedbeds for his new poetry) a thematized summary of the Reverend J. S. Watson's translation of *De Rerum natura* published in 1851 (Gay Wilson Allen, *Solitary Singer*, 139). The catalog rhetoric so conspicuous in Whitman is comparably profuse in the Roman poet. But the single most decisive gift of Lucretius to Whitman, and to the ongoing legacy of composting poetry, is his vision of human life fully absorbed into the atomic fabric of the cosmos, a scene of propagations and admixtures inclusive of all creaturely life, but enfolding it in a plenitude far exceeding the bounds of sentience.

> Time was we were molten, time was we were vapor.
> What set us on fire and what set us revolving
> Lucretius the Epicurean might tell us

This is Frost in "Too Anxious for Rivers." The lines might have been by Jeffers; but Frost too went west with his Lucretius. Asked what book he'd take to a desert island, Frost replied, "Well, once I came out to Monrovia, California, and I brought along a single book you could never guess. It was a book of Lucretius' poems [*sic*] in Latin" (Mertins, 258–59).* What Frost retains from *De Rerum natura* is not the Whitmanian catalog of metamorphoses and interpenetrating life cycles, but the sense of nature as trickster, like the buck ("the embodiment that crashed / In the cliff's talus") that appears peremptorily in answer to the lament of solipsism in "The Most of It":

> He thought he kept the universe alone;
> For all the voice in answer he could wake
> Was but the mocking echo of his own
> From some tree-hidden cliff across the lake.
> Some morning from the boulder-broken beach
> He would cry out on life, that what it wants
> Is not its own love back in copy speech,
> But counter-love, original response.

Like many places in Frost, this is a rehearsal of the Emersonian doctrine of compensation. But Emerson is himself Lucretian in his conviction that "the doctrine of compensation is not the doctrine of indifferency" because, for him as for his Roman predecessor, "The soul is not a compensation, but a life. The soul *is*" ("Compensation").

"West-Running Brook" celebrates the nuptials of a human couple with a brook, including an interlude, a choral hymn of generation and entropy.

> 'Speaking of contraries, see how the brook
> In that white wave runs counter to itself.
> It is from that in water we were from
> Long, long before we were from any creature.
> Here we, in our impatience of the steps,
> Get back to the beginning of beginnings,
> The stream of everything that runs away.

* Frost was prone to make asides about Lucretius. In Mertins's table-talk Frost says of the Roman poet, "he had the atomic theory well in hand" (303). Reading "West-Running Brook" at Rutgers, October 5, 1949, he pauses at "Not just a swerving" and says in an aside, "As in Lucretius"—meaning the primal swerve of the atoms that initiates Creation (Lawrance Thompson, *Robert Frost*, 624 n. 9). Late in life, as an octogenarian, Frost confessed to "covet[ing] a new boundary in education. We need to map out new horizons beyond Lucretius even. As for poetry, I've said somewhere that poetry is a way to take life by the throat. I'll stand by that" (Mertins, 338).

. . . .
. . . runs away
To fill the abyss' void with emptiness.
It flows beside us in this water brook,
But it flows over us. It flows between us
To separate us for a panic moment.
It flows between us, over us, and *with* us.
And it is time, strength, tone, light, life, and love—
And even substance lapsing unsubstantial;
The universal cataract of death
That spends to nothingness—and unresisted,
Save by some strange resistance in itself,
Not just a swerving, but a throwing back,
As if regret were in it and were sacred.

"It is from this in nature we are from. / It is most us," Frost's speaker affirms of "this backward motion toward the source." The swerve. Lucretius's *clinamen atomorum,* "the blows of the atoms," Louis Zukofsky summarizes, "the lag and prophecy of Lucretius' art which attempts to prove the unseen atoms so often by seen things" (*Bottom,* 86). "O Nature, and O soul of man!" Ishmael wails in *Moby-Dick,* "how far beyond all utterance are your linked analogies! not the smallest atom stirs or lives in matter, but has its cunning duplicate in mind" (chap. 70).

Asked by a Tufts student about his philosophy, Robinson Jeffers responded diffidently, "Perhaps a gleam from Lucretius on one side and Wordsworth on the other" (*Selected Letters,* 201). But it is mainly the Lucretian posture Jeffers assumes; one in which the turbulent motion, driven into fecund issue by the *clinamen*—the involuntary if ever so slight swerve of an atom—is supreme. It is a vision of a fully composting cosmos, everything and all manner of things freely exchanged in the cauldron of material destiny*—and at his most pantheistically enthused,

* And before that, it is announced in Empedocles:
There is no self-nature
in anything mortal
. . . .
There is only
the merging, change
and exchange
of things that have merged
and their self-nature is only
a matter of words. (Lombardo translation, 33)

Jeffers celebrates a "Divinely superfluous beauty"—its superfluity running over the attentions of humans, outrunning them, and persisting even beyond their (our) eventual demise. In his final vision of "The unformed volcanic earth, a female thing" (Jeffers's title a reminder that *De Rerum natura* was dedicated to Venus), he finds Lucretius exemplary:

And the passionate human intelligence
Straining its limits, striving to understand itself and the universe to the last galaxy—
Flammantia moenia mundi, Lucretius wrote,
Alliterating like a Saxon—all those Ms mean majesty—
The flaming world-walls, far-flung fortifications of being
Against not-being.

Jeffers is a man who "feel[s] the flesh of the mountain move on its bones in the wet darkness" and is moved then to wonder "Is this more beautiful / Than man's disasters?"

Jeffers dichotomizes the world as human and nonhuman, and his scene of reckoning is invariably "this fate going on / Outside our fates." In human frame, new Jerusalems arise, but "this rock will be here . . . the energies / That are its atoms will still be bearing the whole mountain above: and I many packed centuries ago / Felt its intense reality with love and wonder." "The beauty of things was born before eyes and sufficient to itself; the heart-breaking beauty / Will remain when there is no heart to break for it." This is his "Credo."

As for us:
We must uncenter our minds from ourselves;
We must unhumanize our views a little, and become confident
As the rock and ocean that we were made from.

The "inhumanism" that scandalized Jeffers's Random House editors and the reviewers of *The Double Axe* in 1948 (albeit less volatile than the fiasco of the Library of Congress's Bollingen award to *The Pisan Cantos* the same year*) now seems surprisingly sound, so the controversy illuminates the degree of paranoia in the American historical imagination at the onset of the Cold War. Poets like Pound had been saying nasty things about politicians all along, so it couldn't entirely have been Jeffers'

* On the Pound affair, see Rasula, *The American Poetry Wax Museum*, 98–122. Jeffers's "inhumanism" is incorporated (almost too comfortably) into Max Oelschlaeger's comprehensive survey *The Idea of Wilderness*.

routine slander of militarism that made his publisher nervous. The offense was in putting the species in its place, "a shifting of emphasis and significance from man to not-man; the rejection of human solipsism and recognition of the transhuman magnificence" (*Double Axe,* xxi). "It seems time that our race began to think as an adult does," he adds, "rather than like an egocentric baby or insane person."

Watching killer whales prey on sea lions, Jeffers finds that "Here was death, and with terror, yet it looked clean and bright, it was beautiful." Its beauty is frankly affirmed as a quality of being exempt from human meddling.

> . . . The earth is a star, its human element
> Is what darkens it. War is evil, the peace will be evil, cruelty is evil; death is not evil. But the breed of man
> Has been queer from the start. It looks like a botched experiment that has run wild and ought to be stopped.

"The Answer" (a characteristic title) is "To know that great civilizations have broken down into violence" but to take consolation in the knowledge that "however ugly the parts appear the whole remains beautiful. A severed hand / Is an ugly thing, and man dissevered from the earth and stars and his history . . . / Often appears atrociously ugly." So "It is good for man . . . / To know that his needs and nature are no more changed in fact in ten thousand years than the beaks of eagles."

But Jeffers does have a story to tell, a tale of degeneration and disinheritance; of a "wound . . . in the brain" that "has never healed" where men "learned trembling religion and blood-sacrifice . . . / And hate the world." To hate the haters was Jeffers's personal fate. Reinforced by the spartan clifftop loneliness following wife Una's death, he lost all patience with humanity. "Lucretius felt the change of the world in his time," he writes in "Prescription of Painful Ends," yet

> . . . one builds poems for treasuries, time-conscious poems: Lucretius
> Sings his great theory of natural origins and wise conduct; Plato smiling carves dreams, bright cells
> Of incorruptible wax to hive the Greek honey.

By contrast, our own epoch with its "acids for honey" leaves so little hope in Jeffers's wish for a fully intricated human/nature, that

> . . . one christens each poem, in dutiful
> Hope of burning off at least the top layer of the time's uncleanness, from the acid-bottles.

It's surprising that no one has thought of pairing Jeffers and Pound, each "furious from perception" (Pound's tag for Hitler), dwellers on western coasts (Big Sur and Rapallo) where their visions thrived in monomania.* Surprising because Pound's blockbuster docudrama history *Cantos* of the 1930s are as deeply moralized and openly declared as Jeffers's "little chirping Sirens, alcohol, amusement, opiates" who are "another sign that the age needs renewal." Both men demanded renewal: their poems are like fists pounding the city gates; and they come on with a mean disposition. Crawlin' king snake men.

> While this America settles in the mould of its vulgarity, heavily thickening to empire,
> And protest, only a bubble in the molten mass, pops and sighs out, and the mass hardens,
>
> I sadly smiling remember that the flower fades to make fruit, the fruit rots to make earth.

The Poundian counterparts range throughout the *Cantos*. Here are a few:

> The saccharescent, lying in glucose,
> the pompous in cotton wool
> with a stench like the fats at Grasse,
> the great scabrous arse-hole, shitting flies,
> rumbling with imperialism,
> ultimate urinal, middan, pisswallow without a cloaca
>
> ~
>
> England off there in black darkness,
> Russia off there in black darkness,
> The last crumbs of civilization . . .

Pound's epic begins with the invocation preceding an infernal descent, a *catabasis* or *nekyia*. Descent to Hades, where the ghosts swarm (summoned lipsmack-

*Jeffers is also linked to Charles Olson through the advent of the war. Not that they shared political views (Olson worked for the federal government during the war), but Jeffers's severe repudiation of virtually all political action after the Munich Accord resonates with Olson's post-Hiroshima/post-Buchenwald abdication of a political career and turn to poetry. Jeffers had in some sense undergone a similar turn in the wake of the League of Nations, but by 1945 was too bitter to think that a new sort of poetry might be presaged by the ascendancy of empire. For Jeffers, his art was a site where "pained thoughts found / The honey of peace in old poems."

ing to spilled ram's gore in Homer). The rugged Big Sur coastal setting, blessed with Mediterranean weather suited to the literary disposition of someone trained in classics, was the unchanging scene for Jeffers's longer narrative poems as well as the lyrics. But the American shoreline was "Haunted Country" distinct from Pound's Ligurian coast: "Here the human past is dim and feeble and alien to us / Our ghosts draw from the crowded future."

Ghosts of inner ecology

Imagination is the organ of inner ecology. In the nineteenth-century *volkisch* view, the imagination transcended individuality, giving rise to the notion that great artists "belonged" to a nation, that intensity in an individual brightened the race. This short-circuited into a racial stinginess, a prophylactic urge to preserve the purity of imaginative expression, with nationalism as self-appointed custodian of purportedly "universal" values. The stage was set for the absorption of all cultural activity into a bureaucratic network of filtered "exposure" to "culturally enriching" events. Every citizen is delegated a personal sensibility to cultivate like a suburban backyard garden plot, a *compound* of sensibility, a reservation of privacy, a concentration camp of civility. The milieu is indelibly registered by Samuel Beckett in the cadence of "Imagination Dead Imagine":

> No trace anywhere of life, you say, pah, no difficulty there imagination not dead yet, yes, dead, good, imagination dead imagine. Islands, waters, azure, verdure, one glimpse and vanished, endlessly, omit. Till all white in the whiteness the rotunda. No way in, go in, measure. Diameter three feet, three feet from ground to summit of the vault. Two diameters at right angles AB CD divide the white ground into two semicircles ACB BDA. Lying on the ground two white bodies, each in its semicircle. White too the vault and the round wall eighteen inches high from which it springs. Go back out, a plain rotunda, all white in the whiteness, go back in, rap, solid throughout, a ring as in the imagination the ring of bone. The light that makes all so white no visible source, all shines with the same white shine, ground, wall vault, bodies, no shadow.

This is the ultimate depository of civilization. The vault or cockpit becomes the law, the cocoon of cyborgian command-control options. An entire population can be neutralized, plugged into addictive neurosensory inputs. The hominid neocortex seems porous to this assault: "The rotted man inside, who used to seem archetypal, is biological and his 'language environment' is amniotic and porous to heroin. He is the new wilderness announcement that there no longer is a wilderness which has not been mixed with non-wilderness." Human ecology has been consigned to the manic joyride of History, or the System as it appears to Thomas Pynchon:

> Kekulé dreams the Great Serpent holding its own tail in its mouth, the dreaming Serpent which surrounds the World. But the meanness, the cynicism with which this dream is to be used. The Serpent that announces, "The World is a closed thing, cyclical, resonant, eternally-returning," is to be delivered into a system whose only aim is to *violate* the Cycle. Taking and not giving back, demanding that "productivity" and "earnings" keep on increasing with time, the System removing from the rest of the World these vast quantities of energy to keep its own tiny desperate fraction showing a profit: and not only most of humanity—most of the World, animal, vegetable and mineral, is laid waste in the process. The System may or may not understand that it's only buying time. And that time is an artificial resource to begin with, of no value to anyone or anything but the System, which sooner or later must crash to its death, when its addiction to energy has become more than the rest of the World can supply, dragging with it innocent souls all along the chain of life. Living inside the System is like riding across the country in a bus driven by a maniac bent on suicide. (*Gravity's Rainbow*, 412)

The maniac driver is not an individual; nor is it a collective will; rather, it is an aggregate of behavioral tendencies precipitated by historical growth cycles now reaching the planetary limit. In terms of ancient cosmology, the world has become porous to chaos. The eruption of chaos is psychic event, not messy circumstance: "preformed chaos / strives to form / into play and ploy / plot and lore of discourse," as David Meltzer puts it in his "Biodegradable Prose Specks" on chaos. It may be that chaos was man's initial recognition of himself as twin to the universe, his body a distortion loop through which external unboundedness internalized itself; and this upside-down image (passed through the fovea centralis like a Möbius strip, inside out and upside down en route to turning right-side up again; like Maximus with his head in the ground and feet in the air) came out as soul or psyche.

Psyche is the cabin of a cosmos, a cabinet of that cosmetic that is the makeup of each person (*persona* or mask); make up your mind; make it up as you go along. *Psyche folds logos into itself, exfoliating cosmos.* The trivialization by habitual reference to William Carlos Williams's red wheelbarrow upon which "so much" depends should not disguise the fact that everything *does* depend on this tool for hauling compost. Cosmos too is compost, though its rate of decay and recycling is imperceptible except by analogy. Or by trope: to speak of cosmos as universe is to be reminded that it turns around as words in the mouth, that language is biodegradable, that "what is said of what is said" (myth for Charles Olson) is the whole of the law. The animated imprint, the knowledge (or logos enacted) with which the earth is signed and designed, is what the toss is for—play of the dice. Rollin' and tumblin'. Painting cave wall, incising tablet, staining papyrus, and multiplying human deeds by technology—these archaic impulses constitute a discrete evolutionary ecology, creating spaces in which apparent destinies can be reconsidered, new destinations conceived.

> Hermetic, terrible from joy,
> A rude imagination blazed
> This iconography, not
> To animate the game of nerves
> Nor galvanize a rotting fiber,
> But, as supernatural,
> To lead the florid intellect
> Through lovely glades of calm conceiving
> Until it know its final earth.

The hermetic imagination in every era has reflected not so much a craving for secrecy as an effort to pressurize psychic issue so as to insulate it from assaults on inner ecology. If Greek soil is filled with the blood of soldiers, whose ghosts beg heroes to reimburse them of their spilled essence, then American soil is saturated with implacable spirit exiles sifting through and infecting poetic imagination.

The ghosts of Odysseus's descent to the underworld sift down through the eleventh-century Latin of Andreas Divus, to lie there undisturbed till the blood flows for them in Pound's awakening of Divus into English in Canto I. Contemporaneous with Pound's text is Jeffers's "The Torch-Bearer's Race" with its tribe of lost ghosts:

> Dark and enormous rolls the surf; down on the mystical tide-line under the
> cliffs at moonset

Dead tribes move, remembering the scent of their hills, the lost hunters
Our fathers hunted; they driven westward died the sun's death, they dread the depth and hang at the land's hem,
And are unavenged . . .

Thirty-five years later Olson offers a magnified glimpse of these same ghosts, uncannily risen out of an abandoned vehicle:

As the dead prey upon us,
they are the dead in ourselves,
awake, my sleeping ones, I cry out to you,
disentangle the nets of being!

I pushed my car, it had been sitting so long unused.
I thought the tires looked as though they only needed air.
But suddenly the huge underbody was above me, and the rear tires were masses of rubber and thread variously clinging together

as were the dead souls in the living room, gathered
about my mother, some of them taking care to pass
beneath the beam of the movie projector, some record
playing on the victrola, and all of them
desperate with the tawdriness of their life in hell

I turned to the young man on my right and asked, "How is it,
there?" And he begged me protestingly don't ask, we are poor
poor. And the whole room was suddenly posters and presentations
of brake linings and other automotive accessories, cardboard
displays, the dead roaming from one to another
as bored back in life as they are in hell, poor and doomed
to mere equipments.

Hindrances spread like nets across each plane of being; angels and demons, spectral revenants ascend and descend in a network encompassing both the living and the dead:

The nets we are entangled in. Awake,
my soul, let the power into the last wrinkle
of being, let none of the threads and rubber of the tires
be left upon the earth. Let even your mother
go. Let there be only paradise

The desperateness is, that the instant
which is also paradise (paradise
is happiness) dissolves
into the next instant, and power
flows to meet the next occurrence.

The visiting ghosts in these poems of Pound, Jeffers, and Olson emphasize the historical context with its tacit sense of place. There are numerous similar recountings in poets of subsequent generations that seem more personal, less historical, yet the *place* continues to be concretized by the sightings. Clayton Eshleman's exploration of Paleolithic caves in *Hades in Manganese* is framed by poems concerning the nourishment of dead companions. Several poems in Robert Kelly's *Flesh Dream Book* have a comparable function. In *The Holy Forest,* Robin Blaser takes great care in the placement of commemorative poems (not necessarily elegies) in the concluding sections. Jerome Rothenberg's "Khurbn" opens itself to the unburied plaint of the Nazi death camps. And up the coast from Jeffers's Big Sur, Kenneth Irby is witness to an oceanic visitation. "The table top looked glassy for a few seconds," the setting begins, "shimmered, watery, showing the ocean dimly in the distances, then faded into ordinary wood again." An extensive excerpt is needed to convey the unrest in this overlap between the living and the dead, and how it is as much a function of place (the cosmos, glimmering on ocean marge) as it is of an individual psyche.

> Everything happened instantaneously, as at the end of the Diamond Sutra, with the dream intensity. He could only lengthen it, telling himself later. He knew each of them was dead, with the possible exception of Lenhoff, and all but him suicides, but he couldn't say this to their faces, neither could they ever admit it, and any conversation depended on that, confronting them with their deaths? . . .
>
> What did they all want from him? If he kept looking long enough he'd see everything he ever knew about them. If they all stayed long enough, everyone he'd ever known would show up too. All of them wanted touch again? The earthly again, out of those terrible emptinesses, but not some hand on the knee, as in a dream once he'd leaned forward to reassure David, or around the shoulder, or even a handshake, because they no longer shared any common substantiality. A rag of Sam's sleeve, but not Sam himself. They couldn't return to people they didn't know, only to some love, remembrance, the warmth of shared thought, the touch of some shared attention. Prayer,

he thought, must be about this. They didn't *know,* desperate, wrenched from life, *what* they wanted, but from the living, *release* again, as if here, *here,* they might be free, to *continue,* wherever that went, warmed anew. . . . All his life he'd been learning how to *receive.* What they wanted of him wasn't just what he gave, *his* love, but to *receive* theirs. To be *open,* as he'd told himself for years and years. To enlarge the space of the living. Nothing is lost. Take us when we come, we have no other place to go but those we love.

In the glassy surface of the table waves receded and pounded. He heard the roar of the eucalyptus grove, the wind was up, the door had come ajar and the wind was in cold, the post-alcoholic chill, he thought, it's time to go to bed.

Where are you now? In the house of friends, on the Northern coast of California, in the grip of the elements, altogether alive.

The scene provides a portal for the continuity of *longing* as conditional imprint of the western shore. If Whitman's Atlantic carried him back to boyhood refrains—which Olson continues in Gloucester, feeling himself always the son—then the Pacific gaze looks simultaneously on the immensity of the species' terminus and the "compost line of any mind of any / time to map the world line." The Pacific shore is one end of a land soaked with blood:

> the dark gods
> wait in the blooded underground
>
> their visage is more shapeless
> and more terrible than ever
>
> ~
>
> the hermetic secret floats elegantly among the muddy images
>
> ~
>
> in a place named No-Such-Place,
> burred
> speech of a ghost named
> Not-All-There.

The question, then, posed by such coastal limits:

> which direction now
> does *distance* take
>
> that aches in the feet?

There is—this is the hope in the ache—a way of looking at, attending to, cosmos, that catches the whole arc in the vision of its end, that can perceive in the individual a public yearning, "the Jurassic longing . . . we are the inheritors of that gaze."

Mind exists in the overlap between territory and map, the archaic and the old lore. *Chaos* is the place of, or force behind, this difficult perplexity of betweenness: "it is in the deep mind that wilderness and the unconscious become one" (Gary Snyder, quoted in Eshleman, *Hades in Manganese,* 14). "Let a man look for the permanent in the mutable and fleeting; let him learn to bear the disappearance of things he was wont to reverence without losing his reverence; let him learn that he is here, not to work but to be worked upon" (Emerson, "Montaigne"); or, as Dickinson tells it, to feel the "Omen in the Bone" (no. 532). "I want to see the unknown shine, like a sunrise," wrote William Carlos Williams (in Paul, 192).

k
the letter cutting
a the letter starting
o the alarm
s the snake again

~

All life long
you include something
that includes your life.
You are in the egg.

Origin

Cid Corman's magazine *Origin* helped launch the career of Charles Olson. But what is origin? Isn't origin unthinkable, like the moment of one's birth? Whatever we mean by origin, it always comes back to the earth.

> Not our good luck nor the instant peak and fulfillment of time gives us to see
> The beauty of things, nothing can bridle it.
> God who walks lightning-naked on the Pacific has never been hidden from any
> Puddle or hillock of the earth behind us.

The origin is a daily event, daily evident, each day's evidence all that's needed to "make it new." Not good luck nor the instant peak and fulfillment of time; not *only,* for these are numerous and profound. There is no part of it that does not press its release into the forge of a commanding realization. Primitivism, in Paul Shepard's sagacious definition, is "a reciprocity with origins" ("Post-Historic Primitivism," 88).

In *Lectures in America* Gertrude Stein reflects back on the phases of her writing, discerning not a conceptual itinerary but a series of tableaux, tidepools of feeling and sensation. Her ruminations help us overcome the idea that there are ideas, and make her work available *as palpability,* for this is how she remembers herself, remembers the event of her writing as the uniquely registered perturbation of a proprioceptively animated person. Her *métier* is talking and listening at the same time, during which she finds herself wondering "is there any way of making what I know come out as I know it, come out not as remembering" (181). Decades ahead of schedule, Stein invents projective verse. "Is there repetition or is there insistence" (166): that is the question. And "insistence is different. That is what makes life that the insistence is different" (167). The difference is so consuming that at its most acute it *is* without need of supplement; its figure encompasses and includes the ground on which it might otherwise be expected to stand out. And "if it were possible that a movement were lively enough it would exist so completely that it would not be necessary to see it moving against anything to know that it is moving. This is what we mean by life" (170). Credo: "if anything is alive there is no such thing as repetition" (174). Stein's practice in her portraits is cinematic; "in the Making of Americans, I was doing what the cinema was doing, I was making a continuous succession of the statement of what that person was until I had not many things but one thing" (176–77). Everyday life is extemporaneously creative, so "we have living in moving being necessarily so intense that existing is indeed something, is indeed that thing that we are doing" (182). Significantly, "It is not repetition if it is that which you are actually doing because naturally each time the emphasis is different just as the cinema has each time a slightly different thing to make it all be moving" (179). Stein's sense of "moving" expands here like a sponge to include, along with movement, the emotionally moving. It is moving: it is taking us somewhere. We are in transport, galvanized with the mobilizing insistence of e/motion.

Insistence is just what Charles Olson's own syntax prescribes in "Projective Verse":

> The objects which occur at every given moment of composition (of recognition, we can call it) are, can be, must be treated exactly as they do occur therein and not by any ideas or preconceptions from outside the poem, must be handled as a series of objects in field in such a way that a series of tensions (which they also are) are made to *hold,* and to hold exactly inside the content and the context of the poem which has forced itself, through the poet and them, into being. (*Human Universe,* 56)

All the ingredient contributions to composition by field are here: the tensional legacy of romanticism, the direct perception of (Poundian) modernism, and the inter-transpicuous* claim of New England transcendentalism that spirit is form

* The term "inter-transpicuous" is from Shelley, *Prometheus Unbound* IV, l. 236–61:

And from the other opening in the wood
Rushes, with loud and whirlwind harmony,
A sphere, which is as many thousand spheres,
Solid as crystal, yet through all its mass
Flow, as through empty space, music and light:
Ten thousand orbs involving and involved,
Purple and azure, white, and green, and golden,
Sphere within sphere; and every space between
Peopled with unimaginable shapes,
Such as ghosts dream dwell in the lampless deep,
Yet each inter-transpicuous, and they whirl
Over each other with a thousand motions,
Upon a thousand sightless axles spinning,
And with the force of self-destroying swiftness,
Intensely, slowly, solemnly roll on,
Kindling with mingled sounds, and many tones,
Intelligible words and music wild.
With mighty whirl the multitudinous orb
Grinds the bright brook into an azure mist
Of elemental subtlety, like light;
And the wild odour of the forest flowers,
The music of the living grass and air,
The emerald light of leaf-entangled beams
Round its intense yet self-conflicting speed,
Seem kneaded into one aëreal mass
Which drowns the sense.

Gustaf Sobin revisits the inter-transpicuous: "roll, that it / billow; pierce, that it // burst, for this, this only is / depth, dimension, the / sheer // susceptibility of each elastic, still expanding / emanation."

and doth the body make (Olson's declaration at the Berkeley conference in 1965 "that which exists through itself is its own meaning" [in Creeley, *Contexts of Poetry*, 93] recapitulates Emerson's definition of the spiritual as that which is its own evidence [in "Experience"]). Olson's model of the poem as a vehicle of energies accords with Muriel Rukeyser's contemporaneous view, "Exchange is creation. In poetry, the exchange is one of energy. Human energy is transferred, and from the poem it reaches the reader" (*Life of Poetry*, 185). The poem conceived as a unit of binding energy rather than an artifact moves with animal grace and an atmospheric diffusion of its content into its form, its emanation. Resistance to Olson's propositions and to Stein's practice are similar: the work ("projective" or "moving"), being a species of autopoiesis, corresponds to no prior plan, scheme, blueprint, paradigm, authorizing sanction. *It is its own preview and afterthought.* Western aesthetic sensibility has been so sedulously trained in the dialectic of repetition and recognition—rather than motion and cognition—that it is literally stupefied at the prospect of anything different. The insistent could be recognized only as a rhetorical manner, or as a certain temper of moral probity, not as the measure of the occasion itself. Its form. As for "content": that would be circumstantial as well. In Olson's famous retort to Robert Duncan in "Against Wisdom As Such": "any wisdom which gets into any poem is solely a quality of the moment of time in which there might happen to be wisdoms" (*Human Universe*, 71). An important corollary is that there is no secret archetype or governing *eidos* emanating Idea through the passive plasticity of matter, the mother lode or matrix of manifestation. Everything *of* the "moment of time" is actualized as surface, incarnate in what Michael McClure calls a "momentary system of poetics" (*Scratching the Beat Surface*, 54).

Michel Foucault's insight about origin overlaps significantly with (and, as if to corroborate everything in his thesis, without awareness of) Gertrude Stein and Charles Olson. Foucault views origin as a "thin surface . . . which accompanies our entire existence and never deserts it" (*Order of Things*, 330–31). Every move we make inaugurates a new skin of origin. Foucault is inspired here in part by the Romantic dream that valorizes origin as originality. What could be more original than an utterly contingent and gratuitous gesture, such as that celebrated by William Carlos Williams's poem "Danse Russe" ("Who shall say I am not / the happy genius of my household")? Yet these acts are not accredited any force of originality because they are *too* specific, all too proximate to those special signs, the stigmata, the sort of individuation constituted by mortality and diagnosed by the medical gaze.* Origin is not engaged by originality but by reiteration (a point belabored by Plato and Aristotle in their divergent deliberations on First Cause). Foucault and Derrida converge unwittingly on Stein's repudiation of repetition: all three claim that what superficially looks like a repeat is nonetheless inaugural. The origin is immediate, not remote. This immediacy renders it distinct in kind from depth hypotheses of origin, in which origins are affiliated with a maximal interiority (like Olson, Foucault would find in proprioceptive depth a register of embodiment, not a moral crypt) and interiority is valorized as the inner sanctum of authenticity.† The origin Foucault strives to reclaim is *superficial,* that which (like Poe's purloined

* Foucault leaves no ambiguity on this point, either: the "thin surface" of origin he speaks of, which never deserts us, "not even, indeed especially not, at the moment of death, when, on the contrary, it reveals itself, as it were, naked" (*Order of Things,* 331).

† Jean Starobinski criticizes the urge to seek authenticity in roots, in reservoirs of atavism, in the archaeological depth model; but he also cautions against another, equally invasive model—subjective interiority: "the image of the past preserved *internally* is alluring, so much so that it still holds us in thrall" ("Inside and the Outside," 333). When the two models are combined—the *arche* of history with the *telos* of biology—the self is misconstrued as a "nuclear stronghold . . . where origins persist and endure" (334)—"as if we recalld the nature of the deep," Duncan concurs, "out of what we were." "Making the most remote past coefficient to our most intimate depth is a way of refusing loss and separation, of preserving, in the crammed plenum we imagine history to be, every moment spent along the way. The very image of a 'way' assumes that the past is productive and efficacious, its efficacy corroborated not only by the forward distance traveled, but by the traveler whose nature is fraught with the sum total of antecedent experience. To say that the individual constructed himself through his history is to say that the latter is cumulatively present in him and that even as it was elapsing, it was becoming internal structure. From this idea one cannot but draw an inference and its corollary, the inference being that self-knowledge is anamnesis or rememoration, and the corollary that anamnesis is the recognition of deep layers (often compared to geological strata) of the present-day person. When such a theory, far from limiting itself to the individual's history, redounds upon the entire history of the species in that of the person, it begets an extraordinarily reassuring system: there is nothing of the human past not mine, there is no word in the depths of time that does not concern and shed light upon me. Nothing is *outside,* nothing may be considered foreign (*Nihil humani* . . .). All history sets a mirror before us" (Starobinski, 334). In contrast to the sanguine narcissism of the *cogito,* Foucault labored over a more austere yet fertile prospect. "To think is to fold, to double the outside with a coextensive insight," writes Deleuze, summarizing Foucault. Consequently, "every inside-space is topologically in contact with the outside-space, independent of distance and on the limits of a 'living'; and this carnal or vital topology, far from showing up in space, frees a sense of time that fits the past into the inside, brings about the future in the outside, and brings the two into confrontation at the limit of the living present" (*Foucault,* 118–19).

letter) is transparent, invisible, in its superfluity. (It is only in a context as charged and convoluted as the late chapters of *The Order of Things* or Derrida's *Dissemination* that Stein's infamous iteration "a rose is a rose is a rose" assumes its proper dimensions.) To reiterate Gilles Deleuze: *"the organization of language is not separable from the poetic discovery of surface"* ("Schizophrenic and Language," 285). Brian McHale finds such a prospect handsomely evident in *The Tablets* by Armand Schwerner: "what might have been a 'vertical' structure of transmission, emerging out of archaeological 'deep time' into the light of the present, suffers epistemological erosion and ends up collapsing into a single plane. . . . Nothing wells up from the depths; there **are** no depths under this eroded plane" ("Archaeologies of Knowledge," 249; McHale's boldface).

The babble of origin; the talkative manner in which "origin" is itself a discursive construct to begin with rather than a metaphysical drive; the contingency of origin in acts of perception; means that

> the level of the original is probably that which is closest to man: the surface he traverses so innocently, always for the first time, and upon which his scarcely opened eyes discern figures as young as his own gaze . . . not because they are always equally young [but] because they belong to a time that has neither the same standards of measurement nor the same foundations as him. (*Order of Things*, 330)

Foucault's "surface" is marked by that "collateral contemporaneity" in which William James found the whole universe knocking at the door to be let in. "While I talk and the flies buzz, a sea-gull catches a fish at the mouth of the Amazon, a tree falls in the Adirondack wilderness, a man sneezes in Germany, a horse dies in Tartary, and twins are born in France. What does that mean?" This is the riddle William James posed, asking his audience to consider that "We have no organ or faculty to appreciate the simply given order. The real world as it is given objectively at this moment is the sum total of all its beings and events now. But can we think of such a sum?" (*Will to Believe*, 545, 546). "Yet just such a collateral contemporaneity," he reminded them, referring to his Borgesian list, "is the real order of the world" (546). Furthermore, "The Universe, with every living entity which her resources create, creates at the same time a call for that entity, and an appetite for its continuance,—creates it, if nowhere else, at least within the heart of the entity itself" ("Human Immortality," 1125). By this means the individual is wedded to an imponderable congregation in which the whole appears: the accidents and incidents of the everyday that consecrate the unique, in which an odd torque compels divergence, and "objects will not stay concrete and particular: they fuse themselves into general essences, and they sum themselves into a whole—the universe. And then the object that confronts us, that knocks on our mental door and asks to be let in, and fixed and decided upon and actively met, is just this whole universe itself and its essence" (*Will to Believe,* 549).

The issue of origins and originality is then caught up in the matter—the mutter—of alterity, its looming matrix. One might stress *matter,* since alterity is virtually synonymous with matrices of materiality, signs of an intimate alien leading, etymologically and conceptually, to the *maternal* as source and mark of origin. Even language is gendered in the mother tongue. The figure of the mother as guardian of memory—subtended perhaps by the muses as daughters of memory—indicates something about the labile continuum in which Foucault would find us released to a memory alleviated from depth (and the vertical dimension of status and hierarchy), exonerated from authority, and given over to an erotics of transversality rather than laboring under the weight of symbolic capital and the "universal."* Julia Kristeva gives more credit to the maternal in her figure of the *chora,* the vocal and kinetic plenitude challenging the symbolic order as such. She attributes this challenge specifically to poetry, the function of which is "to introduce through the symbolic that which works on, moves through, and threatens it" (*Revolution in Poetic Language,* 81). Below the armaments of social friction and constraint a deep uncanny persists, an "Occult ferocity of origin" wherein

> Vision closes over vision
> Standpoint melts into open
>
> wanton meteor ensign streaming
>
> ~
>
> not water not air *not* earth not conflux or mixture not number
> not mind not force
>
> it is
>
> both thing and thought
> co-implicate
> singular.

* This is not quite the call to heterogeneous profusion that it might seem, however. The origin may be immediate rather than remote, but its immediacy always threatens to engorge us in our own appetites. This is readily apparent in the continuous appeals to originality, freshness, the unprecedented, and the new in commercial advertising. So the work of maturity (not a term Foucault would use) is to go beyond this immediate apprehension of origin to the recognition of origin (and its immediacy) as *mediated.*

Detritus pathways

"Life will show you masks that are worth all your carnivals. Yonder mountain must migrate into your mind" (Emerson, "Illusions"—reiterated in Aldo Leopold's famous exhortation to think like a mountain). This migration mimics the interplay of real and ideal in the "loom of time": "Illusion, Temperament, Succession, Surface, Surprise, Reality, Subjectiveness—these are threads on the loom of time, these are the lords of life" ("Experience"). The loom is a figure attracting not only Emerson but Melville in "The Mat-Maker" (*Moby-Dick,* chap. 47). In a dreamy stillness aboard the Pequod, Ishmael says, "it seemed as if this were the Loom of Time, and I myself were a shuttle mechanically weaving and weaving away at the Fates." But the very powers of the Fates produce a counterforce: "The weaver-god, he weaves; and by that weaving is he deafened, that he hears no mortal voice; and by that humming, we, too, who look on the loom are deafened. . . . Ah, mortal! then, be heedful; for so, in all this din of the great world's loom, thy subtlest thinkings may be overheard afar" (chap. 102). Such a figure provides the scale and plectrum on which Robert Kelly tunes and turns and untunes tales of an alchemical anatomy in his four-hundred-page poem *The Loom.* The point of a loom is twofold: to make a covering shelter (the counterpane of Queequeg and Ishmael), and as cover or disguise of Penelope's stratagem of delay in the *Odyssey.* Both produce a design, or pattern, and both retain a sense of *having designs.*

In texture we feel the tug of particulars in the claim and counterclaim of the weave. "The web is woven and you have to wear it," intones Wallace Stevens in "The Dwarf."

> It is the mind that is woven, the mind that was jerked
> And tufted in straggling thunder and shattered sun.
>
> It is all that you are, the final dwarf of you,
> That is woven and woven and waiting to be worn,
>
> Neither as mask nor as garment but as a being . . .

Within the parameters of the loom, contraries interpenetrate and form a subtle bond. The loom is a sensible figure for the mind, which never stops concealing its meanings from itself and then unconcealing them in particular increments—alternating/overlapping threads in warp and woof; Heidegger's dialectic of vorhanden/zuhanden; Freud's game of fort/da, "wo es war, soll ich werden" (where *it* is, there I'll be), which becomes Lacan's "locus of speech" in which "The Other is, therefore, the locus in which is constituted the I who already speaks to him who hears, that which is said by the one being already the reply, the other deciding to hear it whether the one has or has not spoken" (*Écrits,* 141). Selfhood; identity; fly in the ointment. Like Tarbaby, the struggle to escape intensifies the grip that retains. Cross purposes, slantwise, refractory: the ties that bind are always the work of a web. A web orders filaments of assimilation. So does a dream.

In a dream reported to me long ago by a friend (whose passing I commemorate in the telling): he was at the top of some steps, where he cupped both hands together, leaving a circle between thumb and forefinger through which to peer. When he looked in, he saw a butterfly sitting calmly, stared into its eyes, which were—he realized at that instant—as fully and momentously alert and penetrating as any human eyes he'd ever seen.

it let me stand
above it ten minutes
watching it quiver
while it did what?

what do souls do?

Organic respiration is synthesized in these wings, prompting a delirium of infinite regress. Cosmos, psyche, logos: to our working plenum of inherited intelligence these words are like mineshafts condensing an *ore* of *lore.* The butterfly dreamt as a soul is a familiar glimpse. In asking of his image "what do souls do?" Robert Kelly presses a finger against the pulse of the wingbeat. It's an image of the psyche of psyche, of psyche *ad infinitum. Psyche folds logos into itself, exfoliating cosmos.*

The dream material appears like this: the logos—a pungency of psyche or soul—is folded by psyche into itself, held in its hands, and the exfoliation as if from a world-tree is leafy, winglike, a thin membrane bounding animate being, clearly and startlingly (to the dreamer) possessed of intelligence. A wing is a sentient web, a "body of paradigmatic fields" in the title of Catherine Webster's poem:

Wooing swallow, quivery hilly wings, shape the eaves.

Hurry the ditchbank wild hair in bloom back to the nest, flurry the crimped in.

Crisscross the porch, waxy bird, pack the soil and the pond back in, opened.

Sink in, flush an ovary, worry the fringes of ditches, vernal pools, whir madly, flash below the flowering cut-leafed daisy's hair, bull thistle,

skinning surface mud,
skin the toothy-margined rothrock, lobes of maiden clover.

Skin a second time the waxy margins, squeeze
the paean sallow, spit the crude back into the nest.

~

detritus pathways. "delayed and complex ways
to pass the food through webs."

maturity. stop and think. draw on the mind's
stored richness. memory, dream, half-digested
image of your life. "detritus pathways"—feed
the many tiny things that feed an owl.
send heart boldly travelling,
on the heat of the dead & down.

The phrase "to have heart" speaks of the courage required to follow "the heat of the dead & down." The heart taken through detritus pathways is an original animus, the "breath that was consciousness in the chest" (Onians, 170)—the cavern of coronary empathy—but eventually the Greeks posited psyche in or of the head, distinguishing it not by its consciousness but by its *vividness.*

The shape of the head reinforced archaic configurations of the soul as circular (the head as seat of the crown, the nut in the halo). Psyche as procreative essence in the body was the manifest serpent of the fluid of Okeanos encircling earth and bathing the stars (Onians, 249). Greek placement of Okeanos at the margin is instructive, suggesting that the generative exceeds human affairs and extends to the cosmos as such. Telos—fate or end—was circular, as time was: the telos of an individual was the circle of a personal destiny, a radius of time and space. To die was not to come to the end of a line but to break the circle, shatter the egg; to vibrate beyond identity, and even beyond entity. The Pythagoreans held Kronos to be *the psyche of the universe.* Kronos's circularity and cyclicity (as time, Chronos) make him another web overlapping with Okeanos, telos, psyche, ouroboros, all images of circulation, all evidence of the conviction that *where soul is in motion a cosmos appears.*

Onians writes that "*chronos* was perhaps originally expressive of that which touched one's surface" (451). That is, as the circle of one's telos came into contact with encircling Okeanos (through psyche's link with Okeanos's incubating compass), Kronos linked each surface with a facing countenance, inside with outside, form and counterform folding and unfolding. On the surfaces of bodies where touch is expressed as kronos (and is chronic), the consequence of circulation is expressed in the word "uni-verse" as a single turn. As Benjamin Blood put it, "the universe is wild—game flavored as a hawk's wing. Nature is miracle all; the same returns not, save to bring the different. The slow round of the engraver's lathe gains but the breadth of a hair, but the difference is distributed back over the whole curve" (in William James, *Will to Believe,* 448).

We can assign the earliest commemoration of cosmic circulation to the encircling walls of Paleolithic caves; and by this, the arousal of psyche and the posing of the question, "What do souls do?" The caves encompass the witness all around; circularity is immediate location, and location is sensation; the walls are webs, detritus pathways, overlays of contact and boundedness (telos, awakening the kronos of fluidity from stone), early expressions of the concept of *an inside* that is not to be confused with subjective interiority. Psyche could come forth only as enactment, only in spatial terms as the attention to sacred location as simultaneously spatial and temporal. The time unfolding in transit through the caves to the painted chambers was echoed in the overlapping images of different times that covered the walls. Paleolithic psyche is not containable within the individual, but is the chemical residuum of images overlaid by generations of application. Psyche, art, and myth are ways of attending to the human by circulating images of the lives of species. The plural is important: for the Paleolithic mind, the human is syncretic, compounded of enabling pluralities of which other species were contributing features. Masks. Applications. Supplicants.

"Paleolithic space appears to be multidirectional, not only a world of broken interrelation where everything is in association, but also a world that is not partitioned from its material by a frame or some other boundary device" (Eshleman, *Antiphonal Swing,* 163). Therio-expulsion created the cosmic hollow of a gnostic gap in matter, Eshleman imagines, and "What we project as abyss, and into it, are the guardians, or sides of boundary, the parietal labor to bear Hermes, to give a limit to evasiveness, to contour meandering, to make connections" ("Paleo-Ecology," 340). Mythic potential, actualized in the framework of humanism, gives us a field manual of applications called Literature. All that we know as "literature" may be the domestication of myth, that formerly wild, autonomous psychic emanation—pulsing between the "unmade boundaries of acts and poems." In the Paleolithic the human had not yet come into focus as a clear receptacle; man tended "to depict animals realistically and himself as a hybrid monster" (Eshleman, "Seeds of Narrative," 45). Human participation in the world was *through* animals or *as* animal, but no image of a clearly human figure emerges until much later. But if, as Foucault maintains*, "l'homme" is the last stopgap in our ongoing Western estimation of the finite, we are on the brink of a return to chaos, facing the unbounded, the pervasive condition in which *we* are the ouroboros biting our own tale. "*Someone,* at this point, must take in hand the task of being everyone, & no one, as the first poets did. Someone must pay attention to the real spiritual needs of both her neighbors (not her poetic peers) & the future" (Notley, *Scarlet Cabinet,* vi). We are free to entertain *scruples* and assess the bounty of the superfluous.

> As species disappear, the paleolithic grows more vivid. As living animals disappear, the first outlines become more dear, not as reflections of a day world, but as the primal contours of psyche, the shaping of the underworld, the point at which Hades was an animal. The new wilderness is thus the spectral realm created by the going out of animal life and the coming in, in our time, of

* "As the archaeology of our thought easily shows, man is an invention of recent date. And one perhaps nearing its end," Foucault famously wrote in *Les Mots et les choses* (*Order of Things,* 387). "Nietzsche rediscovered the point at which man and God belong to one another, at which the death of the second is synonymous with the disappearance of the first, and at which the promise of the super-man signifies first and foremost the imminence of the death of man. . . . It is no longer possible to think in our day other than in the void left by man's disappearance. For this void does not create a deficiency; it does not constitute a lacuna that must be filled. It is nothing more, and nothing less, than the unfolding of a space in which it is once more possible to think" (342). Foucault's diagnosis pertains to the compost library, which in the heat of biorephrasable thought discloses "man" to be of a certain consistency, now subject like papyrus to disintegration. The premonitions are cumulative and reflect the pace of historical acceleration. Nietzsche's proclamation of the death of God predates only slightly Freud's exhumation of the unconscious, which is contemporary with Henry Adams's suggestion that the scope of what must be known of the world is now beyond the capacity of a single individual (reiterated at the opening of Pound's *Guide to Kulchur* three decades later). "Adams applies the rule of phase, the mathematics that describes threshold phenomena—such as water turning to ice—to history. His argument [is that] thought would reach 'the limit of its possibility in the year 1921' " (Byrd, *Poetics of the Common Knowledge,* 157–58). Pound wrote in *Guide to Kulchur* that "Certain ground we have gained and lost since Rabelais's time or since Montaigne browsed over 'all human knowledge.' Certain kinds of awareness mark the live books in our time, in the decade 1930 to 40. Lack of these awarenesses shows in the mass of dead matter printed. No living man knows enough to write: Part I. Method. Part II. Philosophy, the history of thought. Part III. History, that is of action. Part IV. The arts and civilization" (23). Pound's own unhinged pretensions have understandably been construed as hubristic refusal of his own advice.

these primary outlines. Our tragedy is to search further and further back for a common non-racial trunk in which the animal is not separated out of the human while we destroy the turf on which we actually stand.

~

"The brush
May paint the mountains and streams
Though the territory is lost."

Scruples & superstition

Fear and trembling, awe and dread reverberate the archaic animal body in cultural personae. Gorgon and Medusa are such figures, the Muse is another, bringing on shudders, rapture, palsied compliance;* allowing no deviations, her strictness is meter, pulse, *rhythmos.* She is part of a tide of intercultural drift, a detritus like glacial boulders. But in cultural morphology—what Guy Davenport calls the geography of the imagination—there are forces of distribution and distillation that have little to do with human boundaries, historical or social. He describes the geography as a map:

* For more on the legacy of the Muse, see Rasula, "Poetry's Voice-Over" and "Gendering the Muse." Black Mountain and Beat writers conspicuously gendered the Muse in private life, now increasingly disclosed in biographies and published documents. No wonder Alice Notley can ask " 'Was' / 'the human psyche' 'made of women' 'turned to stone?' " No one may be better situated to reflect on this legacy than Anne Waldman, who knows the ups and downs of male idolatry complexly infused with misogyny (and this is clearly one incentive behind her multivolume epic study of maleness, *Iovis*); but she knows another level of complexity as a woman poet for whom the Muse is nonetheless female: "She was my fixed star for a time of heart & I was perpetual motion too. I catch her as best I can/could through scent & ambiguity of verse. The pronouns you find us in in here are a relationship to secret notebooks and hallucinated masks. A relationship to a web of emptiness dotted with long molecules held near one another by the action of invisible forces . . . The 'shes' in it are our relationship. I am the mother most frequently & she too. And we are both daughters standing between the lines. And as children we both put on the shields like Amazons" (*Kill or Cure,* 127). Like H. D. and Virginia Woolf, Waldman is an advocate of a pan-gendered writing: "I propose a utopian creative field where we are defined by our *energy,* not by gender. I propose a transsexual literature, a hermaphroditic literature, a transvestite literature, and finally a poetics of transformation beyond gender" (145).

> Such a map would presumably display such phenomena as the contours of the worship of Demeter and Persephone, coinciding with grain-producing terrain, and with the contours of Catholicism. This would not surprise us. It might also show how the structure of psychology and drama nourished by grain-producing cultures persists outside that terrain, continuing to act as if it were inside, because its imaginative authority refuses to abdicate. (*Geography of the Imagination,* 10–11)

Out of such obscure persistence we seek the recovery of a terminological tool kit. Certain words come to hand: soul, psyche, logos, cosmos, anthropos, physis, and more. They are all archaic insofar as we can regard them with—and behold them in—*superstition.*

We are of a moment in which the "imaginative authority" of the image of man in his uniquely human potential "refuses to abdicate." We still seek a psychology that is *humanistic* (instead of animistic—vegetable, mineral, animal); we hanker after an art and literature that is "imaginative" yet possessed of "authority"—wondering, like Anne Waldman, "Was the agreement that words shine like sun, / or glint as weapons in moonlight?" We want authorities, not authors. This "we" is of course one I would prefer to disengage. Yet disaffiliation now—even from that which oppresses—results in exile into a worldview spooked by dread of chaos, driven astray in search of an autonomy that often turns out to camouflage authority and privilege:

> Now I subtract myself from the industrial
> white hive, a worker slinking off
> from my queen valve position,
>
> letting it spurt, knowing that in a moment
> another will be plugged in my place.
> It is Soweto miners whose 115 degree eyes
>
> gleam from the neighboring houseside,
> the studs supporting our king-sized bed.
> I subtract myself while I add up
>
> the multiplication that I am part of,
> the scorpion-tail cornucopia that,
> with nature disappearing, the earth is becoming.

As in Kafka's story of the Great Wall, only the nomads are in a position to know how extensive the wall is, how close to completion, how irreparable the consequences. "With the growth of military skill and political suspicion, the wall might turn into a complicated system" (Mumford, *City in History*, 66). What Gilles Deleuze calls nomad thought best approximates this state of superstition poets have maintained in the face of an expanding wall. In wreading this composting poetry, we see that *all* human production needs urgently to be deglamorized, unframed the instant it appears, each saying bound up with its unsaying. The classical image of civilized citizen allows only certainties. Charles Olson, following Keats, proclaims the necessity of *persisting in doubts and uncertainties.* Robert Duncan said of Olson, "He wanted not only a crisis in consciousness but a crisis in the unconscious" ("As an Introduction," 82). What we have at hand now is a need to reimagine the archaic (*soul:* the archaic word for human) so that it includes logos (certitude, sign) but is not dominated by it, leaving room also for psyche (our personal bit of chaos, which daily and nightly delivers a recycled portion of our "faculty of tact as members of life"). The Great Wall is now not a construct but the gap in biodiversity looming before us: impenetrable as a wall because, once the diversity lapses, nothing imaginable within the total time frame of human experience can repair it. Psyche is the only receptacle deep enough to make the consequences palpable:

> . . . where drought is the epic then there must be some
> who persist, not by species-betrayal
> but by changing themselves
>
> minutely, by a constant study
> of the price of continuity
> a steady bargain with the way things are.

Psychosm

If the logos—locked in dogma by authority of a book—is an image of centrality, mythos might be seen not as peripheral (i.e., subordinate or secondary to the center) but as *centrifugal.* Myth is the centrifugal suction pulling centers apart into other circles, new centers, rings, circles within circles expanding and contracting in a "steady bargain with the way things are." What Derrida calls "arche-writing" is, ostensibly, composting poetry: nonlinear, denoting the transcendental signified of the Book, deferring all questions of origin and originality, yet referring them *to writing* as the disseminating medium that at once constitutes the book and leaks or even gushes from it. It is a problem of ostensible unity, addressed by Charles Stein in terms of monism.

> Plato [and the Neo-Platonists after him and the Christians, Jews, and Moslems along with and after *them,* and much of the scientism after *them*] mistook the Parmenidean Vision of Undivided Being for a Doctrine of the One. This productive error afforded hierarchy in everything, and the finally gruesome spectacle of *degrees* of Being: you were with or in or possessed of Being just so much as you participated in a transcendent Unity. Thus has our UNIverse grown littered with Qliphotic existences deficient in being: shells, shards, leftovers, junk, weeds, outcasts, inappropriate subject matters, inadmissible behaviors, *personae non gratae,* inadmissible poems.
>
> The spiritual praxis of the One aimed to advance beyond Being to a Good purified of contingency; the poetic work became a practice of exclusion that celebrated the hypertrophy of Unity: valorized ideal forms and universal, ideal voices. ("For Gerrit Lansing," 41; brackets are in Stein)

Stein celebrates Lansing's "genial occultism" as "an address from the contingency of intimate care that touches us not where we are Everyman—but where we are ourselves." He takes such work to be instructively Parmenidean in affirming that "Being exceeds the One" and that "Unity is a function of experience, not what funds it"; so, for Lansing, "concerns are not authorized by anything but the tropisms of a vitalized attention, and the work of setting to rights the exclusions of western history is quietly and quite subversively accomplished" (41).

A problem remains: what do we do with the logos embedded in our words for disciplined research: archaeology, sociology, geology, psychology? The root, the social, the earth and psyche are subject to a logos, a generalization or common denominator imposed on them. But what is it? The word *mythology* is a conspicuous misnomer (or names a presumptuous science), but it affords a clue to one way around the dilemma. For the word mythology reminds us that myth, too, has its logos. As Heraclitus insisted, logos is common: speech joins us each by each. The points of contact become mutually interpenetrating inversions, one model of which is the alchemical figure of the double pelican:

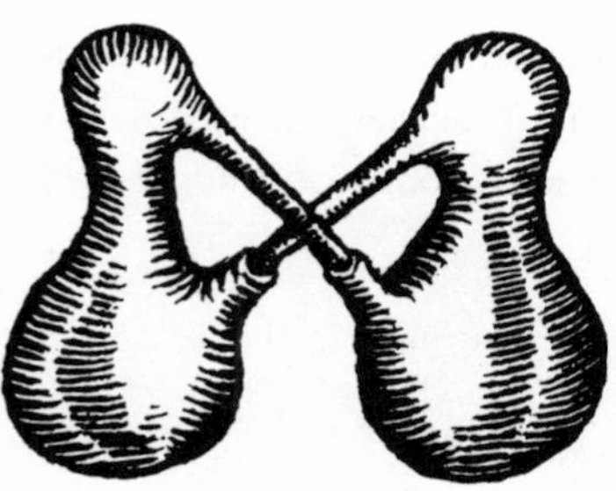

Giambattista Vico's description of this state is especially pungent. Drawing on his foundational axiom, "Because of the indefinite nature of the human mind, wherever it is lost in ignorance man makes himself the measure of all things" (*New Science,* para. 120), Vico argues that

> as rational metaphysics teaches that man becomes all things by understanding them (*homo intelligendo fit omnia*), this imaginative metaphysics shows that man becomes all things by *not* understanding them (*homo non intelligendo fit omnia*); and perhaps the latter proposition is truer than the former, for when man understands he extends his mind and takes in the things, but when he does not understand he makes the things out of himself and becomes them by transforming himself into them (para. 405).

From Vico's imaginative metaphysics it is not much of a leap to Heidegger, whose etymological reveries exemplify Vico's insight. Heidegger's essay on the logos seeks to restore a common dimension to the word: the logos is "the Laying that gathers"—a phrase that is itself a laying out of bait, an invitation to play, like laying down a line in jazz, fizzing up melodic alignments from the syncopated nudge. Heidegger's language is not logical but tropological; his meditation here is guided by the overlapping stimulation of the German verbs *lesen* (to read, to gather) and *legen* (to lay, which he traces to the Greek *legein* from which *logos* comes).* The world passes through the mouth and this transit is the logos. The vitality of the term has practically vanished, because the logos of each scholarly discipline is held to be the special terminology setting it apart from the common. Confined in use to a suffix of specialization, the logos—which should be simply the word as available to all—is lost to thought, and only poets take thought in common *words,* finding that words commonly disclose the uncommon.

* See "Logos," in Heidegger, *Early Greek Thinking,* 59–78.

Conveniently, a poet coined the word *psychosm,* conjoining psyche and cosmos.* A psychosm would be a plexus of energy by which the universe is pivoted in mind, and psyche integrates a material world extending to cosmos—

that,
through us, the
hazel
might ripen, and the stars
into their
fall quadrants
drift.

Superfluity

Myth arises, reputedly, as participatory response: the interjected *mu* of onlookers in a circle around a performance or recitation. The mu of myth is the oracle of circularity: myth is psyche affirming a circulation and is as innate to the individual as the distinctive whorl of fingerprint by which we are identified: an implicating fold, a personal labyrinth, a diagram of detritus pathways. The very notions of psyche and myth are unambiguously concentric in their bias. Jacques Derrida's critique of logocentrism couples the image of centrality with the logos, that traditional antithesis of myth. In *Of Grammatology* Derrida covertly addresses the collapsed legacy of the ouroboros in terms of the infinite regression of the signifier, which is a variant of the *perpetuum mobile* of Zeno's paradox. The lapse of outer circumference, fatigued beyond repair, boomerangs as binding indecision in the slippage of "différance"—that syncopation of distress that, from another perspective, becomes the sound of a startled pounding heart.

Myth—the nigredo of artifact, smelted into tale or image—has long been the "content" of art, and art attests to a profusion of life exceeding any single time

* In *NeoLogos,* a mimeo circular (1975), Charles Stein defined *psycosm* as: "1. A soul-world or soul's world. 2. The world specified within any consensual realm. There would be a 'psycosm' for any group or persons participating in a common system of reality. 3. Any representation of a soul's world, as in a poem or other work of art. 4. A breath world: the field of consciousness arising and vanishing with the duration of any specified unit of temporal consciousness." My altered spelling adds a psychological torque, a nudge in the direction of inner ecology.

or place. "The transformations of culture do not take place in history, they take place in myth. It is because the individual cannot perceive in the limits of his own lifetime such transformations as the Neolithic or Industrial revolutions that we have need of myth" (William Irwin Thompson, *Falling Bodies,* 135). To reiterate Robert Duncan's point from *The Truth and Life of Myth,* "To inherit or to evolve is to enter mythic existence" (59). Myth is amorphous and protean because it so freely changes hands or mouths. Myth is the legacy of biodegradable thought, compost rumination. Myth comes to mouth to make apparent what the eye can't see. It is a means of giving scope to idiosyncrasy and gratuitous bounty—the bounty of gratuity. The preponderance of indirection in poetry acknowledges drift—as does Thoreau's "saunter" (from, he says, *sans terre*), the Situationist *derive,* and the clinamen of Lucretius. "God said, 'Let meanings move,' and there was poetry." It is Robinson Jeffers's "Divinely superfluous beauty"; the "high superfluousness" by which we "know / Our God."

> . . . to fling
> Rainbows over the rain
> And beauty above the moon, and secret rainbows
> On the domes of deep sea-shells,
> And make the necessary embrace of breeding
> Beautiful also as fire,
>
> . . . .
>
> There is the great humaneness at the heart of things,
> The extravagant kindness, the fountain . . .

~

> The great Mind passes by its own
>   fine-honed thoughts,
>   going each way.
>
> Rainbow hanging steady
>   only slightly wavering with the
>   swing of the whole spill,
>   between the rising and the falling,
>   stands still.
>
> I stand drenched in crashing spray and mist,
> and pray.

Superfluity sharpens the edge of awareness. The prayer combines wonder and danger; the gist of any prayer is a poet's question. Muriel Rukeyser asks, "Do I move toward form, do I use all my fears?" This is a presentiment of *duende,* the Spanish uncanny that (playing off the German sense of *unheimlich* as unhomely) Federico García Lorca found in New York, sensing himself "not a man, not a poet, not a leaf, / only a wounded pulse that probes the things of the other side." "A certain arch and/or ache and/or ark of duress, the frazzled edge of what remains 'unsung,' " as Nathaniel Mackey puts it. "An undertow / of whir im- / mersed in / words": "it is human nature to stand in the middle of a thing / but you cannot stand in the middle of this" (wrote Marianne Moore of the ocean), "in which dropped things are bound to sink— / in which if they turn and twist, it is neither with volition nor consciousness."

Feeling herself superfluous, "too old to be useful" in London during the blitz, H. D. came into a premonition of superfluity as bounty and began to reanimate the tangible threads of hermetic ancestry latent in her art:

we are the keepers of the secret,
the carriers, the spinners

of that rare intangible thread
that binds all humanity

to ancient wisdom,
to antiquity;

our joy is unique to us,
grape, knife, cup, wheat

are symbols in eternity,
and every concrete object

has abstract value, is timeless
in the dream parallel

whose relative sigil has not changed
since Nineveh and Babel.

This glimpse of detritus pathways through the old lore sustained H. D. to the end of her life through her major works: *Trilogy, Helen in Egypt* and *Hermetic Definition.* She was part of a "home front" scattered over battleground Earth during the war, recuperating by occult measures a civilization shattered into pure symbol-detritus, a compost heap from which archaic values could be gleaned. Eliot, like H. D. in London during the blitz, affirmed an equally ancestral if less occult heritage, as he acknowledged "the communication / Of the dead is tongued with fire beyond the language of the living." In his search for the "crowned knot of fire" where "the fire and the rose are one" in Christian concord, Eliot could find no place for war.

> Where is the point at which the merely individual
> Explosion breaks
>
> In the path of an action merely typical
> To create the universal, originate a symbol
> Out of the impact?

Poetry is a life, Eliot found, whereas "War is not a life: it is a situation."

William Carlos Williams had a different view, accepting war as the manifestation of an essential reality.* Poetry "*is* the war or part of it, merely a different sector of the field," he wrote in preface to *The Wedge* (1944). The field was kinetic energy, "its movement is intrinsic, undulant," evident equally in the subjects of the book's first four poems: the saxifrage ("my flower that splits / the rocks"), a woman giving birth ("The new opens / new ways beyond all known ways"), the falls of the Passaic River in Paterson ("the empty / ear struck from within, roaring"), and in the rollicking dancers of Brueghel's painting, *The Kermess.*

> What is war,
> the destroyer
> but an appurtenance
>
> to the dance?
> The deadly serious
> who would have us suppress
>
> all exuberance
> because of it
> are mad. When terror blooms—

* Robert Duncan proves himself most deeply indebted to H. D. and Williams in his lifelong preoccupation with war as primal strife. The first volume of *Ground Work* is subtitled *Before the War,* not as a temporal marker but a posture of physical address, like the body before a mirror—war as mirror in which Duncan attempted to reflect on himself as early as in "An Essay at War," written during the Korean War:

> The war is a mineral perfection, clear,
> unambiguous evil   within which
> our delite, our life,   is the flaw,
> the contradiction?

leap and twist
whirl and prance

"The vision of exuberance requires identification with the exuberant life of the whole," wrote Norman O. Brown after the fall of the Berlin wall (*Apocalypse and/or Metamorphosis*, 198). But the whole, being full of energy, is strife and discord. "The science of enjoyment is also a science of death," for "it is a universal principle of biological life that growth leads to excess: and excess leads to laceration and loss" (194). But loss is also passing on; it is the extravagant abandonment of the torch bearer's race commemorated by Jeffers. Transmission is a conflagration, and "The book sets the reader on fire. The meaning is the fresh creation, the eruption of poetry; meaning is always surplus meaning, an excess extracted" (193). "Burning up myself, I would leave fire behind me" (Blaser, "The Fire," 236).

The empty house

Jorie Graham poses a question in the form of a delicately hanging mobile:

Is the house empty?
Is the emptiness housed?

Paleolithic cave art represents approximately twenty thousand years of applied human perception. Hunting-gathering cultures made this graffiti panorama in the form of outlines, stains, dots, and meanders, in abstract and cryptic as well as recognizably mimetic figures. This was all produced well after hominid evolution had resulted in people like us, but with slightly larger cranial capacity. A relatively undocumented period followed, probably linked to deglaciation. This time—between the Gravettian, Solutrean, and Magdalenian cultures of the late Paleolithic, 14,000 B.C., and the early food-producing Mesolithic communities of 9000 B.C.—is a psychic blank. We know little of what went on, but it is during this period that humans became sedentary, developing a new relation to food resources.

With animals domesticated for their meat and other products as well as for sacrificial ritual, and plants domesticated for fruit, seeds, and leaves, "food" became an expedient generalization for what had formerly been utterly specific: *every* animal taken in the hunt is explicitly singular. It is an auspiciously mortal drama.

Domestication breeds animals exempt from the existential drama of the hunt, and men lose contact with the dramatic privilege of their skill as hunters. In the sedentary state, the world is broken up into anthropocentric spaces, understood less and less in terms of animal partners, biospheric conditions, weather, migration routes, and the old star lore. However, with the stimulation of energies in social congregation on a metropolitan scale, a tremendous flowering of human capability occurs. In the space of about four thousand years: an agricultural urban-based trading and shipping economy develops, with utilization and transportation of a prodigious variety of materials, sophisticated tools and boats, "status kit" prestige burials, mining of copper around 5500 B.C., and a fuller metallurgy by 4600 B.C.

In the foothills of the Zagros Mountains and along the Mesopotamian flood plain, all those forces finally concretize into the first megalopolis, from which emanate the earliest myths, lore, laws, and social customs of which there is evidence. And from there—the Sumerians down to the early Minoans—we have a full two thousand years, out of which we retain Mediterranean civilization as our self-declared origin. Charles Olson took Americans to be "the last 'first' people," meaning the last to feel themselves—however presumptuously—first-comers.* In the same way we can regard the Greeks as "the first *last* people": the earliest crisis-cult hubristic civilization, and earliest battleground of cultural syncretism. Mesopotamian civilizations, like Rome much later, simply adopted or colonized alien myth and lore. The Greek tension (fantasized as a "synthesis" in eighteenth-century neoclassicism) is described by Weston LaBarre:

> Greek religion was a compost of shamanistic nature gods of people from the north and the old fertility rituals of the native country folk. Despite the differences, however, the two were rooted in the same animistic world view, with no intrinsic factor impeding a tolerable amalgamation. But the fusion was never quite successful because, to a degree, the two traditions ran side by side on different social levels. On one, that of Ionian philosophy, the nature gods were subjected to increasingly refined and rationalized statements of the nature of reality, and the man-like was gradually driven out of nature—an intellectual movement toward science imperfect only in certain limitations of

* "An American, properly speaking, is an exception," writes Robert Pogue Harrison on Thoreau. "Perhaps it is in his knowledge that he could not find in his country's national destiny the meaning of what it means to be American that Thoreau remains most radically American." So, "America will forever be what it did not become, and *Walden* will remain its empty house" (*Forests,* 221, 232).

> method that were in essence socio-political. On the other level, folk religion continued to dramatize, by analogy and symbol, recurrent seasonal events in nature that, misconstrued as "immortality" when applied to man, came into violent contradiction with the other tradition. The Ghost Dance catastrophe of this unstable acculturation was in the end as much socio-political as it was philosophico-religious. (*Ghost Dance,* 477)

To LaBarre's account here we might add Hyams, in *Soil and Civilization,* addressing the social and religious disintegration of Greek culture through soil abuse, as much our legacy as democracy and Ionian philosophy.

LaBarre finds in Plato an imprint of the Ghost Dance: Plato, he writes, "has polytheized the One into an indefinite number of noetic Ideas, each Idea being the pattern for the appropriate species of particulars" (546). "Like every metaphysical system it is an unwitting statement of the misunderstood facts of life; it confounds the communication of organic pattern with the communication of patterns in speech" (547). Abandoning the cyclic vitality inherent in traditional chthonic worship, anthropocentrism referred all authority to human prestige; and once the polis becomes the measure of all things, politics emerges as the measure of affairs, commodifying nature as the standing reserve of man's bidding. For twenty-five hundred years Hellenistic legacy has been accepted as the "seed" from which civilization grew. But as the modern Greek poet George Seferis put it, "We are the seed that dies. And I went into my empty house."

The times promised

Facing American derelictions of surplus meaning becoming global fate, Olson laments:

> The individual
> has become divided
> from the Absolute, it is the times promised
> by the poets.

~

> I've seen it all go in other directions
> and heard a man say why not
> stop ocean's tides

and not even more than the slow
loss of a small piece of time, not any more vibration
than the normal wobble of the earth on its present axis

. . . .

. . . He is only valuable
to himself—ugh, a species
acquiring
distaste
for itself.

~

. . . One even, at this date begins to look on man as
a pure decline from
Paleolithic, so animal—or as birds make love—is
the human eye, when, inside, it does not know
any more than what it can express by living &
that sight be in this man's eye is the expression we call love . . .

The following poem is quoted in full:

<u>Same day, Later</u>

Contemplating my Neolithic
neighbors, Mother and Son, while Son mows
noisily, with power mower the grass & Ma
hangs over the fence simply
watching—and Maiden, or Unmarried Sister
comes around the corner to see him,
too
& if you let the ape-side out the eyes
have died or become so evolutionary
and <u>not</u> cosmological (vertical
not the eyes any longer of the distinctness
of species but of their connections
And then Nature is a pig-pen or
swill, and any improvement or increase
[including the population] of <u>goods</u>—things,
in the genetic sense, plural, and probable,
in <u>that</u> lottery—are then what human beings

get included in, by themselves as well as by any
administrative or service conditions such as contemporary
States find the only answer, the ticketing or studying of
—or selling of—family relations among contemporary Americans and
not Africans but of the baboons as a kin group in
Africa: I prefer my boundary of
land literally adjacent & adjoining mid Mesozoic at
the place of the parting of the seams of all the Earth.

These passages of late *Maximus Poems* recapitulate most of my themes. From his early formulation "polis is / eyes," Charles Olson comes twenty years later to "if you let the ape-side out the eyes / have died"; we are a species acquiring a distaste for itself, and our eyes no longer register the omnivorousness with which we devour the biological and ecological basis of our condition. "The universe is filld with eyes then, intensities . . . / benemaledictions of the dead." It's only within a framework like that of Maximus—proposed as the enlarged image of human capability—that Olson manages to pinpoint *homo sapiens* as transhistorical fatality.

The wars and brutalities of the twentieth century are unique, but still characteristic of a much longer time span in which the degradation of the human is the final chapter in a terrestrial legacy of despoliation. We face a dilemma unprecedented in the entire epoch of Christian moralism or the preceding age of Greek pride: the danger is no longer wicked tyrants and evildoers, it is the cumulative byproduct of normality, with its increasing disinterest in plants and animals, the earth and the stars; its marginal awareness of economic and political dereliction; and a corresponding hyperattention to mass-mediated fame and fortune. In the new world of "infotainment" and "reality programming," the traditional figure of (Vitruvian) "man" is itself a blank integer, a joker in the pack—in response to which Don Byrd has coined an integrally inquisitive word to replace this generality: *whoman* (which includes woman as well as man and human and embodies them in the imperative of open identity: *who*). "Whomans / in the whosmos" emerge from humans when "history is a leaky ball-point, / fouling the pocket." But

History cannot end as history;
for it to end, beat
as history
it must exceed itself,
drt drt.

The nature of this prospect is not the Hegelian one of self-overcoming, but a tropologistical *excess* unimaginable to planning commissioners and rights activists alike. The challenge is not "monumental" (the term displays its misplaced imperial honorific): it is the unnamable pressure on every articulation of global prospects.

> The World
> has become divided
> from the Universe. Put the three Towns
> together

So begins Olson's fable of the three towns, as viewed from the heavenly tree growing downward (Gerrit Lansing) or Maximus's feet in the air (Olson): head in the earth, human in humus, a foothold on the stars. In Olson's projection the three towns are like Blakean states, permutations in chaos that form human propensities (the third town, for instance, of which men know the least, is overpopulated). The Dialogue of the second town begins only after the collapse of the use of reason. In this state, as in Hesiod, "The earth / shall have preceded love." In the first town there is communication without need of the explicit. The three towns—which must be recovered ("without three Towns / there is no Society, there is no / known / Absolute")—compose an image of necessity or *ananke* that is archetypal in the vital sense: ignored with peril.

Olson's "The Festival Aspect" is based on an Indian tale of cosmic tyranny. The tyrant Maya welds his three fortresses into "a single, prodigious center of demon-chaos and world-tyranny, practically unassailable" (Zimmer, 185). The Jungian attraction to mandalas predisposes archetype to idealism and its rules of symmetry. But in Olson's case, the *type* is literally on the page, materialized (mothered) in the mask of a typeface. The text is a threnody on tyrannical conditions, conditions exceeding the span of the witness (Olson) who draws on a tradition of reference (muthologistics) to substantiate the diagnosis, recasting it into gnosis. His use of such materials suggests that they are not sources but resources. The poet seizes on a text *as* the here and now of the poem; in this sense, one could claim there are no "references" in *The Maximus Poems.* Archetypal vitality is preserved only in the *sense* of type—singular, but not hypostatized as *the* or *an.* In restoring the sense of archetype through Maximus—the figure of the large, the impending, not necessarily human at all—Olson resumes an ability of the species fallen into neglect millennia before: the capacity to trace our boundedness and discern our limits. Reread *"Same day, Later"* with its contemplation of Neolithic neighbors: the poem revitalizes archetype by beginning with the comedy appropriate to archetypes, concretizing images in the immensity of geological time, "literally adjacent," to which we act and finally "come to rest." A comedy in Dante's sense: the spectacle of where we all, each by each, end up. And are upended.

Trope is conceded in the word "universe," which speaks of one turn—taking a turn on the dance floor—and calls it a verse. Trope is also friction, a rotation of heat bound to the sun, around which the earth migrates:

> Migration in fact (which is probably
> as constant in history as any <u>one</u> thing: migration
>
> is the pursuit by animals, plants & men of a suitable
> —and gods as well—& preferable
>
> environment; and leads always to a new center.

The in-spiritus, the "Animus" of the new centered occasion is

> . . . that the Mind or Will always
>
> successfully opposes & invades the Previous, This
> is the rose is the rose is the rose   of the World.

Change, turbulence, power, catastrophe, beauty: these features of the poem make up a face or mask through which we still peer out, observing the accidents and subtle surprises of what will fit and what will work in the ever-expanding persistence of difference.

In Olson's continental drift poem "Astride / the Cabot / fault" (printed atilt on the page), central images of continental migration, the Diorite Stone, and the polar icecap come together mysteriously in the phrase "Frances Rose-Troup Land." True to the fortuitousness of accidental fit, this phrase names the historian of early Cape Ann on whose work Olson consistently relied for *The Maximus Poems,* yet in doing so he discovers that the name itself undergoes a fault or slippage by which it is embedded in "the rose is the rose is the rose of the World," which is part of Gertrude Stein's trope of "uni-verse"—and by a turn of emphasis in the mouth Olson's historian is rose-trope, circulating its contingencies in the accidental essential.

The uninterrupted tissue

The old question recurs: in this trope of universe, what is our place?

Ficino had the idea
life circulates from the earth
to the stars
"*in order to constitute the uninterrupted*
tissue of the whole of nature."

But what if *we* are the interruption, the clog; we are the discord, festering the scales of the serpentine ouroboros?

There is no life that does not rise
melodic from the scales of the marvelous.

To which our grief refers.

If Ficino's vision of an "uninterrupted tissue of the whole of nature" marks the Renaissance (in its unique preservation of mediaeval cosmology filtering a recovered Hellenism), it is the *interruption* that has proven mesmerizing in modernity, favoring History as "a declaration of independence from the deep past" (Shepard, "Post-Historic Primitivism," 46). The previous fifteen hundred years had been devoted to examining the tissue called Jesus and Mary, Jehovah and Holy Ghost, Moses and Aaron, Saul and David. Yet traditions persisted—hermetic, sealing their preserves tight—that spoke of Zeus and Hera, Apollo and Dionysus, Isis and Osiris, Pan, Mithra.

. . . theft of what the heart desired
made so beautifully by theft's magic that
men still remember the walls of Troy,
the horse-traders' town; and young boys have heroic affinities,
immune by the Mother-Dragon's blood,
except that Eros marks one spot to be betrayd as His,
close upon Death.

All that we've lived obscured truth on these pages.

The elemental man is a humpt bank where
the hair grows, heapt up of time,

folded upon fold, lifted up from what he was,
a depth of silt, into this height
above sea level.

Compressions, oppressions—the horde gathering
in the poorest lands,
shifting the weight of continents. And continents
are only what giants must be

Theosophists teach that primeval man is a vast dispersed being,
having as much intelligence in the sweep of his tail
as in his claws or those ravening jaws, back of whose
row on row of teeth ripping the meat
a brain like a child's fist pushing those eyes;

and see the force of intellectual hunger
focus, ravening towards such rest
a diamond has in structure, sustained by pressure. Man
so exclusively defined he is
a figure of light.

To be restored to light is no easy thing, though it falls from the sky each day, as Whitman aspired to judge his own time: the poet, he declared in his 1855 preface to *Leaves of Grass,* "judges not as the judge judges but as the sun falling around a helpless thing"; and Dickinson grapples with that "Light a newer Wilderness / My Wilderness has made" (no. 1233). The light of the Orient of theophanic apprehension, the light of *Xvarnah,** the tag "All things are lights" of Erigena, is beckoned by Pound in Canto XCIV, in his quest

* "Xvarnah" is the primal energy source in the *Zend-Avesta,* the Zoroastrian scripture, translated as Light of Glory. Henry Corbin elaborates: "That Light of Glory, which is the archetype-Image of the Mazdean soul, is in fact the organ by which the soul perceives the world of light that is of the same nature as itself, and through which, originally and directly, the soul effects the transmutation of physical data, the very data which for us are 'positive,' but which for the soul would be 'insignificant.' This is the very Image that the soul projects into beings and things, raising them to the incandescence of that victorial Fire with which the Mazdean soul has set the whole of creation ablaze. . . . In short, it is by this projection of its own Image that the soul, in effecting the transmutation of the material Earth, also establishes from the beginning an *Imago Terrae* that reflects and announces its own Image to the soul, that is to say, an Image whose *Xvarnah* is also the soul's own *Xvarnah.* It is at that point—in and by this double reflection of the same Light of Glory—that the Angel of

"To build light

 jih

 hsin

said Ocellus.

Howard McCord's *Gnomonology* includes Rudolf Steiner's analogy: "The mind is related to thought as the eye is to light." The Chinese Taoist *Secret of the Golden Flower* that was crucial to Charles Olson is on "the circulation of Light." "Heaven is not the wide blue sky, but the place in which the body is made in the house of the creative" (Wilhelm, 25). The light is what *circulates;* its currency is more pervasive than coin, its credit not interest but pure gift. Gratuitously everlasting,

> these lights never die whose embers glow wilder
> than wilderness at the beginning of words
> to catch the ring of stars.

The transfiguring principle of light permits us to speak of a *human nature* reciprocal with nature, an ecology enfolding person and world. The heaven of exaltation that soaks into the earth in the *Golden Flower* is the heavenly flower that grows downward. The light in man spreads down through breath (conceivably one of the book's attractions for Olson, with his emphasis on breath units in prosody). The two invariable conditions, Master Lu Tzu says, are breath and image. "Should a man have no images in his mind? One cannot do without images. Should one not breathe? One cannot do without breathing" (*Wilhelm,* 44). "The elk mind moves its antlers / flourishing the trees."

In later *Cantos* Pound hovered like a bee around an elemental perception: the circulation of light established in ecological tact cultivates a psychosm. "A man's paradise is his good nature"; while "to perambulate the bounds of cosmos" is Olson's sense of the determinable good of one's nature. Space is unframed, and cosmos comes unwound like a lute string, if it is not knitted into coextensive reverence and habitation. In some cosmologies the brain, in the "heights" of the spine, is the end of a drawstring that tunes the place by orienting the individual within

---

the Earth is revealed to the mental sight, that is to say, that the Earth is perceived in the *person* of its Angel" (*Spiritual Body and Celestial Earth,* 14–15).

the Orient of destiny. This is the telos of one's contact with the encircling serpent of light. The string spans the length of an instrument stretching from earth to heaven—heaven as both the astronomical field and the paradise of "good nature," an ecological state as deftly woven with interdependent modes of energy as a climax forest.

> In a climax situation a high percentage of the energy is derived not from grazing off the annual production of biomass, but from recycling dead biomass, the duff on the forest floor, the trees that have fallen, the bodies of dead animals. Recycled. Detritus cycle energy is liberated by fungi and lots of insects. I would then suggest: as climax forest is to biome, and fungus is to the recycling of energy, so "enlightened mind" is to daily ego mind, and art to the recycling of neglected inner potential. When we deepen or enrich ourselves, looking within, understanding ourselves, we come closer to being like a climax system. Turning away from grazing on the "immediate biomass" of perception, sensation, and thrill; and re-viewing memory, internalized perception, blocks of inner energies, dreams, the leaf-fall of day-to-day consciousness, liberates the energy of our own sense-detritus. Art is an assimilator of unfelt experience, perception, sensation, and memory for the whole society. When all that compost of feeling and thinking comes back to us then, it comes not as a flower, but—to complete the metaphor—as a mushroom: the fruiting body of the buried threads of mycelia that run widely through the soil, and are intricately married to the root hairs of all the trees. "Fruiting"—at that point—is the completion of the work of the poet, and the point where the artist or mystic reenters the cycle: gives what she or he has done as nourishment and as spore or seed spreads the "thought of enlightenment," reaching into personal depths for nutrients hidden there, back to the community. The community and its poetry are not two. (Snyder, *Real Work*, 173–74)

William James would concur with such ecological imperatives. "I am against bigness & greatness in all their forms," he declared, "and with the invisible molecular moral forces that work from individual to individual, stealing in through the crannies of this world like so many soft rootlets or like the capillary oozing of water" (*Correspondence of William James*, 8:546). Communities of exchange exist like root hairs. When that realization is dormant, and knowledge dissociated from practice, the art of living atrophies.

For centuries, the term "America" has meant an intuited vertigo of the social body, signifying throughout much of the world a perplexing combination of *opportunity* and *abuse*. This trope on a man's name is not so much a nation as a word for an image in time. Speaking the word is myth. No matter what we *do*, myth precedes us. The circulation of images in time is myth. Or, in the image of the *Heavenly Flower*, myth circulates through the two indispensable features of Anthropos: image and breath, taking myth as *mu* to mean breath expelled in the exchange of images. The biological insistence of organic analogies has been evident from the earliest Paleolithic art. We are axiomatically and unavoidably organic in our possession of a treasury—but nothing more efficient than a *heap*—of recycled lore, images, desires, attractions, fascinations, dilations. Biodegradable thought. Myth is the image of the image. The eye confirms the passage of light even if the object is unfamiliar.

The poets in *This Compost* have affirmed the poem as a space possessed of a nature, which absorbs "symbol detritus" like the photosynthesis of light in chlorophyll. They confirm the poem as a passage, akin to the elaborate cave passages leading to Paleolithic image sanctuaries, leaving the temporality of the wreader's experience of it *as* the orientation, as the Orient of one's own good nature stands revealed. Such poetry is esoteric in this time when nature is no longer analogous to inner ecology, in this space where the topos of the tropics is not inclined to trope or apprehend anything other than opportunistically.

In ancient gnosticism of the Near East, the circulation of images convenes a visionary topology through which one moves with the agency of a Guide. Psyche is not the Guide, but the agency of Light through which the Guide is apprehended. As the history of the Americas instructs: inner ecology *is* outer; psyche without cosmos is an illness: it ceases to be psychosm, totem, Pole Star. But there is still an Orient where the sun we circulate comes to warm us in the beds of our composting minds. It is a *hieros gamos*, a sacred wedding. By being born, by descending among the company of the living in these tropics of American compost, we are *exalted game*, a sacrificial occasion that had better be sanctified, because a

> . . . philosophic wedding
> seeps down to the heart
>
> & we find ourselves married to the fact of it,
> married to all of us!
>
> one flesh of world & no divorce!

The philosophical wedding commends the real to the transtemporal figuration that is myth. Ronald Johnson, by suspending two words and postponing a third, gives us a Jung disposed to reveal the pivot of the full weight of the world in the head:

> Jung: "There are unconscious aspects of our perception of reality. The first is the fact that even when our senses react to real phenomena, sights, and sounds, they are somehow translated from the real of reality into that of the mind. Within the mind they become psychic events, whose ultimate
>
> nature is

Psychic events, whose ultimate "nature is"—: "An Inlet of Reality, or Soul," in which the tiny words that mean so much pour more and more meaning out through such open and simple vessels as ear and eye, mouth and skin; and "whatever might chafes away under the peel, the body eats away at the seeming." "From the ape at my shoulderblade I see angels. Our embryo dreamt the fishes' sleep, became a ripple, leap-frogged itself, and later a mammal: perception is a slingshot drawn back to first plasm."

Pound and his tribe of composting poets remain first instructors in how a poetics of history can be a poetics of light. The loosening or unbinding Pound proposed in the "rag bag" of the long poem could begin to include anything of use (and by the *Pisan Cantos* obviously all that was *necessary*). Engaging poetry as bricolage (not simply the juxtaposition of collage, but the activated working assembly of refractory materials), the poet is of necessity a bricoleur, a language-handyman for whom all written and spoken matter is readymade, spare parts, data, testimony; and the poem is "the contingent result of all the occasions there have been to renew or enrich the stock or to maintain it with the remains of previous constructions or destructions" (Lévi-Strauss, *Savage Mind*, 17). *"The poem is the Gestalt of what it can assimilate"* (Kenner, 185). The strength peculiar to subsequent American poetry is its wreaderly inclination, opening the poem to the full textual compost of the written record of the old lore and its imaginal overlap with an emergent sense of the archaic. It has meant the reanimation of a working space within language where the *mundus imaginalis* is transparent to history, where the individual is accountable to the species, where logos can be extracted from psyche and soul restored to cosmos, that interpersonal charm against the unbounded. The poetry I've been wreading here enacts myth as carnal movement of words within words, seeds of image and story, feeling and thinking, emerging from the muthologistical certainty of all the evidence we can lay claim to as the centrifugal force of our inner inherence. Net and web, ring and circle, coil and labyrinth, whorl and cup: all shapes, forms, insignia of nature, as Pound's "Secretary of Nature" John Heydon put it. Finding or "experiencing" nature makes no difference at all without the sense of *good nature* that stamps all force and form with grace and tact.

Citations

Gilgamesh

papyrus / jungle sandhill : Zukofsky, *"A"* 23, p. 539.
Praise! . . gill . . gam . . mesh : Zukofsky, *"A"* 23, p. 540.
I outlived a flood : Zukofsky, *"A"* 23, p. 543.
Ain't pleasant to work at the compost : Lansing, "The Compost," *Heavenly Tree,* 158.

The library

{ footnote } "Celestial Flowers of Glacier Park" : Lindsay, *Going-to-the-Stars,* 88–101.
As things decay : Spicer, "After Lorca," *Collected Books,* 34.
go into all the places you're frightened of : Schwerner, "Tablet VIII," *The Tablets,* 29.
Out there somewhere / a shrine for the old ones : Snyder, "Old Bones," *Mountains and Rivers Without End,* 10.
Not one but many energies shape the field : Duncan, "Passages 33," *Ground Work,* vol. 1:23.
There is a mound in the poet's mind : Ammons, *Garbage,* 20.
heaven's fire : Johnson, *RADI OS,* book 1.
Selected Listings from the Western Carolina Telephone Company's Directory : Jonathan Williams, *Blues & Ruets.*
Limits / are what any of us : Olson, *Maximus Poems,* vol 1:17.

Generation

somehow a man must lift himself : William Carlos Williams, *Paterson,* book 3, sect. 3, p. 135.
as there is always / a thing he can do : Olson, "In Cold Hell, In Thicket," *The Distances,* 27.
he / is already also : Olson, "In Cold Hell, In Thicket," *The Distances,* 31.
Or, if it is me : Olson, "In Cold Hell, In Thicket," *The Distances,* 27.
polis is / eyes : Olson, *Maximus Poems,* vol. 1:26.
Because of the agora America is : Olson, *Maximus Poems,* vol 1:62.

The tropics, & the trope

Isolated person in Gloucester : Olson, *Maximus Poems,* vol. 1:12.
Thousands and thousands of miles hence : Whitman, "A Thought of Columbus."
as they are fed and grow, this nest : Olson, "The Kingfishers," *The Distances,* 6.
To be in different states without a change : Olson, "The Kingfishers," *The Distances,* 8.

Nota: man is the intelligence of his soil : Stevens, "The Comedian as the Letter C," *The Palm at the End of the Mind,* 58.
It was a flourishing tropic he required : Stevens, "The Comedian as the Letter C," *Palm,* 65.
the blissful liaison : Stevens, "The Comedian as the Letter C," *Palm,* 64.
the fecund minimum : Stevens, "The Comedian as the Letter C," *Palm,* 65.
Nota: his soil is man's intelligence : Stevens, "The Comedian as the Letter C," *Palm,* 66.
A still new continent : Stevens, "The Comedian as the Letter C," *Palm,* 66.
the purpose of his pilgrimage : Stevens, "The Comedian as the Letter C," *Palm,* 66–67.
Beauty is natures coyn : Milton, *Comus,* lines 739–45.
Green barbarism turning paradigm : Stevens, "The Comedian as the Letter C," *Palm,* 61.
flourishing tropic : Stevens, "The Comedian as the Letter C," *Palm,* 65.
All din and gobble : Stevens, "The Comedian as the Letter C," *Palm,* 73.
Delivered with a deluging onwardness : Stevens, "The Comedian as the Letter C," *Palm,* 74.
Making gulped potions : Stevens, "The Comedian as the Letter C," *Palm,* 75.
the honey bearing chaos : Rexroth, "When We With Sappho," *Collected Shorter Poems,* 139.
gigantic quavers of its voice : Stevens, "The Comedian as the Letter C," *Palm,* 63.
connoisseur of elemental fate : Stevens, "The Comedian as the Letter C," *Palm,* 63.
blissful liaison : Stevens, "The Comedian as the Letter C," *Palm,* 64.
The plum survives its poems : Stevens, "The Comedian as the Letter C," *Palm,* 70.
The wheel survives the myths : Stevens, "The Sense of the Sleight-of-Hand Man," *Palm,* 168.
The wheel, the lever, the incline : Rexroth, "Gas or Novocain," *Collected Shorter Poems,* 151.

Cinders

bee-loud glade : Yeats, "The Lake Isle of Innisfree," *Collected Poems,* 39.
the movement of men was to the west : Johnson, "When Men Will Lie Down as Gracefully & as Ripe," *Valley of the Many-Colored Grasses,* 44.
In the machinery of injustice : Howe, "Thorow," *Singularities,* 49.
They were sentenced to observe : Dorn, "The Slipping of the Wheel," *Recollections of Gran Apacheria.*
understory of anotherword : Howe, "Thorow," *Singularities,* 50.
the share of language is a yearning : Irby, "For Marcel Weinreich," manuscript.
How long did it last, that Paradise? : Irby, "(After Sauer)" *Catalpa,* 84.
one-armed explorer : Merwin, "The Gardens of Zuñi," *Carrier of Ladders,* 49.
the alien world : Duncan, "Up Rising," *Bending the Bow,* 82.
Here is a map of our country : Rich, "Atlas of the Difficult World," *Atlas,* 6.
The magic we have : McCord, "A Day's Journey with Geoffrey Young," *Fables & Transfigurations,* 6.
one's forced / considering America : Olson, *Maximus Poems,* vol. 1:134–35.
7 years & you cld carry cinders in yr hand : Olson, *Maximus Poems,* vol 3:41.

A noise in the head of the prince : Spicer, “The Holy Grail” (“Book of the Death of Arthur”), *Collected Books,* 213.

where some outcast people find a place : Dorn, “Inauguration Poem #2,” *Collected Poems,* 101.

or of how we might / plead our case : Dorn, “A Letter, in the Meantime, Not to be Mailed, Tonight,” *Collected Poems,* 99.

disposal so complete : Dorn, “The Land Below,” *Collected Poems,* 68.

how many waves / of hell and death : Olson, *Maximus Poems,* vol. 3:120.

o my people, where shall you find it : Olson, *Maximus Poems,* vol. 1:2.

in a society like America energy if it is not moral : Olson, *Maximus Poems,* vol. 3:89.

I don't want to know : Rich, “Atlas of the Difficult World,” *Atlas,* 4.

The cars run in a void of utensils : Oppen, “Route,” *Collected Poems,* 191.

With tire song lulling like love : R. P. Warren, “Going West,” *New and Selected Poems,* 93.

And by this we are carried : Oppen, “Route,” *Collected Poems,* 195.

Strange to be here, strange for them also : Oppen, “Route,” *Collected Poems,* 196.

hygienic of / views not viable to this soil : Dorn, “Idaho Out,” *Collected Poems,* 120.

The dust of intolerable social conditions : Lamantia, “Ship of Seers,” *Meadowlark,* 12.

Grimed tributaries : Crane, “The Bridge [The River],” *Complete Poems,* 68.

One can be looted, burned : Creeley, “One World,” *Mirrors,* 16.

How much of it is still true : Clarke, “Christmas Eve,” *In the Analogy,* 237.

Total war / has been uninstructive : Dorn, “The North Atlantic Turbine,” *Collected Poems,* 188.

the gathered gestures of historic particulars : Irby, *A Set,* 4.

We will produce no sane man again : Oppen, “Route,” *Collected Poems,* 184.

Vomito cogito

This kind of speaking : DuPlessis, “Draft 19: Working Conditions,” *Drafts,* 121.

{ footnote } the white-toothed black flag of Vomito Negro : Césaire, “Gunnery Warning,” *Collected Poetry,* 89.

my total is ever lengthened : Césaire, “Notebook of a Return to the Native Land,” *Collected Poetry,* 79.

and our limbs vainly disjointed : Césaire, “Notebook of a Return to the Native Land,” *Collected Poetry,* 65.

And this land screamed for centuries that we are bestial brutes : Césaire, “Notebook of a Return to the Native Land,” *Collected Poetry,* 61.

Drunken start, drowned / Atlantean root : Mackey, “Out Island,” *School of Udhra,* 50.

Whoever would not understand me : Césaire, “Notebook of a Return to the Native Land,” *Collected Poetry,* 45.

But who misleads my voice? : Césaire, “Notebook of a Return to the Native Land,” *Collected Poetry,* 55.

If your voice could crack : Rich, "Atlas of the Difficult World," *Atlas,* 18.
anagrammatic / ythm, anagrammatic myth : Mackey, "Alphabet of Ahtt," *School of Udhra,* 43–44.
{ footnote } To the outer / principalities of Onem : Mackey, "Song of the Andoumboulou: 20," *Whatsaid Serif,* 22.
No one / has loved the west I came into : Dorn, "The Sense Comes Over Me . . ." *Collected Poems,* 156.
Only the Illegitimate are beautiful : Dorn, "The North Atlantic Turbine," *Collected Poems,* 179.
expressing with broken // brain : W. C. Williams, "The pure products of America," *Collected Poems,* vol. 1:218.
blows with her every skill : Rich, "Atlas of the Difficult World," *Atlas,* 23.
Rolled a / joint with gunpowder : Mackey, "Degree Four," *School of Udhra,* 33.
THOSE WHO ARE BEAUTIFUL : Rothenberg, "Khurbn," *Khurbn,* 20.
"practice your scream" I said : Rothenberg, "Khurbn," *Khurbn,* 11.
Where shall the scream stick? : Graham, "Manifest Destiny," *Dream of the Unified Field,* 185.
Let a great pain come up into your legs : Rothenberg, "Khurbn," *Khurbn,* 33.
Write this. We have burned all their villages : Palmer, "Sun," *Sun,* 83.

That origin which is act . . . that riddle which is awe

the pure form / Of the cutting edge : Rexroth, "The Phoenix and the Tortoise," *Collected Longer Poems,* 81.
{ footnote } gnostic import : Mackey, "Song of the Andoumboulou: 35," *Whatsaid Serif,* 108.
The dead in via / in vita nuova : Olson, "La Préface," *In Cold Hell, In Thicket,* 9.
Each word a / flash-pod correspondent : Sanders, "Hieroglyphs," *Thirsting for Peace,* 99.
{ footnote } "Books" "books ruined us" : Notley, *The Descent of Alette,* 70.
as if our condition now is / hugely umbilical : Eshleman, "Permanent Shadow," *Hades in Manganese,* 83.
where the dead walked / and the living were made of cardboard : Pound, *Cantos,* no. CXV, p. 794.

The archaic and the old lore

male dominion, gangrape : Rich, "The Spirit of Place," *Wild Patience,* 45.
There is no proposal the imagination cannot assimilate : Eshleman, "Liberation Footage," *From Scratch,* 110.
{ footnote } Us critters : Snyder, "Old Woodrat's Stinking House," *Mountains and Rivers Without End,* 119.

Think of wings pushing through shoulders : Brandi, "This Language Isn't Speech," *Heartbeat Geography*, 177.
The past is not a husk : Rich, "For Memory," *Wild Patience*, 22.
oak powers renewing : Lamantia, "The Marco Polo Zone," *Meadowlark*, 43.

Indian skin

big masculine history / on tap : Waldrop, "Chapter XIII: Of the Weather," *A Key into the Language of America*, 28.
Darkness is another kind of light : McCord, "The Rim of the Great Basin," *Maps*, 11.
what history is longing for : Irby, *Antiphonal*, 1.
for solitude and grieving : Irby, *Antiphonal*, 7.

On the extremest verge

The road between Europe and Asia : Whitman, "Passage to India," no. 3.
the earth to be spann'd : Whitman, "Passage to India," no. 2.
His mother came to the laundry : Reznikoff, *Testimony*, vol. 1:210.
you whose fine mouth : Spicer, "Some Notes on Whitman for Allen Joyce," *One Night Stand*, 81.
install'd amid the kitchen ware! : Whitman, "Song of the Exposition," no. 3.
Not to repel or destroy so much as to accept : Whitman, "Song of the Exposition," no. 1.
thy rapid patents : Whitman, "Song of the Exposition," no. 8.
wide geographies, manifold, different, distant : Whitman, "Song of the Exposition," no. 8.
Earth's modern wonder, history's seven outstripping : Whitman, "Song of the Exposition," no. 5.
this and these, America : Whitman, "Song of the Exposition," no. 6.
the joiner, he sees how they join: Whitman, "Song of the Answerer," no. 1.
Southward there I screaming : Whitman, "Our Old Feuillage."
In Kanadian forests the moose : Whitman, "Our Old Feuillage."
A / darkness there / like tar : Mackey, "Waters," *Eroding Witness*, 3.

The rim, the sediment

Now I am terrified at the Earth : Whitman, "This Compost," no. 2.
Whereto answering, the sea : Whitman, "Out of the Cradle Endlessly Rocking."
half in love with easeful Death : Keats, "Ode to a Nightingale."
my dusky demon and brother : Whitman, "Out of the Cradle."
husky pantings through clench'd teeth: Whitman, "Not Heaving from my Ribb'd Breast Only."

Beautiful dripping fragments : Whitman, "Spontaneous Me."

Love-thoughts, love-juice, love-odor : Whitman, "Spontaneous Me."

The limpid liquid within the young man : Whitman, "Spontaneous Me."

I too but signify at the utmost a little wash'd up drift : Whitman, "As I Ebb'd with the Ocean of Life," no. 2.

The waves of the sea fall through / Our each others : Rexroth, "Past and Future Turn About," *Collected Shorter Poems,* 171.

Me and mine, loose windrows, little corpses : Whitman, "As I Ebb'd," no. 4.

Let the paper remain on the desk unwritten : Whitman, "Song of the Open Road," no. 15.

Held by this electric self out of the pride : Whitman, "As I Ebb'd," no. 1.

all the water and all the land of the globe : Whitman, "As I Ebb'd," no. 1.

Hissing melodious : Whitman, "Out of the Cradle."

The rim, the sediment that stands for all : "Whitman, "As I Ebb'd," no. 1.

Copulation is no more rank to me than death is : Whitman, "Song of Myself," no. 24.

forbidden voices / Voices of sexes and lusts : Whitman, "Song of Myself," no. 24.

The sea and a crescent strip of beach : Oppen, "Some San Francisco Poems," no. 3, *Collected Poems,* 217.

Fascinated, my eyes reverting from the south : Whitman, "As I Ebb'd," no. 1.

A cold wind chills the beach : Stevens, "The Auroras of Autumn," no. 2, *Palm,* 308.

the lines through these words : Palmer, "Sun," *Sun,* 78.

The sum of all that will ever be deciphered : Ashbery, "Fragment," *Double Dream of Spring,* 94.

where not a single single thing endures : Ammons, "Saliences," *Collected Poems,* 155.

I allow myself eddies of meaning : Ammons, "Corson's Inlet," *Collected Poems,* 148.

to fasten into order enlarging grasps of disorder : Ammons, "Corson's Inlet," *Collected Poems,* 151.

an order held / in constant change : Ammons, "Corson's Inlet," *Collected Poems,* 150.

the possibility of rule as the sum of rulelessness : Ammons, "Corson's Inlet," *Collected Poems,* 150.

I've often said that a poem in becoming generates the laws : Ammons, "Essay on Poetics," *Collected Poems,* 315.

real change occurs along the chromosomes : Ammons, "Essay on Poetics," *Collected Poems,* 316.

What does not change/is the will to change : Olson, "The Kingfishers," *The Distances,* 5.

we want to change without changing : Ammons, *Sphere,* 12.

We change to keep all else the same : Koller, "We change . . ." *Poems for the Blue Sky,* 83.

Watch out for unity as you age : Eshleman, "Yachats, the Shore," *From Scratch,* 72.

I'm a little boy in my glandbox : Eshleman, "Yachats, the Shore," *From Scratch,* 72.

Mallarmé's throw still tumbling : Eshleman, "Yachats, the Shore," *From Scratch,* 72.

Necropoetics

These things I would record : Duncan, "The Performance We Wait For," *Opening of the Field,* 57.

runes upon the sand from sea-spume : Duncan, "Food for Fire, Food for Thought," *Opening of the Field,* 95.

They are dead. That is they do not answer : Kelly, "Alchemical Journal," *Alchemist to Mercury,* 56.

green kelp waves arms : Zukofsky, *"A"* 22, p. 533.

death also / can still propose the old labors : Creeley, "Heroes," *Collected Poems,* 192.

white white white : Duncan, "A Storm of White" *Opening of the Field,* 74.

Like the pieces of a totally unfinished puzzle : Spicer, "Heads of the Town" ("Textbook of Poetry"), *Collected Books,* 176.

you must excuse us if we scratch each other's / backs : Olson, "Letter for Melville 1951," *The Distances,* 47.

The realized / is dung of the ground : Duncan, "Nor Is the Past Pure," *Opening of the Field,* 41.

We have broken through into the meaning of the tomb : Ashbery, *Three Poems,* 5.

spelling light for hymn to day recast : Grenier, "Rose Appellate Project (Entwurf)," *Phantom Anthems.*

To have the whole outline in mind : Ashbery, *Three Poems,* 25.

intimations of the secret Mover : Duncan, "Nor Is the Past Pure," *Opening of the Field,* 42.

It is only the midden heap, Beauty : Duncan, "Nor Is the Past Pure," *Opening of the Field,* 43

"Cole's Island" : Olson, *Maximus Poems,* vol. 3:69.

The upshot is : Olson, *Maximus Poems,* vol. 1:55.

Diadem of fox teeth : Snyder, "Under the Hills Near the Morava River," *Mountains and Rivers Without End,* 96.

A deer skull : McCord, "Signs and Gifts," *The Fire Visions.*

a sheepskull forehead : Snyder, "Arctic Midnight Twilight," *Mountains and Rivers Without End,* 93.

Muses' archetext

And then went down to the ship : Pound, *Cantos,* no. I, p. 3.

Off-shore, by islands hidden in the blood : Olson, *Maximus Poems,* vol. 1:1.

A / round of fiddles : Zukofsky, *"A"* 1, p. 1.

He neigh ha lie low h'who : Zukofsky, *"A"* 15, p. 359.

Art is to show other people : Kelly, "Women of the Bois de Boulogne," *Kill the Messenger,* 62.

Isolated person in Gloucester : Olson, "Letter 3," *Maximus Poems,* vol. 1:12.

The hand holds no chalk : Ashbery, "Self Portrait in a Convex Mirror," *Self Portrait,* 83.
the voice is recognizable : Blaser, "Image-Nation," no. 5, *Holy Forest,* 116.
the language, older : Blaser, "Image-Nation," no. 10, *Image-Nations,* 36.
but language is other than ourselves : Blaser, "Image-Nation," no. 12, *Image-Nations,* 42.
ecstatic / contorting / of the / soul : Grenier, "Easter Roses," *Phantom Anthems.*
To begin a song : Zukofsky, *"A"* 12, p. 140.
here is the table : Palmer, "Baudelaire Series," *Sun,* 11.
B says, the real table does not exist : Palmer, "Sun," *Sun,* 66.
through its drafts : Sobin, "Article of Faith," *Breath's Burials,* 60.
a draft, a stroke : DuPlessis, "Draft 4: In," *Drafts,* 25.
An intake / of breath : Mackey, "Alphabet of Ahtt," *School of Udhra,* 45.
the Muse / is the "fate" of the poem : Olson, "Prajna," *Olson,* no. 9, p. 42.

A skin of mouths

How can I leave you be in me : Charles Stein, "Pages from *First Forest,*" *Hat Rack Tree,* 17.
I attempt the discontinuities : Duncan, "The Breaking Up of Cold Clouds," *Derivations,* 91.
Around my life / an animal paces : Kelly, *The Loom,* 393.
what, anyway / was that sticky infusion : Kinnell, "The Bear," *Body Rags,* 63.
I, too, have eaten : Kinnell, *Book of Nightmares,* 29.
My father . . . his / crowned eye : Duncan, "A Set of Romantic Hymns," *Roots and Branches,* 109.
I would be a falcon and go free : Duncan, "My Mother Would Be a Falconress," *Bending the Bow,* 54.
and so the stain uniquely gives consent : Lansing, "Thinking of the Eyebrows of My Lord," *Heavenly Tree,* 60.
The owls shiver down : Duncan, "The Sentinels," *Ground Work,* vol. 2:39.
The vowels are physical / corridors : Duncan, "An Owl Is an Only Bird of Poetry," *Derivations,* 132.
we are strange and deep : McClure, *Ghost Tantras,* 73.
always another one walking beside you : Eliot, *The Waste Land,* line 362.
It goes without saying that / To have it make sense : Ashbery, "Litany," left column, *As We Know,* 55.
Space and Time the saliva : Olson, *Maximus Poems,* vol. 3:47.
the dirty filthy whining ultimate thing : Olson, *Maximus Poems,* vol. 3:33–34.
through this hole / at the bottom of the cavern : Williams, *Paterson,* book 5, sect. 1, p. 210
I heard words : Creeley, "The Language," *Collected Poems,* 283.
the jack-hammer jabs : Lowell, "Colloquy in Black Rock," *Selected Poems,* 5.
Poets die adolescents : Lowell, "Fishnet," *Selected Poems,* 221.
I heard / The birds inside me : Lowell, "Thanksgiving's Over," *Selected Poems,* 50.
[glyphs] : Schwerner, *The Tablets,* 72.

I lie without sleeping, remembering : Kinnell, *Book of Nightmares,* 30.
{ footnote } I was once   another man's heart : Blaser, "Image-Nation," no. 9, *Holy Forest,* 127.

The vessel

Language is the only genetics : Kelly, "Against the Code," *Mill of Particulars,* 11.
Gravelly hill was 'the source and end (or boundary' : Olson, *Maximus Poems,* vol. 2:161.
the Greeks / made much of *chros* : Kelly, "Jealousy," *Finding the Measure,* 91.
Laminated marl—fret changes : Zukofsky, *"A"* 22, pp. 512–13.
not / superficial but a visible core : Ashbery, "Self Portrait in a Convex Mirror," *Self Portrait,* 70.
bright life needles every clod : Rexroth, "Ice Shall Cover Nineveh," *Collected Shorter Poems,* 131.
earth is interesting : Olson, *Maximus Poems,* vol. 2:9.
tropical forests / hardened to coal : Metcalf, *Apalache,* in *Collected Works,* vol. 1:464.
I became aware / That beneath me : Rexroth, "Adonis in Summer," *Collected Shorter Poems,* 160.
the faithfulness I can imagine would be a weed : Rich, "When We Dead Awaken," *Diving into the Wreck, 6.*
the tree, the cup, the star, the bird : Duncan, "Epilogos," *Bending the Bow,* 136.
more keeps getting included : Ashbery, "Self Portrait in a Convex Mirror," *Self Portrait,* 72.
I cannot explain the action of leveling : Ashbery, "Self Portrait in a Convex Mirror," *Self Portrait,* 71.
the greater the water you add : Olson, *Maximus Poems,* vol. 2:10.
You were fluid then, a network of soul : Duncan, "Adam's Way," *Roots and Branches,* 147.
The gods / broken into the pieces that are us : Kelly, "Texts: 25 [The Philosopher's Stone]," *Kill the Messenger,* 167.
why that was you that / is how you weather division : Zukofsky, *"A"* 22, p. 508.
might have been. / Certainly these ashes : Duncan, "This Place Rumord to Have Been Sodom," *Opening of the Field,* 22.
wind space and rain space : Pound, *Cantos,* no. LXXVI, p. 452.
the life / That is fluent in even the wintriest bronze : Stevens, "Sleight-of-Hand Man," *Palm,* 168.
which in the midst of summer stops : Stevens, "The Auroras of Autumn," no. 7, *Palm,* 313.
For the listener, who listens in the snow : Stevens, "The Snow Man," *Palm,* 54.
in the shattering of the cup : Duncan, "Epilogos," *Bending the Bow,* 137.
wrist high unwearing bent, cosmos : Zukofsky, *"A"* 22, p. 524.
The Cosmos / begins at the end of yourself : Olson, "Watered Rock," *Olson* 9:33.
The wickedness / for man : Olson, "Watered Rock," *Olson* 9:33.
Jack Clarke's "we are under image" : Blaser: "Image-Nation," no. 9, *Holy Forest,* 128.

Nigredo

All things move toward / the light : Niedecker, "Paean to Place," *The Granite Pail,* 74–75.
I passed through the lens : Berry, "Elegy," *Collected Poems,* 234.
The descent to a level plain : Irby, "Cahokia," *Catalpa,* 96.
strong like a puddle's ice : Olson, *Maximus Poems,* vol. 2:5.
150,000 years ago : Olson, *Maximus Poems,* vol. 3:140.
Continents of water and of earth : Duncan, "The Continents," *Roots and Branches,* 175.
The war of Africa against Eurasia : Olson, *Maximus Poems,* vol. 2:1.
There is only / the one continent : Duncan, "The Continents," *Roots and Branches,* 176.
In the mind the bone pile grows : Webster, "Hominid Activity," *Thicket Daybreak,* 26.
sarcophagus of we know not whom : Duncan, "Passages 30," *Bending the Bow,* 131.
tomorrow rustles in yesterday's corpse : Lansing, "Soluble Forest," *Heavenly Tree,* 203.
Not lost battles or even defeated people : Spicer, "The Holy Grail" ("Book of the Death of Arthur"), *Collected Books,* 212.
downward / to darkness : Olson, *Maximus Poems,* vol. 2:162.
The dreams pursue us over the snow : Kelly, "The Wall," *Flesh Dream Book,* 93.
the whole mystery, the lush squeeze : Ammons, *Sphere,* 12–13.
supraliminal language-field is body-field : Lansing, "Soluble Forest," *Heavenly Tree,* 200–201.
to call up the dead from dreams : Irby, "Offertory," *Catalpa,* 101.
but along the edge of the wall : Irby, "Offertory," *Catalpa,* 101.
yolk openings in the hand : Irby, "Offertory," *Catalpa,* 101.
crows on Tufts Hill : Irby, "Offertory," *Catalpa,* 101.
and now there will be a footstep uncovering a rock in the mud : Irby, "Offertory," *Catalpa,* 102.
where / From huddle of trash : Warren, "Looking Northward, Aegeanward: Nestlings on Seacliff," *New and Selected Poems,* 91.
dripping fetid mass : Olson, "The Kingfishers," *The Distances,* 6.
The Visitors—Resters : Olson, "The Lordly and Isolate Satyrs," *The Distances,* 84–85.
In any case the whole sea was now a hemisphere : Olson, "The Lordly and Isolate Satyrs," *The Distances,* 83.
gnostic reminder of / world-rut : Mackey, "Song of the Andoumboulou: 19," *Whatsaid Serif,* 20.
Hail them solely that they have the seeds : Olson, "A Newly Discovered 'Homeric' Hymn," *The Distances,* 73.

From Saturn to Demeter

Boulders blunted like an old bear's teeth : Jeffers, "Apology for Bad Dreams," *Collected Poetry,* vol. 1:210.

He brays humanity in a mortar : Jeffers, "Apology for Bad Dreams," *Collected Poetry*, vol. 1:210–11.

We have flowed out of ourselves : Loy, "The Dead," *Lost Lunar Baedeker*, 72.

We splinter into Wholes : Loy, "The Dead," *Lost Lunar Baedeker*, 72.

I am the centre / Of a circle of pain : Loy, "Parturition," *Lost Lunar Baedeker*, 4.

The open window is full of a voice : Loy, "Parturition," *Lost Lunar Baedeker*, 5.

Stir of incipient life : Loy, "Parturition," *Lost Lunar Baedeker*, 6.

There is a climax in sensibility : Loy, "Parturition," *Lost Lunar Baedeker*, 5–6.

The was—is—ever—shall—be : Loy, "Parturition," *Lost Lunar Baedeker*, 7.

Milk light

art is not construction, artifice : Blaser, "Image-Nation," no. 12, *Image-Nations*, 45.

These stars / are fragrant : Duncan, "Dante Études ('To Speak My Mind')," *Ground Work*, vol. 1:100.

Sex on earth is rhymed angelic motion : Lansing, "Stanzas of Hyparxis," *Heavenly Tree*, 170.

But the solar heart defines the blood : Lansing, "Stanzas of Hyparxis," *Heavenly Tree*, 171.

pressing a knee or elbow : Kinnell, *Book of Nightmares*, 5.

The sweet virile hair : Rexroth, "When We With Sappho," *Collected Shorter Poems*, 140.

before us gods goddesses at the ends of words : Blaser, "Image-Nation," no. 12, *Image-Nations*, 43.

A transparent base / shuddering : Johnson, "Letters to Walt Whitman," *Valley*, 95.

The ringing in your ears : Snyder, "The Hump-Backed Flute Player," *Mountains and Rivers*, 82.

Freedom. It isn't once : Rich, "For Memory," *Wild Patience*, 22.

atavistic two-headed / beast : Mackey, "Amma Seru's Hammer's Heated Fall," *School of Udhra*, 39.

{ footnote } ta'wīl said to've been sown : Mackey, "Song of the Andoumboulou: 18," *Whatsaid Serif*, 16.

"mu" more related to miss : Mackey, "Song of the Andoumboulou: 27," *Whatsaid Serif*, 64.

room in Poitiers where one can stand : Pound, *Cantos*, no. XC, p. 605.

to see the world focused back at us : Johnson, "When Men Will Lie Down as Gracefully & as Ripe," *Valley*, 47.

After a long time of light, there began to be eyes : Johnson, *Ark, the Foundations*, Beam 4.

The floor of the upside down

Only the sun / in the morning : Olson, *Maximus Poems*, vol. 2:6.

I tell you solemnly / That I was sorry : Jeffers, "Vulture," *Collected Poetry*, vol. 3:462.

The calyx of death's bounty : Crane, "At Melville's Tomb," *Complete Poems*, 34.

anything / nature puts in the sea : Olson, *Maximus Poems,* vol. 1:127.
afternoon Manatee of my mind? : Olson, *Maximus Poems,* vol. 2:13.
Work the old images from the hoard : Duncan, "The Question," *Opening of the Field,* 55.
The pageant, growing ever more curious : Ashbery, "Voyage in the Blue," *Self Portrait in a Convex Mirror,* 25.
All night long / I was a Eumolpidae : Olson, *Maximus Poems,* vol. 2:157.
upside-down trees / and sky : Blaser, "Image-Nation," no. 12, *Holy Forest,* 140.
That closed and open sounds : Zukofsky, *"A"* 12, pp. 138–39.
Who bury the dead : Lansing, "The Heavenly Tree Grows Downward," *Heavenly Tree,* 4.
for 'the / blossoms to / fall up' : Zukofsky, *"A"* 14, p. 326.
Only when the Flower : Olson, *Maximus Poems,* vol. 3:74–75.
as if the earth under our feet : W. C. Williams, "The pure products of America," *Collected Poems,* vol. 1:218.
The eyes, clamped shut, squeeze to a star : Sobin, "All Octaves Simultaneous," *Wind Chrysalid's Rattle.*
those stars in beautiful cosmology : Waldman, *Iovis,* vol. 2:191.
head full of stars : Ammons, "Concerning the Exclusions of the Object," *Collected Poems,* 200.
how / can I expel these roomy stars? : Ammons, "Concerning the Exclusions of the Object," *Collected Poems,* 200.
The immense stellar phenomenon : Rexroth, "The Phoenix and the Tortoise," *Collected Longer Poems,* 90.
The orders / are elaborate : Kelly, *The Loom,* 91.
I looked up and saw / its form : Olson, *Maximus Poems,* vol. 2:173.
no tomb / is solid : Kelly, *The Loom,* 224.
can it be said to have come forth from the tomb? : Kelly, "Easter," *Kill the Messenger,* 178.
When I am dead in the empty ear : Zukofsky, *"A"* 18, p. 393.
Tell us of excess : Duncan, "The Propositions," *Opening of the Field,* 35.

The starry horizon

This language is a horizon : Brandi, "This Language Isn't Speech," *Heartbeat Geography,* 177.
I went out on my cabin porch : Rexroth, "The Signature of All Things," *Collected Shorter Poems,* 179.
"the shape of heaven   is as confused : Blaser, "Image-Nation," no. 13, *Holy Forest,* 142–43.
The vast onion of the actual : Rexroth, "The Phoenix and the Tortoise," *Collected Longer Poems,* 77–78.
Off-shore, by islands hidden in the blood : Olson, *Maximus Poems,* vol. 1:1.
starting from fish-shape Paumanok : Whitman, "Starting from Paumanok," no. 1.
running around arranging / things : Blaser, "Image-Nation," no. 12, *Holy Forest,* 138.
action is, perhaps, the magnitude : Blaser, "Image-Nation," no. 10, *Holy Forest,* 134.

The impatient dead go out : Mackey, "Passing Thru," *Eroding Witness,* 79.

Libyans and Egyptians entered the Mississippi : Metcalf, U.S. Dept. of the Interior, *Collected Works,* vol. 2:229.

So the Jews, we now / from Tennessee inscriptions : Irby, "Jesus," *To Max Douglas.*

A band of seduction : Irby, "Delius," no. 8, *To Max Douglas.*

Nebula, whirlpool, mist & cloud : Johnson, "Four Orphic Poems," *Valley,* 29.

For "where the figure is, the answer is" : Johnson, "Four Orphic Poems," *Valley,* 30.

The frozen being

Looking at a Nation herself untaken : Olson, *Maximus Poems,* vol. 3:106.

When the ancient wisdom is folded : Jeffers, "The Torch-Bearer's Race," *Collected Poetry,* vol. 1:101.

The cosmos will not / dissolve its orders : Duncan, "Passages 24," *Bending the Bow,* 79.

The tides are in our veins : Jeffers, "Continent's End," *Collected Poetry,* vol. 1:16–17.

some part of us always / out beyond ourselves : Rich, "The Spirit of Place," *Wild Patience,* 45.

Emanation

they look up at the sky they see : Rothenberg, "A History of Surrealism in Cattaraugus County," *Seneca Journal,* 107.

{ footnote } Twenty men crossing a bridge : Stevens, "Metaphors of a Magnifico," *Palm,* 35.

the limited body : Zukofsky, *"A"* 12, pp. 202–3.

My bikini is worth yr/raft : Pound, *Cantos,* no. XCV, p. 645.

What is / hisses like a serpent : Duncan, "The Law," *Roots and Branches,* 30.

monster husband . . . Serpent Desire : Duncan, "Poem Beginning with a Line by Pindar," *Opening of the Field,* 67.

brought to her / insect instructor : Duncan, "Poem Beginning with a Line by Pindar," *Opening of the Field,* 65.

when the mind swings : Pound, *Cantos,* no. LXXXIII, p. 533.

It begins with the root of the tongue : Waldman, "Makeup on Empty Space," *Helping the Dreamer,* 133.

Memoranda and signatures

An apparent confusion if lived with long enough : Johnson, "The Different Musics," *Valley,* 85.

to find, out of the design : Johnson, "When Men Will Lie Down as Gracefully & as Ripe," *Valley,* 47–48.

All things / are engaged in writing their history : Johnson, "When Men Will Lie Down as Gracefully & as Ripe," *Valley,* 49.
{ footnote } history the dark crumble : Rich, "The Spirit of Place," *Wild Patience,* 41.
that poems / might be made as Harry Partch makes / music : Johnson, "Of Circumstance, The Circum Stances," *Valley,* 69.
engrossed // "between a miscroscopic & a telescopic / world" : Johnson, "Four Orphic Poems," *Valley,* 24.
My whole life / needs to be here : Duncan, "Dante Études ('To Speak My Mind')," *Ground Work,* vol. 1:99–100.
My life / in the leaves and on water : Niedecker, "Paean to Place," *Granite Pail,* 70.
rich friend / silt : Niedecker, "Along the River," *Granite Pail,* 5.
And what might have been : Rexroth, "Lyell's Hypothesis Again," *Collected Shorter Poems,* 181.
Tiny red marks on your flanks : Rexroth, "Lyell's Hypothesis Again," *Collected Shorter Poems,* 181.
And a kind of greening speech comes : Johnson, *Book of the Green Man,* 59.
Each leaf is an encyclopedia : Rexroth, "Death, Judgment, Heaven, Hell," *Collected Shorter Poems,* 61.
So goes: first, shape : Zukofsky, *"A"* 12, p. 126.
the cave wall socket : Eshleman, "Placements," *Hades in Manganese,* 29.
THEN I KNOW I AM NATURE : McClure, *Rare Angel,* 39.
THE PREDATORS MAKE PATTERNS : McClure, *Rare Angel,* 82.
WE ARE STICK FIGURES : McClure, *Rare Angel,* 92.
yours was the mouth of the wish : Duncan, "Circulations of the Song," *Ground Work,* vol. 1:169.
{ footnote } I wanted . . . a *Guneaform* : Strickland, "On First Looking into Diringer's *The Alphabet: A Key to the History of Mankind,*" *True North,* 5.
John of the Oak was here : Kelly, "Arnolfini's Wedding," *Mill of Particulars,* 121.
monumenta. In nature are signatures : Pound, *Cantos,* no. LXXXVII, p. 573.

Proprioception

How can a body be made from the word? : Blaser, "Image-Nation," no. 25, *Holy Forest,* 370.
boldly traveling, / on the heat of the dead : Snyder, "Toward Climax," *Turtle Island,* 84.
It is dangerous to leave written that which is badly written : Williams, *Paterson,* book 3, sect. 3, p. 129.
This is how we came to resume writing : Silliman, *Tjanting,* 109.
Get mind to hand or add tongue to eye : Silliman, *Tjanting,* 99.
The act of jotting down these marks : Silliman, *Tjanting,* 108.
These words jump around like fleas : Silliman, *Tjanting,* 42.
This is typical is an orange sentence : Silliman, *Tjanting,* 189.

Conversing lazily over espresso : Silliman, *Tjanting,* 176.
Reading rewrites this : Silliman, *Tjanting,* 40.
Rewriting reads this : Silliman, *Tjanting,* 91.
While you read this you continue thinking : Silliman, *Tjanting,* 47.
This text might be a guide : Silliman, *Tjanting,* 158.

Vertigo

Dante in my dream : Kelly, "Arnaut Daniel," *Flesh Dream Book,* 108.
Tape recorder—tape reason : Zukofsky, *"A"* 13, p. 288.
This living hand, now warm : Olson, *Maximus Poems,* vol. 3:177 [original in Keats, *Poems,* 438].
A hundred years ago I made a book : Palmer, "Baudelaire Series," *Sun,* 9.
the unnamable draws from us a world / of names : Duncan, "The Five Songs," *Ground Work,* vol. 2:79.
{ footnote } In the poem he learns to turn : Palmer, "Notes for Echo Lake 3," *Notes for Echo Lake,* 17.
{ footnote } would live against sentences : Palmer, "Notes for Echo Lake 10," *Notes for Echo Lake,* 62.
{ footnote } Prose is a sentence : Coolidge, "The Walls Have Ears in Mind: On First Receiving *Notes for Echo Lake,*" *Solution Passage,* 179.
It is a site where language hangs : DuPlessis, "Draft 33: Deixis," *Drafts,* 223.
It is an illusion that we were ever alive : Stevens, "The Rock," *Palm,* 362.
I wonder, have I lived a skeleton's life : Stevens, "As You Leave the Room," *Palm,* 396.
& where is wisdom : Kelly, "Arnaut Daniel," *Flesh Dream Book,* 109.

Characters

The problem of personality : Rexroth, "The Phoenix and the Tortoise," *Collected Longer Poems,* 70.
it's gonna be hot soon : Dorn, *Gunslinger,* 58.
I too had been struck from the float : Whitman, "Crossing Brooklyn Ferry," no. 5.
Straight man. / 1000 percent : Dorn, *Gunslinger,* 60.
What then, if we make I / a receptacle : Dorn, *Gunslinger,* 60.
The choice is simply, / I will : Creeley, "The Finger," *Collected Poems,* 387.
In which these painfully small / endings : Creeley, "Echoes," *Echoes,* 98.
Here now you are : Creeley, "Like a man committed to searching," *Collected Poems,* 428.
scatter be / my name : Mackey, "Songs of the Andoumboulou: 34," *Whatsaid Serif,* 103.
You never know what name : Giscombe, *Giscome Road,* 69.
a negro miner : Giscombe, *Giscome Road,* 17.
the blood as if it too were out there : Giscombe, *Giscome Road,* 59.
the same old story : Giscombe, *Giscome Road,* 49.

the story's the same old edge : Giscombe, *Giscome Road,* 34.
the longest song bends away : Giscombe, *Giscome Road,* 64.
His they their / we : Mackey, "Irritable Mystic," *School of Udhra,* 25.

Language obeyed

Like translations : DuPlessis, "Draft 33: Deixis," *Drafts,* 219.
the work of Art to set words : Duncan, "Passages 33," *Ground Work,* vol. 1:19.
the line / [is] a trial : Duncan, "Passages 33," *Ground Work,* vol. 1:22.
The common air includes / Events : Zukofsky, *"A"* 6, pp. 26–27.
Of and Or are snails, repeat vegetable lessons : Duncan, "Structures of Rime VIII," *Opening of the Field,* 70.
Language obeyd flares tongues in obscure matter : Duncan, "Food for Fire, Food for Thought," *Opening of the Field,* 95.
eye net I / quoin own me : Zukofsky, *"A"* 23, p. 549.
For example / The poem does not know : Spicer, "Heads of the Town" ("Homage to Creeley"), *Collected Books,* 123.
Our image shrinks to a morpheme : Spicer, "Language" ("Morphemics"), *Collected Books,* 235.
For the blue wash of sound drawn back to its shores : Duncan, "Structure of Rime X," *Opening of the Field,* 72.
Hello and goodbye : McNaughton, "For Peter," *Shit On My Shoes.*
The verb divides us evenly : Palmer, "Tomb of Baudelaire," *Without Music,* 43.
the touch breaks / who touches : Kelly, *Book of Persephone,* no. 14.
would have to be mmmmm : Spicer, "Heads of the Town" ("A Fake Novel about the Life of Rimbaud"), *Collected Books,* 161.
A design Thoreau saw : Johnson, "When Men Will Lie Down as Gracefully & as Ripe," *Valley,* 47.
Then ache cue test his air earth : Zukofsky, *Catullus,* no. 64.
Song's fateful. Crime / fulfills the law : Duncan, "The Law," *Roots and Branches,* 27.
Language obeyd flares tongues in obscure matter : Duncan, "Food for Fire, Food for Thought," *Opening of the Field,* 95.

Pestilence

mill of particulars : Kelly, "The Mill," *The Mill of Particulars,* 96–97.
Spreading over the world : Rexroth, "Strength through Joy," *Collected Shorter Poems,* 156.
Tomb of Donald Duck : Eshleman, *Fracture,* 91–102.
you must now take into consideration : Eshleman, "The Aurignacian Summation," *Fracture,* 128.
For what we cannot accomplish : Williams, *Paterson,* book 2, sect. 3, p. 79.
The ear / catches rime like pangs of a disease : Duncan, "Passages 11," *Bending the Bow,* 32.

And if I know not my wound : Duncan, "The Regulators ('In Blood's Domaine')," *Ground Work,* vol. 2:69.

Mind comes into this language : Duncan, "After Passage," *Ground Work,* vol. 2:69.

There is no ecstasy of beauty : Duncan, "The Regulators ('In Blood's Domaine')," *Ground Work,* vol. 2:69.

enemies . . . whose whispers prickle the spirit : Stevens, "Examination of the Hero in a Time of War," *Palm,* 199.

not men but / heads and armors of the worm : Duncan, "Passages 21," *Bending the Bow,* 73.

the / hollow coil of our own dark scribbles : Sobin, "Under the Bright Orchards," *Towards the Blanched Alphabets,* 5.

nothing's written, in effect, that's not underwritten : Sobin, "Premises," *Towards the Blanched Alphabets,* 8.

all this garbage! : Ammons, *Garbage,* 75.

Posses led by a promising girl : Dorn, "Home on the Range, February, 1962," *Collected Poems,* 44.

I am bent on fathoming : Rich, "Atlas of the Difficult World," *Atlas,* 22.

Actually the stirrings now of man faced / with a wall : Olson, *Maximus Poems,* vol. 3:155.

To unmean with moaning : Mackey, "Aspic Surmise," *School of Udhra,* 76.

Tellus old earth : Lamantia, "The Mysteries of Writing in the West," *Meadowlark,* 53.

recalling the Jew / in the pit : Williams, *Paterson,* book 5, sect. 2, p. 221.

De rerum natura: *epic's lyric absolute*

this poem / Of the phoenix and the tortoise : Rexroth, "The Phoenix and the Tortoise," *Collected Longer Poems,* 64.

Fragments of its inexhaustible / Life : Rexroth, "The Phoenix and the Tortoise," *Collected Longer Poems,* 63.

bumping / In a sharl of kelp : Rexroth, "The Phoenix and the Tortoise," *Collected Longer Poems,* 64.

And, out of his drained gray flesh : Rexroth, "The Phoenix and the Tortoise," *Collected Longer Poems,* 64.

the organization / Of the evil instincts : Rexroth, "The Phoenix and the Tortoise," *Collected Longer Poems,* 74.

Its goal is the achievement : Rexroth, "The Phoenix and the Tortoise," *Collected Longer Poems,* 80–81.

The assumption of history : Rexroth, "The Phoenix and the Tortoise," *Collected Longer Poems,* 76.

The vast onion of the actual : Rexroth, "The Phoenix and the Tortoise," *Collected Longer Poems,* 77–78.

Endurance, novelty, and simple / Occurrence : Rexroth, "The Phoenix and the Tortoise," *Collected Longer Poems,* 71–72.

the thing that falls away is myself : Rexroth, "The Phoenix and the Tortoise," *Collected Longer Poems,* 72.

The squirming facts exceed the squamous mind : Stevens, "Connoisseur of Chaos," *Palm,* 167.

one more / Element in the immense disorder of truths : Stevens, "Connoisseur of Chaos," *Palm,* 167.

a plentiful waste : Ammons, *Garbage,* 103.

A. A violent order is disorder : Stevens, "Connoisseur of Chaos," *Palm,* 166.

There is an exquisite movement, like it were chaos : Johnson, *Valley,* 25.

prosper / o / cell : Johnson, "Beam 25, A Bicentennial Hymn," *Ark, the Foundations.*

beckoned by pungencies : Johnson, "The Unfoldings," *Valley,* 106.

are nothing / but an immense swarm : Johnson, "The Unfoldings," *Valley,* 108.

Without dimension : Johnson, *RADI OS,* book 2.

Time was we were molten : Frost, "Too Anxious for Rivers," *Collected Poems,* 343.

the embodiment that crashed : Frost, "The Most of It," *Collected Poems,* 307.

He thought he kept the universe alone : Frost, "The Most of It," *Collected Poems,* 307.

Speaking of contraries, see how the brook : Frost, "West-Running Brook," *Collected Poems,* 237–38.

Divinely superfluous beauty : Jeffers, "Divinely Superfluous Beauty," *Collected Poetry,* vol. 1:4.

And the passionate human intelligence : Jeffers, "The unformed volcanic earth," *Collected Poetry,* vol. 3:431.

Is this more beautiful / Than man's disasters? : Jeffers, "Night without Sleep," *Collected Poetry,* vol. 2:559.

this fate going on / Outside our fates : Jeffers, "Oh Lovely Rock," *Collected Poetry,* vol. 2:546.

this rock will be here : Jeffers, "Oh Lovely Rock," *Collected Poetry,* vol. 2:547.

The beauty of things was born before eyes : Jeffers, "Credo," *Collected Poetry,* vol. 1:239.

As for us: / We must uncenter our minds : Jeffers, "Carmel Point," *Collected Poetry,* vol. 3:399.

Here was death, and with terror : Jeffers, "Orca," *Collected Poetry,* vol. 3:206.

The earth is a star : Jeffers, "Orca," *Collected Poetry,* vol. 3:206.

To know that great civilizations have broken down : Jeffers, "The Answer," *Collected Poetry,* vol. 2:536.

It is good for man : Jeffers, "The Beaks of Eagles," *Collected Poetry,* vol. 2:537.

learning trembling religion and blood-sacrifice : Jeffers, "The unformed volcanic earth," *Collected Poetry,* vol. 3:433.

Lucretius felt the change of the world : Jeffers, "Prescription of Painful Ends," *Collected Poetry,* vol. 3:14.

one builds poems for treasuries : Jeffers, "Prescription of Painful Ends," *Collected Poetry,* vol. 3:14.

one christens each poem : Jeffers, "Prescription of Painful Ends," *Collected Poetry,* vol. 3:14.

furious from perception : Pound, *Cantos,* no. XC, p. 606.

little chirping Sirens : Jeffers, "The Sirens," *Collected Poetry,* vol. 3:4.

While this America settles in the mould : Jeffers, "Shine, Perishing Republic," *Collected Poetry,* vol. 1:15.

{ footnote } pained thoughts found / The honey peace : Jeffers, "To the Stone-Cutters," *Collected Poetry,* vol. 1:5.

The saccharescent, lying in glucose : Pound, *Cantos,* no. XV, p. 64.

England off there in black darkness : Pound, *Cantos,* no. XXVII, p. 129.

Here the human past is dim and feeble : Jeffers, "Haunted Country," *Collected Poetry,* vol. 1:111.

Ghosts of inner ecology

No trace anywhere of life, you say : Beckett, "Imagination Dead Imagine," *Complete Short Prose,* 182.

The rotted man inside, who used to seem archetypal : Eshleman, "Narration Hanging from the Cusp of the Eighties," *Hades in Manganese,* 96.

preformed chaos / strives to form : Meltzer, "K-K-K-A-O-S: Lecture Notes (Biodegradable Prose Specks)," *Arrows,* 186.

Hermetic, terrible from joy : Lansing, "Graffiti, Ancient and Modern," *Heavenly Tree,* 9.

Dark and enormous rolls the surf : Jeffers, "The Torch-Bearer's Race," *Collected Poetry,* vol. 1:99.

As the dead prey upon us : Olson, "As the Dead Prey Upon Us," *The Distances,* 74.

The nets we are entangled in : Olson, "As the Dead Prey Upon Us," *The Distances,* 77.

The table top looked glassy for a few seconds : Irby, "September," *Catalpa,* 56.

Everything happened instantaneously : Irby, "September," *Catalpa,* 56–57.

compost line of any mind : Irby, "To Max Douglas," *To Max Douglas.*

the dark gods / wait in the blooded underground : Irby, "To Max Douglas," *To Max Douglas.*

the hermetic secret floats : Lamantia, "West," *Meadowlark,* 8.

in a place named No-Such-Place : Mackey, "Song of the Andoumboulou: 24," *Whatsaid Serif,* 43.

which direction now / does distance take : Irby, "To Max Douglas," *To Max Douglas.*

the Jurassic longing : Irby, "To Max Douglas," *To Max Douglas.*

k / the letter cutting : Meltzer, "K-K-K-A-O-S: Lecture Notes (Biodegradable Prose Specks)," *Arrows,* 185.

All life long / you include something : Lansing, "The Great Form is Without Shape," *Heavenly Tree,* 13.

Origin

Not our good luck nor the instant peak : Jeffers, "Not Our Good Luck," *Collected Poetry,* vol. 1:12.

{ footnote } roll, that it / billow : Sobin, "Called It Space," *Towards the Blanched Alphabets,* 122.

Who shall say I am not / the happy genius : Williams, "Danse Russe," *Collected Poems,* vol. 1:87.

{ footnote } as if we recalld the nature of the deep : Duncan, "An Alternate Life ('Supplication')," *Ground Work,* vol. 2:9.

occult ferocity of origin : Howe, "Articulation of Sound Forms in Time," *Singularities,* 30.

Detritus pathways

The web is woven : Stevens, "The Dwarf," *Palm,* 152.

It is the mind that is woven : Stevens, "The Dwarf," *Palm,* 152–53.

it let me stand / above it : Kelly, "Swallowtail," *Kill the Messenger,* 206.

wooing swallow : Webster, "A Body of Paradigmatic Fields," *Thicket Daybreak,* 1.

detritus pathways : Snyder, "Toward Climax," *Turtle Island,* 84.

unmade boundaries of acts and poems : Rukeyser, "The Book of the Dead," *Muriel Rukeyser Reader,* 48.

As species disappear, the paleolithic grows more vivid : Eshleman, "Placements," *Hades in Manganese,* 29.

"The brush / May paint" : Snyder, "Logging," no. 15, *Myths and Texts,* 15.

Scruples & superstition

{ footnote } "Was" / "the human psyche" "made of women" : Notley, *Descent of Alette,* 71.

Was the agreement that words shine : Waldman, "Suppose a Game," *Kill or Cure,* 2.

Now I subtract myself : Eshleman, "The Aurignacians Have the Floor," *Hades in Manganese,* 88.

where drought is the epic : Rich, "The Desert as Garden of Paradise," *Time's Power,* 27.

Psychosm

that, / through us, the / hazel / might ripen : Sobin, "The Earth as Air: An Ars Poetica," *The Earth as Air,* 102.

Superfluity

God said, "Let meanings move" : Rukeyser, "The Sixth Night: Waking," *Muriel Rukeyser Reader,* 196.
high superfluousness : Jeffers, "The Excesses of God," *Collected Poetry,* vol. 1:4.
to fling / Rainbows over the rain : Jeffers, "The Excesses of God," *Collected Poetry,* vol. 1:4.
The Great Mind passes by : Snyder, "The Flowing," *Mountains and Rivers Without End,* 71.
Do I move toward form : Rukeyser, "Double Ode," *Muriel Rukeyser Reader,* 274.
not a man, not a poet : García Lorca, "Double Poem of Lake Eden," *Poet in New York,* 79.
A certain arch and/or ache : Mackey, "Song of the Andoumdoulou: 7," *Eroding Witness,* 54.
An undertow / of whir : Mackey, "Waters / wet the / mouth," *Eroding Witness,* 3.
it is human nature to stand in the middle of a thing : Moore, "A Grave," *Observations,* 60.
we are keepers of the secret : H. D., "The Walls Do Not Fall," no. 15, *Trilogy,* 24.
the communication / of the dead : Eliot, "Little Gidding," no. 1, *Complete Poems,* 192.
crowned knot of fire : Eliot, "Little Gidding," no. 5, *Complete Poems,* 198.
where is the point : Eliot, "A Note on War Poetry," *Complete Poems,* 202.
war is not a life : Eliot, "A Note on War Poetry," *Complete Poems,* 202.
{ footnote } The war is a mineral perfection : Duncan, "An Essay at War," *Derivations,* 23.
is the war or part of it : Williams, "Author's Introduction," *Collected Poems,* vol. 2:53.
my flower that splits / the rocks : Williams, "A Sort of Song," *Collected Poems,* vol. 2:55.
The new opens / new ways : Williams, "Catastrophic Birth," *Collected Poems,* vol. 2:56.
the empty / ear : Williams, "Paterson: The Falls," *Collected Poems,* vol. 2:58.
The Kermess : Williams, "The Dance," *Collected Poems,* vol. 2:58.
what is war : Williams, "War, the Destroyer!" *Collected Poems,* vol. 2:43.

The empty house

Is the house empty? : Graham, "The Phase after History," *Dream of the Unified Field,* 155.
We are the seed that dies : Seferis, "Memory I," *Collected Poems,* 359.

The times promised

The individual / has become divided : Olson, *Maximus Poems,* vol. 3:73.
I've seen it all go in other directions : Olson, *Maximus Poems,* vol. 3:155.
One even, at this date begins to look on man : Olson, *Maximus Poems,* vol. 3:163.
Same day, Later : Olson, *Maximus Poems,* vol. 3:166.
polis is / eyes : Olson, *Maximus Poems,* vol. 1:26.
The universe is filld with eyes : Duncan, "The Law I Love Is Major Mover," *Opening of the Field,* 10.
Whomans in the whosmos : Byrd, *Great Dimestore Centenniel,* 98.

History cannot end as history : Byrd, *Great Dimestore Centennial,* 61.
The World / has become divided : Olson, *Maximus Poems,* vol. 3:73.
The earth / shall have preceded love : Olson, *Maximus Poems,* vol. 3:74.
without three Towns / there is no Society : Olson, *Maximus Poems,* vol. 3:73.
Migration in fact (which is probably / as constant : Olson, *Maximus Poems,* vol. 3:176.
that the Mind or Will always / successfully opposes : Olson, *Maximus Poems,* vol. 3:176.
Astride / the Cabot / fault : Olson, *Maximus Poems,* vol. 3:37.
Frances Rose-Troup Land : Olson, *Maximus Poems,* vol. 3:37.

The uninterrupted tissue

Ficino had the idea : Duncan, "Apprehensions," *Roots and Branches,* 31.
There is no life that does not rise / melodic : Duncan, "Apprehensions," *Roots and Branches,* 43.
theft of what the heart desired : Duncan, "Apprehensions," *Roots and Branches,* 35–36.
To build light : Pound, *Cantos,* no. XCIV, p. 642.
these lights never die : Lamantia, "There," *Meadowlark,* 70.
The elk mind moves its antlers : Stein, "Later Poems from 'The Sad World,'" *Hat Rack Tree,* 93.
A man's paradise is his good nature : Pound, *Cantos,* no. XCIII, p. 623.
to perambulate the bounds of cosmos : Olson, *Maximus Poems,* vol. 3:133.
philosophic wedding : Kelly, "Arnolfini's Wedding," *Mill of Particulars,* 122.
Jung: "There are unconscious aspects" : Johnson, *Ark, the Foundations,* Beam 26.
An Inlet of Reality, or Soul : Lansing, *Heavenly Tree,* 40.
whatever might chafes away under the peel : Webster, "Anthropophagy 1928," *Thicket Daybreak,* 67.
From the ape at my shoulderblade : Johnson, *Ark, the Foundations,* Beam 12.

Bibliography

Abram, David. *The Spell of the Sensuous: Perception and Language in a More-than-Human World.* New York: Vintage, 1997.

Alcosser, Sandra. *Except by Nature.* Saint Paul: Graywolf Press, 1998.

Alexander, Will. "Nathaniel Mackey: 'An ashen finesse.'" *Callaloo* 23, no. 2 (2000): 700–702.

Allen, Donald M., and Warren Tallman, eds. *The Poetics of the New American Poetry.* New York: Grove Press, 1973.

Allen, Gay Wilson. *The Solitary Singer: A Critical Biography of Walt Whitman.* New York: Macmillan, 1955.

Ammons, A. R. *Collected Poems, 1951–1971.* New York: Norton, 1972.

———. *Garbage.* New York: Norton, 1993.

———. *Sphere: The Form of a Motion.* New York: Norton, 1974.

Andrews, Bruce. *Lip Service.* Toronto: Coach House, 2001.

———. *Paradise & Method: Poetics & Praxis.* Evanston, Ill.: Northwestern University Press, 1996.

Arnold, Matthew. *Selected Prose.* Ed. P. J. Keating. New York: Penguin, 1980.

Arvin, Newton. *Whitman.* New York: Macmillan, 1938.

Ashbery, John. *As We Know.* New York: Viking, 1979.

———. *The Double Dream of Spring.* New York: Dutton, 1970.

———. *Self-Portrait in a Convex Mirror.* New York: Viking, 1975.

———. *Three Poems.* New York: Viking, 1972.

Atlan, Henri. "Uncommon Finalities." In *Gaia,* ed. William Irwin Thompson, 110–27.

Bateson, Gregory. *Steps to an Ecology of Mind.* San Francisco: Chandler, 1972.

Beckett, Samuel. *The Complete Short Prose, 1929–1989.* Ed. S. E. Gontarski. New York: Grove Press, 1995.

Bernstein, Charles. *Content's Dream: Essays, 1975–1984.* Los Angeles: Sun & Moon Press, 1986.

———. *My Way: Speeches and Poems.* University of Chicago Press, 1999.

———. *A Poetics.* Cambridge: Harvard University Press, 1992.

Berry, Wendell. *Collected Poems, 1957–1982.* San Francisco: North Point Press, 1985.

———. *Recollected Essays, 1965–1980.* San Francisco: North Point Press, 1981.

———. *Standing by Words.* San Francisco: North Point Press, 1983.

Blaser, Robin. "The Fire." In *The Poetics of the New American Poetry,* ed. Donald M. Allen and Warren Tallman, 235–46. New York: Grove Press, 1973.

———. *The Holy Forest.* Toronto: Coach House, 1993.

———. *Image-Nations 1–2 & The Stadium of the Mirror.* London: Ferry Press, 1974.

Bloom, Harold. *Agon: Towards a Theory of Revisionism.* New York: Oxford University Press, 1982.

Boer, Charles, trans. *The Homeric Hymns.* Chicago: Swallow Press, 1970.

Bohm, David. *Wholeness and the Implicate Order.* London: Routledge and Kegan Paul, 1980.

Borges, Jorge Luis. *Labyrinths.* Ed. Donald A. Yates and James E. Irby. New York: New Directions, 1964.

———. *Selected Non-Fictions.* Ed. Eliot Weinberger. New York: Viking, 1999.

Brandi, John. *Heartbeat Geography: Selected and Uncollected Poems, 1966–1994.* Fredonia, N.Y.: White Pine, 1995.

———. *That Back Road In: Selected Poems, 1972–1983.* Berkeley: Wingbow, 1985.

Brown, G. Spencer. *Laws of Form.* New York: Bantam, 1973.

Brown, Norman O. *Apocalypse and/or Metamorphosis.* Berkeley: University of California Press, 1991.

Browne, Sir Thomas. *The Prose of Sir Thomas Browne.* Ed. Norman J. Endicott. New York: Anchor Books, 1967.

Byrd, Don. "Getting Ready to Read 'A.'" *Boundary 2* 10, no. 2 (1982): 291–308.

———. *The Great Dimestore Centennial.* Barrytown, N.Y.: Station Hill Press, 1986.

———. *The Poetics of the Common Knowledge.* Albany: SUNY Press, 1994.

Calasso, Roberto. *The Marriage of Cadmus and Harmony.* Trans. Tim Parks. New York: Knopf, 1993.

Césaire, Aimé. *The Collected Poetry.* Trans. Clayton Eshleman and Annette Smith. Berkeley: University of California Press, 1983.

Clarke, John. *From Feathers to Iron: A Concourse of World Poetics.* Bolinas, Calif.: Tombouctou/Convivio, 1987.

———. *In the Analogy.* Toronto: Shuffaloff, 1997.

Claus, David B. *Toward the Soul: An Inquiry into the Meaning of ψυχή before Plato.* New Haven, Conn.: Yale University Press, 1981.

Coolidge, Clark. *Solution Passage.* Los Angeles: Sun & Moon Press, 1986.

Corbin, Henry. *Avicenna and the Visionary Recital.* Trans. Willard Trask. New York: Pantheon, 1960.

———. *Creative Imagination in the Sufism of Ibn 'Arabi.* Trans. Ralph Manheim. Princeton: Princeton University Press, 1969.

———. *The Man of Light in Iranian Sufism.* Trans. Nancy Pearson. Boulder: Shambhala, 1978.

———. "*Mundus Imaginalis* or The Imaginary and the Imaginal." In *Spring 1972,* 1–19.

———. *Spiritual Body and Celestial Earth.* Trans. Nancy Pearson. Princeton: Princeton University Press, 1977.

Crane, Hart. *The Complete Poems and Selected Letters and Prose.* Ed. Brom Weber. New York: Doubleday Anchor, 1966.

Creeley, Robert. *The Collected Essays.* Berkeley: University of California Press, 1989.

———. *The Collected Poems, 1945–1975.* Berkeley: University of California Press, 1982.

———. *Contexts of Poetry: Interviews, 1961–1971.* Ed. Donald Allen. Bolinas, Calif.: Four Seasons, 1973.

———. *Echoes.* New York: New Directions, 1994.

———. *Mirrors.* New York: New Directions, 1983.

Crosby, Alfred W. *Germs, Seeds, and Animals: Studies in Ecological History.* Armonk, N.Y.: M. E. Sharpe, 1994.

Davenport, Guy. *Every Force Evolves a Form.* San Francisco: North Point Press, 1987.

———. *The Geography of the Imagination.* San Francisco: North Point Press, 1981.

Deleuze, Gilles. *The Fold: Leibniz and the Baroque.* Trans. Tom Conley. Minneapolis: University of Minnesota Press, 1993.

———. *Foucault.* Trans. Seán Hand. Minneapolis: University of Minnesota Press, 1988.

———. "He Stuttered." Trans. Constantin V. Boundas. In *Gilles Deleuze and the Theater of Philosophy,* ed. Constantin V. Boundas and Dorothea Olkowski, 23–29. New York: Routledge, 1994.

———. "Nomad Thought." In *The New Nietzsche,* ed. David B. Allison, 142–49. New York: Dell, 1977.

———. *Proust and Signs.* Trans. Richard Howard. New York: Braziller, 1972.

———. "The Schizophrenic and Language: Surface and Depth in Lewis Carroll and Antonin Artaud." In *Textual Strategies,* ed. Josué V. Harari, 277–95. Ithaca, N.Y.: Cornell University Press, 1979.

Deleuze, Gilles, and Félix Guattari. *Anti-Oedipus: Capitalism and Schizophrenia.* Trans. Robert Hurley, Mark Seem, and Helen R. Lane. New York: Viking, 1977.

———. *A Thousand Plateaus: Capitalism and Schizophrenia.* Trans. Brian Massumi. Minneapolis: University of Minnesota Press, 1987.

DeLillo, Don. *White Noise.* New York: Viking, 1985.

Derrida, Jacques. *Dissemination.* Trans. Barbara Johnson. Chicago: University of Chicago Press, 1981.

———. *Of Grammatology.* Trans. Gayatri Spivak. Baltimore: Johns Hopkins University Press, 1976.

———. "White Mythology." Trans. F. C. T. Moore. *New Literary History* 6 (autumn 1974): 5–74.

Dickinson, Emily. *The Complete Poems.* Ed. Thomas H. Johnson. Boston: Little, Brown, 1960.

———. *Selected Letters.* Ed. Thomas H. Johnson. Cambridge: Harvard University Press, 1986.

Doria, Charles, and Harris Lenowitz, eds. and trans. *Origins: Creation Texts from the Ancient Mediterranean.* New York: Anchor Books, 1976.

Dorn, Edward. *The Collected Poems, 1956–1974.* Bolinas, Calif.: Four Seasons, 1975.

———. *Gunslinger.* Durham, N.C.: Duke University Press, 1989.

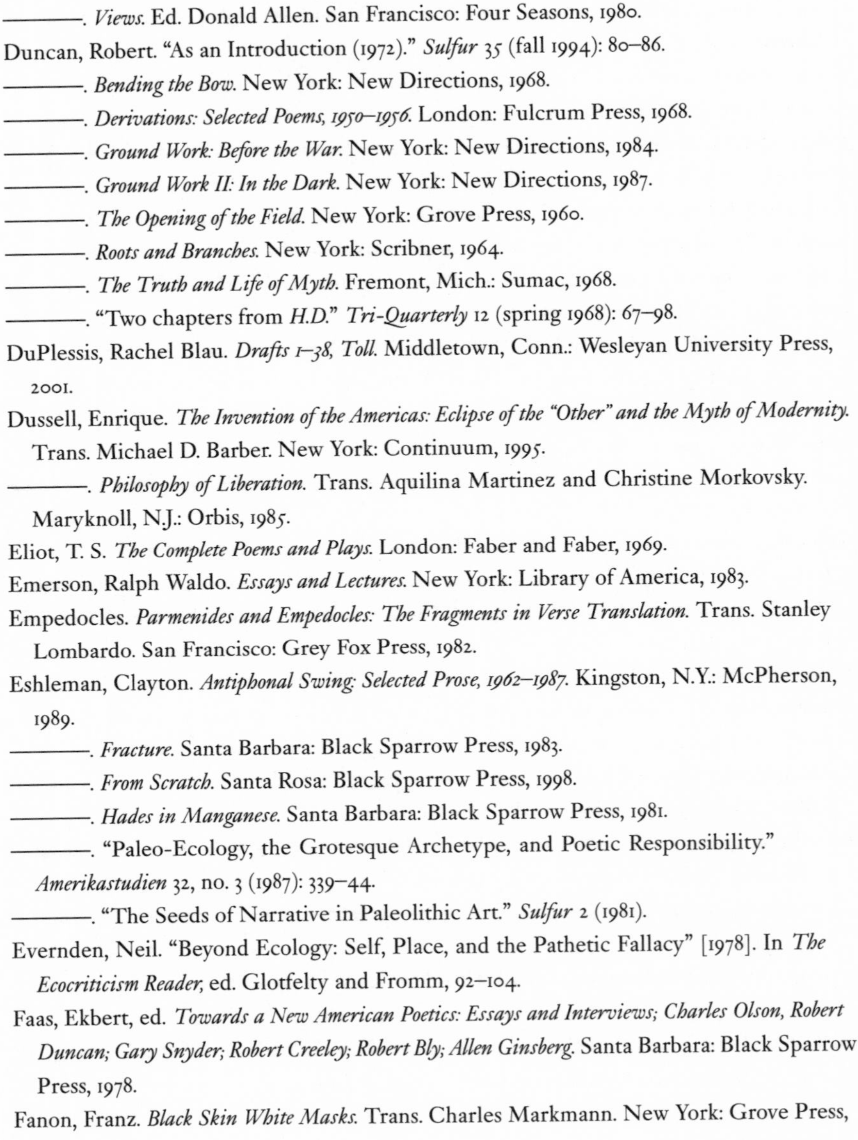

———. *Recollections of Gran Apachería.* San Francisco: Turtle Island, 1974.

———. *Views.* Ed. Donald Allen. San Francisco: Four Seasons, 1980.

Duncan, Robert. "As an Introduction (1972)." *Sulfur* 35 (fall 1994): 80–86.

———. *Bending the Bow.* New York: New Directions, 1968.

———. *Derivations: Selected Poems, 1950–1956.* London: Fulcrum Press, 1968.

———. *Ground Work: Before the War.* New York: New Directions, 1984.

———. *Ground Work II: In the Dark.* New York: New Directions, 1987.

———. *The Opening of the Field.* New York: Grove Press, 1960.

———. *Roots and Branches.* New York: Scribner, 1964.

———. *The Truth and Life of Myth.* Fremont, Mich.: Sumac, 1968.

———. "Two chapters from *H.D.*" *Tri-Quarterly* 12 (spring 1968): 67–98.

DuPlessis, Rachel Blau. *Drafts 1–38, Toll.* Middletown, Conn.: Wesleyan University Press, 2001.

Dussell, Enrique. *The Invention of the Americas: Eclipse of the "Other" and the Myth of Modernity.* Trans. Michael D. Barber. New York: Continuum, 1995.

———. *Philosophy of Liberation.* Trans. Aquilina Martinez and Christine Morkovsky. Maryknoll, N.J.: Orbis, 1985.

Eliot, T. S. *The Complete Poems and Plays.* London: Faber and Faber, 1969.

Emerson, Ralph Waldo. *Essays and Lectures.* New York: Library of America, 1983.

Empedocles. *Parmenides and Empedocles: The Fragments in Verse Translation.* Trans. Stanley Lombardo. San Francisco: Grey Fox Press, 1982.

Eshleman, Clayton. *Antiphonal Swing: Selected Prose, 1962–1987.* Kingston, N.Y.: McPherson, 1989.

———. *Fracture.* Santa Barbara: Black Sparrow Press, 1983.

———. *From Scratch.* Santa Rosa: Black Sparrow Press, 1998.

———. *Hades in Manganese.* Santa Barbara: Black Sparrow Press, 1981.

———. "Paleo-Ecology, the Grotesque Archetype, and Poetic Responsibility." *Amerikastudien* 32, no. 3 (1987): 339–44.

———. "The Seeds of Narrative in Paleolithic Art." *Sulfur* 2 (1981).

Evernden, Neil. "Beyond Ecology: Self, Place, and the Pathetic Fallacy" [1978]. In *The Ecocriticism Reader,* ed. Glotfelty and Fromm, 92–104.

Faas, Ekbert, ed. *Towards a New American Poetics: Essays and Interviews; Charles Olson, Robert Duncan; Gary Snyder; Robert Creeley; Robert Bly; Allen Ginsberg.* Santa Barbara: Black Sparrow Press, 1978.

Fanon, Franz. *Black Skin White Masks.* Trans. Charles Markmann. New York: Grove Press, 1967.

Flannery, Tim. *The Eternal Frontier: An Ecological History of North America and Its Peoples.* New York: Atlantic Monthly Press, 2001.

Foucault, Michel. *The Order of Things.* New York: Pantheon, 1970.

Franklin, Wayne. *Discoverers, Explorers, Settlers.* Chicago: University of Chicago Press, 1979.

Frost, Robert. *Collected Poems, Prose, and Plays.* New York: Library of America, 1995.

Fussell, Edwin. *Frontier: American Literature and the American West.* Princeton: Princeton University Press, 1965.

———. *Lucifer in Harness.* Princeton: Princeton University Press, 1973.

García Lorca, Federico. *Deep Song and Other Prose.* Ed. and trans. Christopher Maurer. New York: New Directions, 1980.

———. *Poet in New York.* Rev. ed. Ed. Christopher Maurer and trans. Greg Simon and Steven F. White. New York: Noonday Press, 1998.

Gardner, Thomas. *Regions of Unlikeness: Explaining Contemporary Poetry.* Lincoln: University of Nebraska Press, 1999.

Ginsberg, Allen. *The Fall of America: Poems of These States, 1965–1971.* San Francisco: City Lights, 1972.

Ginzburg, Carlo. "Morelli, Freud and Sherlock Holmes: Clues and Scientific Method." Trans. Anna Davin. *History Workshop* 9 (spring 1980): 5–36.

Giscombe, C. S. *Giscome Road.* Normal, Ill.: Dalkey Archive, 1998.

Glotfelty, Cheryll, and Harold Fromm, eds. *The Ecocriticism Reader: Landmarks in Literary Ecology.* Athens: University of Georgia Press, 1996.

Goldbarth, Albert. *Adventures in Ancient Egypt.* Columbus: Ohio State University Press, 1996.

———. *The Gods.* Columbus: Ohio State University Press, 1993.

Goody, Jack, ed. *Literacy in Traditional Societies.* Cambridge: Cambridge University Press, 1968.

Graham, Jorie. *The Dream of the Unified Field: Selected Poems, 1974–1994.* New York: Ecco Press, 1995.

Grenier, Robert. "On Speech." In *In the American Tree,* ed. Ron Silliman, 496–97. Orono, Maine: National Poetry Foundation, 1986.

———. *Phantom Anthems.* Oakland: O Books/Trike Press, 1986.

Grossinger, Richard. "Origin of the Human World: A Chronicle." In *An Olson-Melville Sourcebook, Volume II: The Mediterranean,* ed. Richard Grossinger, 5–91. Plainfield, Vt.: North Atlantic Books, 1976.

Harrison, Jane Ellen. *Themis.* Cambridge: Cambridge University Press, 1927.

Harrison, Robert Pogue. *Forests: The Shadow of Civilization.* Chicago: University of Chicago Press, 1992.

H.D. *Trilogy.* New York: New Directions, 1973.

Heidegger, Martin. *Early Greek Thinking.* Trans. David Farrell Krell. New York: Harper & Row, 1975.

———. *Poetry, Language, Thought.* Trans. Albert Hofstader. New York: Harper & Row, 1971.

Heinzelman, Kurt. *The Economics of the Imagination.* Amherst: University of Massachusetts Press, 1980.

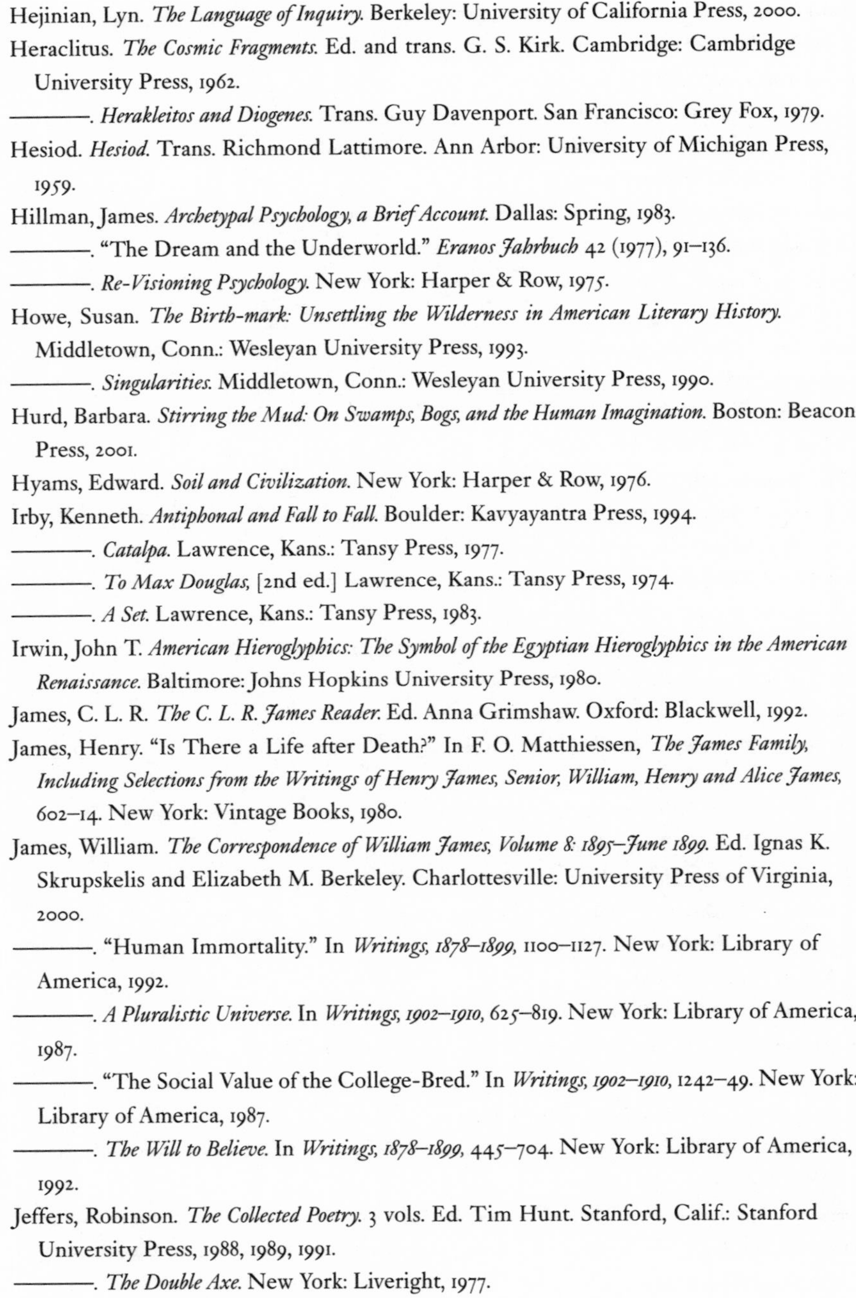

Hejinian, Lyn. *The Language of Inquiry.* Berkeley: University of California Press, 2000.

Heraclitus. *The Cosmic Fragments.* Ed. and trans. G. S. Kirk. Cambridge: Cambridge University Press, 1962.

———. *Herakleitos and Diogenes.* Trans. Guy Davenport. San Francisco: Grey Fox, 1979.

Hesiod. *Hesiod.* Trans. Richmond Lattimore. Ann Arbor: University of Michigan Press, 1959.

Hillman, James. *Archetypal Psychology, a Brief Account.* Dallas: Spring, 1983.

———. "The Dream and the Underworld." *Eranos Jahrbuch* 42 (1977), 91–136.

———. *Re-Visioning Psychology.* New York: Harper & Row, 1975.

Howe, Susan. *The Birth-mark: Unsettling the Wilderness in American Literary History.* Middletown, Conn.: Wesleyan University Press, 1993.

———. *Singularities.* Middletown, Conn.: Wesleyan University Press, 1990.

Hurd, Barbara. *Stirring the Mud: On Swamps, Bogs, and the Human Imagination.* Boston: Beacon Press, 2001.

Hyams, Edward. *Soil and Civilization.* New York: Harper & Row, 1976.

Irby, Kenneth. *Antiphonal and Fall to Fall.* Boulder: Kavyayantra Press, 1994.

———. *Catalpa.* Lawrence, Kans.: Tansy Press, 1977.

———. *To Max Douglas,* [2nd ed.] Lawrence, Kans.: Tansy Press, 1974.

———. *A Set.* Lawrence, Kans.: Tansy Press, 1983.

Irwin, John T. *American Hieroglyphics: The Symbol of the Egyptian Hieroglyphics in the American Renaissance.* Baltimore: Johns Hopkins University Press, 1980.

James, C. L. R. *The C. L. R. James Reader.* Ed. Anna Grimshaw. Oxford: Blackwell, 1992.

James, Henry. "Is There a Life after Death?" In F. O. Matthiessen, *The James Family, Including Selections from the Writings of Henry James, Senior, William, Henry and Alice James,* 602–14. New York: Vintage Books, 1980.

James, William. *The Correspondence of William James, Volume 8: 1895–June 1899.* Ed. Ignas K. Skrupskelis and Elizabeth M. Berkeley. Charlottesville: University Press of Virginia, 2000.

———. "Human Immortality." In *Writings, 1878–1899,* 1100–1127. New York: Library of America, 1992.

———. *A Pluralistic Universe.* In *Writings, 1902–1910,* 625–819. New York: Library of America, 1987.

———. "The Social Value of the College-Bred." In *Writings, 1902–1910,* 1242–49. New York: Library of America, 1987.

———. *The Will to Believe.* In *Writings, 1878–1899,* 445–704. New York: Library of America, 1992.

Jeffers, Robinson. *The Collected Poetry.* 3 vols. Ed. Tim Hunt. Stanford, Calif.: Stanford University Press, 1988, 1989, 1991.

———. *The Double Axe.* New York: Liveright, 1977.

———. *The Selected Letters of Robinson Jeffers, 1897–1962*. Ed. Ann N. Ridgeway. Baltimore: Johns Hopkins University Press, 1968.

Johnson, Ronald. *Ark, The Foundations*. San Francisco: North Point Press, 1980.

———. *The Book of the Green Man*. New York: Norton, 1967.

———. "From Hurrah for Euphony." *Chicago Review* 42, no. 1 (1996): 25–31.

———. *RADI OS*. Berkeley: Sand Dollar, 1977.

———. *Valley of the Many-Colored Grasses*. New York: Norton, 1969.

Jolas, Eugene. "Workshop." *Transition* 23 (July 1935): 97–106.

Jonas, Hans. *The Gnostic Religion: The Message of the Alien God and the Beginnings of Christianity*. Boston: Beacon Press, 1963.

Jung, C. G. *Aion: Researches into the Phenomenology of the Self*. Vol. 9 of *Collected Works*, 2nd ed., part II. Princeton: Princeton University Press, 1968.

Keats, John. *The Poems of John Keats*. Ed. G. W. Garrod. London: Oxford University Press, 1956.

Kelly, Robert. *The Alchemist to Mercury*. Ed. Jed Rasula. Richmond: North Atlantic Books, 1981.

———. *The Book of Persephone*. New Paltz, N.Y.: Treacle Press, 1978.

———. *Finding the Measure*. Los Angeles: Black Sparrow Press, 1968.

———. *Flesh Dream Book*. Los Angeles: Black Sparrow Press, 1971.

———. *In Time*. West Newbury, Mass.: Frontier Press, 1971.

———. *Kill the Messenger*. Santa Barbara: Black Sparrow Press, 1979.

———. *The Loom*. Los Angeles: Black Sparrow Press, 1975.

———. *The Mill of Particulars*. Los Angeles: Black Sparrow Press, 1973.

Kenner, Hugh. *A Homemade World: The American Modernist Writers*. New York: Knopf, 1975.

Kinnell, Galway. *Body Rags*. Boston: Houghton Mifflin, 1968.

———. *The Book of Nightmares*. Boston: Houghton Mifflin, 1971.

Kirk, G. S., and J. E. Raven, eds. *The Presocratic Philosophers: A Critical History with a Selection of Texts*. Cambridge: Cambridge University Press, 1963.

Klibansky, Raymond, Erwin Panofsky, and Fritz Saxl. *Saturn and Melancholy*. London: Nelson, 1964.

Koller, James. *Poems for the Blue Sky*. Santa Barbara: Black Sparrow Press, 1976.

Krell, David Farrell. *Lunar Voices: Of Tragedy, Poetry, Fiction, and Thought*. Chicago: University of Chicago Press, 1995.

Kristeva, Julia. *Revolution in Poetic Language*. Trans. Margaret Waller. New York: Columbia University Press, 1984.

Kroeber, Karl. *Ecological Literary Criticism: Romantic Imagining and the Biology of Mind*. New York: Columbia University Press, 1994.

Kuberski, Philip. *The Persistence of Memory: Organism, Myth, Text*. Berkeley: University of California Press, 1992.

Kyger, Joanne. *Just Space: Poems, 1979–1989*. Santa Rosa: Black Sparrow Press, 1991.

LaBarre, Weston. *The Ghost Dance*. New York: Dell, 1972.

Lacan, Jacques. *Écrits: A Selection*. Trans. Alan Sheridan. New York: Norton, 1977.

Lacarriere, Jacques. *The Gnostics*. Trans. Nina Rootes. New York: Dutton, 1977.

Lamantia, Philip. *Meadowlark West*. San Francisco: City Lights, 1986.

Lansing, Gerrit. "The Burden of Set." *Caterpillar* 10 (January 1970): 82–93; also in *Io* 12 (1972).

———. *Heavenly Tree Soluble Forest*. Jersey City: Talisman House, 1995.

Leopold, Aldo. *The River of the Mother of God and Other Essays*. Ed. Susan L. Flader and J. Baird Callicott. Madison: University of Wisconsin Press, 1991.

Levinas, Emmanuel. *Otherwise than Being or Beyond Essence*. Trans. Alphonso Lingis. Dordrecht, Holland: Kluwer, 1991.

Lévi-Strauss, Claude. *The Savage Mind*. Chicago: University of Chicago Press, 1966.

Lezama Lima, José. "*Orbita* Interview." Trans. James Irby. *Sulfur* 24 (1989): 172–83.

Lindsay, Vachel. *Going-to-the-Stars*. New York: Appleton, 1926.

Lowell, Robert. *History*. London: Faber & Faber, 1973.

———. *Selected Poems*. Rev. ed. New York: Noonday Press, 1977.

Loy, Mina. *The Lost Lunar Baedeker*. Ed. Roger L. Conover. New York: Farrar, Straus and Giroux, 1996.

Mackey, Nathaniel. *Discrepant Engagement: Dissonance, Cross-Culturality, and Experimental Writing*. New York: Cambridge University Press, 1993.

———. *Eroding Witness*. Urbana: University of Illinois Press, 1985.

———. "From Gassire's Lute: Robert Duncan's Vietnam War Poems." In *Reading Race in American Poetry: "An Area of Act,"* ed. Aldon Lynn Nielsen, 209–23. Urbana: University of Illinois Press, 2000.

———. *School of Udhra*. San Francisco: City Lights, 1993.

———. *Whatsaid Serif*. San Francisco: City Lights, 1998.

Martin, Calvin L. *In the Spirit of the Earth: Rethinking History and Time*. Baltimore: Johns Hopkins University Press, 1992.

———. *Keepers of the Game: Indian-Animal Relationships and the Fur Trade*. Berkeley: University of California Press, 1978.

Maturana, Humberto, and Francisco Varela. *The Tree of Knowledge: The Biological Roots of Human Understanding*. Boston: Shambhala, 1987.

McCaffery, Steve. "Blaser's Deleuzian Folds." In *The Recovery of the Public World: Essays on Poetics in Honour of Robin Blaser*, ed. Charles Watts and Edward Byrne, 373–92. Vancouver: Talonbooks, 1999.

McClure, Michael. *Ghost Tantras*. San Francisco: Four Seasons Foundation, 1969.

———. *Rare Angel*. Los Angeles: Black Sparrow Press, 1974.

———. *Scratching the Beat Surface*. San Francisco: North Point Press, 1982.

McCord, Howard. *Fables & Transfigurations*. San Francisco: Kayak, 1967.

———. *The Fire Visions*. San Francisco: Twowindows Press, 1970.

———. *Gnomonology.* Berkeley: Sand Dollar, 1971.

———. *Maps.* Santa Cruz: Kayak, 1971.

McHale, Brian. "Archaeologies of Knowledge: Hill's Middens, Heaney's Bogs, Schwerner's Tablets." *New Literary History* 30 (1999): 239–62.

McNaughton, Duncan. *Shit on My Shoes.* Bolinas, Calif.: Tombouctou, 1979.

Meine, Curt. "The Utility of Preservation and the Preservation of Utility: Leopold's Fine Line." In *The Wilderness Condition,* ed. Oelschlaeger, 131–72.

Meltzer, David. *Arrows: Selected Poetry, 1957–1992.* Santa Rosa: Black Sparrow Press, 1994.

Melville, Herman. *Moby-Dick.* Ed. Harrison Hayford and Hershel Parker. New York: Norton, 1967.

Mertins, Louis. *Robert Frost, Life and Talks-Walking.* Norman: University of Oklahoma Press, 1965.

Merwin, W. S. *The Carrier of Ladders.* New York: Atheneum, 1970.

Metcalf, Paul. *Collected Works, Volume One: 1956–1976.* Minneapolis: Coffee House Press, 1996.

———. *Collected Works, Volume Two: 1976–1986.* Minneapolis: Coffee House Press, 1997.

Milton, John. *The Poetical Works of John Milton.* Ed. Helen Darbshire. London: Oxford University Press, 1958.

Moore, Marianne. *Observations.* 2nd ed. New York: The Dial Press, 1925.

Mumford, Lewis. *The City in History.* New York: Harcourt, Brace, 1961.

———. *The Lewis Mumford Reader.* Ed. Donald L. Miller. New York: Pantheon, 1986.

———. *Values for Survival.* New York: Harcourt, Brace, 1946.

Naylor, Paul. "An Interview with Nathaniel Mackey." *Callaloo* 23, no. 2 (2000): 645–63.

Niedecker, Lorine. *The Granite Pail: The Selected Poems.* Ed. Cid Corman. San Francisco: North Point Press, 1985.

Nietzsche, Friedrich. *The Gay Science.* Trans. Walter Kaufman. New York: Random House, 1973.

Noël, Bernard. "The Outrage against Words." Trans. Glenda George. *Curtains* 18–21 (1978): 5–12.

Norris, Margot. *Beasts of the Modern Imagination: Darwin, Nietzsche, Kafka, Ernst, and Lawrence.* Baltimore: Johns Hopkins University Press, 1985.

Notley, Alice. *The Descent of Alette.* New York: Penguin, 1996.

———. *The Scarlet Cabinet.* London: Scarlet Editions, 1992.

Oelschlaeger, Max. *The Idea of Wilderness: From Prehistory to the Age of Ecology.* New Haven, Conn.: Yale University Press, 1991.

———. "Wilderness, Civilization, and Language." In *The Wilderness Condition,* ed. Oelschlaeger, 271–308.

———., ed., *The Wilderness Condition: Essays on Environment and Civilization.* San Francisco: Sierra Club, 1992.

O'Gorman, Edmundo. *The Invention of America.* Bloomington: Indiana University Press, 1961.

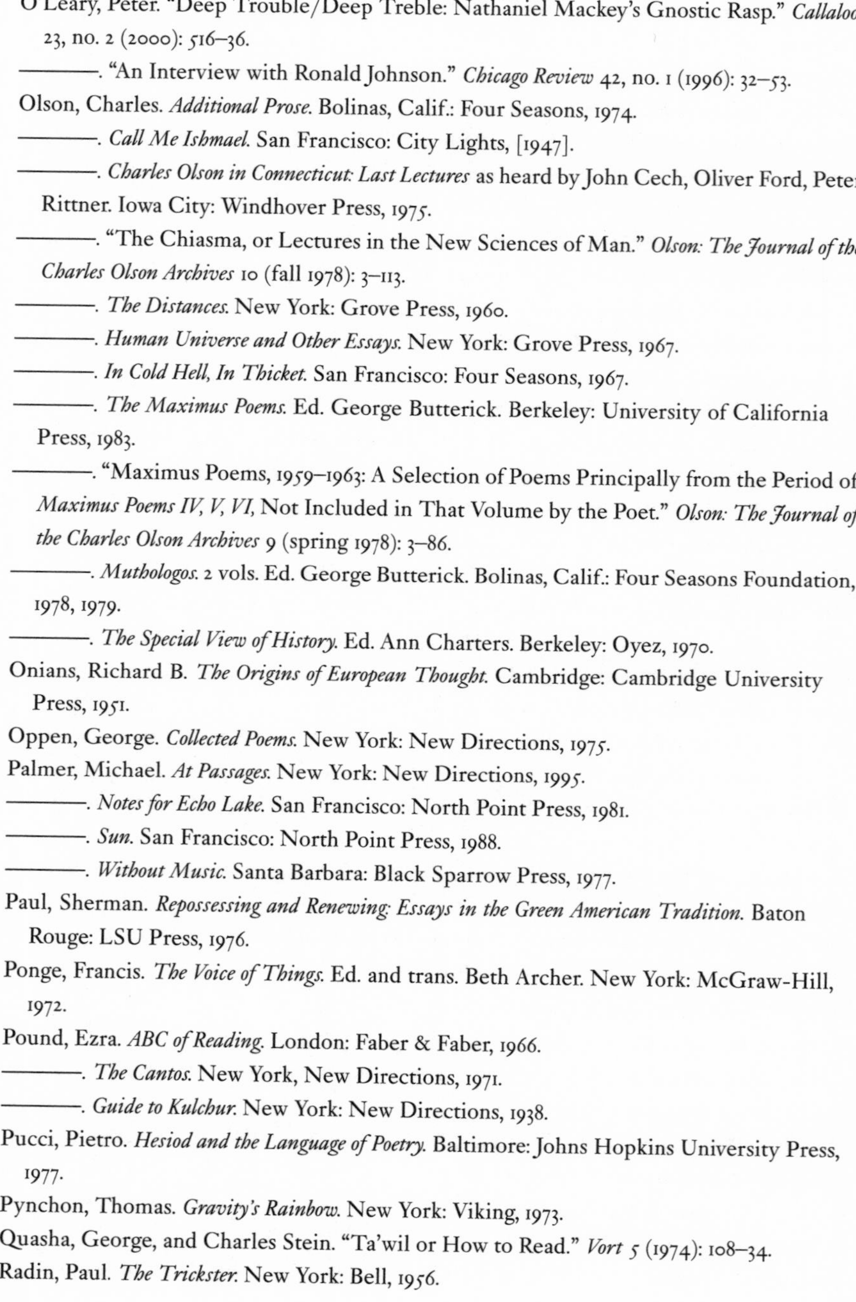

O'Leary, Peter. "Deep Trouble/Deep Treble: Nathaniel Mackey's Gnostic Rasp." *Callaloo* 23, no. 2 (2000): 516–36.

———. "An Interview with Ronald Johnson." *Chicago Review* 42, no. 1 (1996): 32–53.

Olson, Charles. *Additional Prose.* Bolinas, Calif.: Four Seasons, 1974.

———. *Call Me Ishmael.* San Francisco: City Lights, [1947].

———. *Charles Olson in Connecticut: Last Lectures* as heard by John Cech, Oliver Ford, Peter Rittner. Iowa City: Windhover Press, 1975.

———. "The Chiasma, or Lectures in the New Sciences of Man." *Olson: The Journal of the Charles Olson Archives* 10 (fall 1978): 3–113.

———. *The Distances.* New York: Grove Press, 1960.

———. *Human Universe and Other Essays.* New York: Grove Press, 1967.

———. *In Cold Hell, In Thicket.* San Francisco: Four Seasons, 1967.

———. *The Maximus Poems.* Ed. George Butterick. Berkeley: University of California Press, 1983.

———. "Maximus Poems, 1959–1963: A Selection of Poems Principally from the Period of *Maximus Poems IV, V, VI,* Not Included in That Volume by the Poet." *Olson: The Journal of the Charles Olson Archives* 9 (spring 1978): 3–86.

———. *Muthologos.* 2 vols. Ed. George Butterick. Bolinas, Calif.: Four Seasons Foundation, 1978, 1979.

———. *The Special View of History.* Ed. Ann Charters. Berkeley: Oyez, 1970.

Onians, Richard B. *The Origins of European Thought.* Cambridge: Cambridge University Press, 1951.

Oppen, George. *Collected Poems.* New York: New Directions, 1975.

Palmer, Michael. *At Passages.* New York: New Directions, 1995.

———. *Notes for Echo Lake.* San Francisco: North Point Press, 1981.

———. *Sun.* San Francisco: North Point Press, 1988.

———. *Without Music.* Santa Barbara: Black Sparrow Press, 1977.

Paul, Sherman. *Repossessing and Renewing: Essays in the Green American Tradition.* Baton Rouge: LSU Press, 1976.

Ponge, Francis. *The Voice of Things.* Ed. and trans. Beth Archer. New York: McGraw-Hill, 1972.

Pound, Ezra. *ABC of Reading.* London: Faber & Faber, 1966.

———. *The Cantos.* New York, New Directions, 1971.

———. *Guide to Kulchur.* New York: New Directions, 1938.

Pucci, Pietro. *Hesiod and the Language of Poetry.* Baltimore: Johns Hopkins University Press, 1977.

Pynchon, Thomas. *Gravity's Rainbow.* New York: Viking, 1973.

Quasha, George, and Charles Stein. "Ta'wil or How to Read." *Vort* 5 (1974): 108–34.

Radin, Paul. *The Trickster.* New York: Bell, 1956.

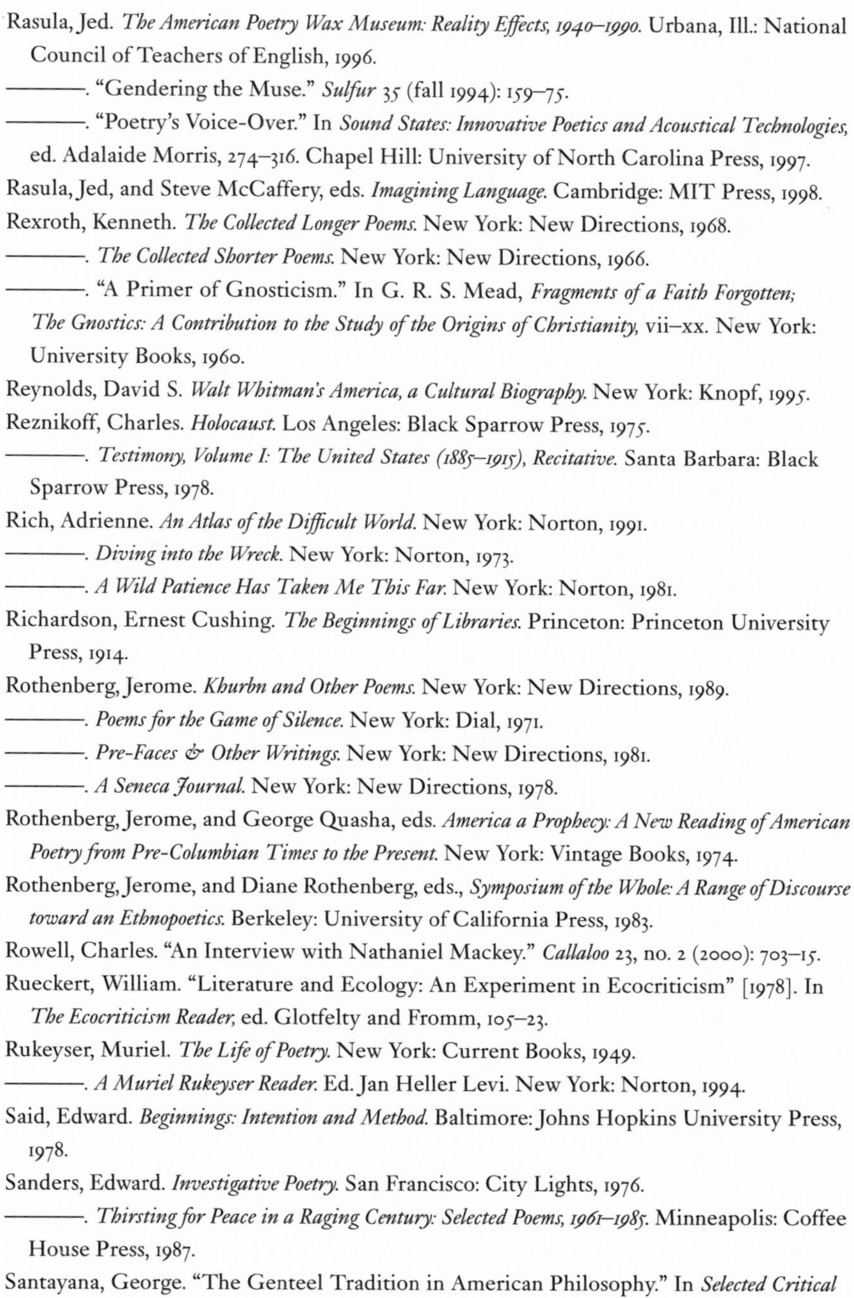

Rasula, Jed. *The American Poetry Wax Museum: Reality Effects, 1940–1990.* Urbana, Ill.: National Council of Teachers of English, 1996.

———. "Gendering the Muse." *Sulfur* 35 (fall 1994): 159–75.

———. "Poetry's Voice-Over." In *Sound States: Innovative Poetics and Acoustical Technologies,* ed. Adalaide Morris, 274–316. Chapel Hill: University of North Carolina Press, 1997.

Rasula, Jed, and Steve McCaffery, eds. *Imagining Language.* Cambridge: MIT Press, 1998.

Rexroth, Kenneth. *The Collected Longer Poems.* New York: New Directions, 1968.

———. *The Collected Shorter Poems.* New York: New Directions, 1966.

———. "A Primer of Gnosticism." In G. R. S. Mead, *Fragments of a Faith Forgotten; The Gnostics: A Contribution to the Study of the Origins of Christianity,* vii–xx. New York: University Books, 1960.

Reynolds, David S. *Walt Whitman's America, a Cultural Biography.* New York: Knopf, 1995.

Reznikoff, Charles. *Holocaust.* Los Angeles: Black Sparrow Press, 1975.

———. *Testimony, Volume I: The United States (1885–1915), Recitative.* Santa Barbara: Black Sparrow Press, 1978.

Rich, Adrienne. *An Atlas of the Difficult World.* New York: Norton, 1991.

———. *Diving into the Wreck.* New York: Norton, 1973.

———. *A Wild Patience Has Taken Me This Far.* New York: Norton, 1981.

Richardson, Ernest Cushing. *The Beginnings of Libraries.* Princeton: Princeton University Press, 1914.

Rothenberg, Jerome. *Khurbn and Other Poems.* New York: New Directions, 1989.

———. *Poems for the Game of Silence.* New York: Dial, 1971.

———. *Pre-Faces & Other Writings.* New York: New Directions, 1981.

———. *A Seneca Journal.* New York: New Directions, 1978.

Rothenberg, Jerome, and George Quasha, eds. *America a Prophecy: A New Reading of American Poetry from Pre-Columbian Times to the Present.* New York: Vintage Books, 1974.

Rothenberg, Jerome, and Diane Rothenberg, eds., *Symposium of the Whole: A Range of Discourse toward an Ethnopoetics.* Berkeley: University of California Press, 1983.

Rowell, Charles. "An Interview with Nathaniel Mackey." *Callaloo* 23, no. 2 (2000): 703–15.

Rueckert, William. "Literature and Ecology: An Experiment in Ecocriticism" [1978]. In *The Ecocriticism Reader,* ed. Glotfelty and Fromm, 105–23.

Rukeyser, Muriel. *The Life of Poetry.* New York: Current Books, 1949.

———. *A Muriel Rukeyser Reader.* Ed. Jan Heller Levi. New York: Norton, 1994.

Said, Edward. *Beginnings: Intention and Method.* Baltimore: Johns Hopkins University Press, 1978.

Sanders, Edward. *Investigative Poetry.* San Francisco: City Lights, 1976.

———. *Thirsting for Peace in a Raging Century: Selected Poems, 1961–1985.* Minneapolis: Coffee House Press, 1987.

Santayana, George. "The Genteel Tradition in American Philosophy." In *Selected Critical*

Writings, Volume II, ed. Norman Henfrey, 85–107. Cambridge: Cambridge University Press, 1968.

———. *Three Philosophical Poets.* Cambridge: Harvard University Press, 1910.

Santillana, Giorgio de, and Hertha von Dechend. *Hamlet's Mill.* Boston: Gambit, 1969.

Sauer, Carl. *Land and Life.* Ed. John Leighly. Berkeley: University of California Press, 1963.

Saussure, Ferdinand de. *Course in General Linguistics.* Trans. Roy Harris. London: Duckworth, 1987.

Scalapino, Leslie. *The Public World/Syntactically Impermanence.* Middletown, Conn.: Wesleyan University Press, 1999.

Schwerner, Armand. *The Tablets.* Orono, Maine: National Poetry Foundation, 1999.

Seferis, George. *Collected Poems, 1924–1955.* Trans. Edmund Keeley and Philip Sherrard. London: Jonathan Cape, 1969.

Serres, Michel. *Hermes: Literature, Science, Philosophy.* Ed. Josué V. Harari and David F. Bell. Baltimore: Johns Hopkins University Press, 1982.

Shelley, Percy Bysshe. *Poetical Works.* Ed. Thomas Hutchinson. New ed. corrected by G. M. Matthews. London: Oxford University Press, 1970.

Shepard, Paul. *Coming Home to the Pleistocene.* Ed. Florence R. Shepard. Washington, D.C.: Island Press, 1996.

———. *The Others: How Animals Made Us Human.* Washington, D.C.: Island Press, 1996.

———. "A Post-Historic Primitivism." In *The Wilderness Condition,* ed. Oelschlaeger, 40–89.

———. *The Tender Carnivore and the Sacred Game.* New York: Scribner, 1973.

Silliman, Ron. *The New Sentence.* New York: Roof, 1987.

———. *Tjanting.* Berkeley: The Figures, 1981.

Slovic, Scott. "Nature Writing and Environmental Psychology: The Interiority of Outdoor Experience." In *The Ecocriticism Reader,* ed. Glotfelty and Fromm, 351–70.

Snyder, Gary. *Earth House Hold.* New York: New Directions, 1969.

———. *Mountains and Rivers Without End.* Washington, D.C.: Counterpoint, 1996.

———. *Myths and Texts.* New York: Totem/Corinth, 1960.

———. *The Old Ways.* San Francisco: City Lights, 1977.

———. *A Place in Space: Ethics, Aesthetics, and Watersheds.* Washington, D.C.: Counterpoint, 1995.

———. *The Practice of the Wild.* San Francisco: North Point Press, 1990.

———. *The Real Work: Interviews and Talks, 1964–1979.* New York: New Directions, 1980.

———. *Turtle Island.* New York: New Directions, 1974.

Sobin, Gustaf. *Breath's Burials.* New York: New Directions, 1995.

———. *The Earth as Air.* New York: New Directions, 1982.

———. *Luminous Debris: Reflecting on Vestige in Provence and Languedoc.* Berkeley: University of California Press, 1999.

———. *Towards the Blanched Alphabets.* Jersey City: Talisman House, 1998.

———. *Wind Chrysalid's Rattle.* New York: Montemora, 1980.

Spicer, Jack. *The Collected Books.* Ed. Robin Blaser. Los Angeles: Black Sparrow Press, 1975.

———. *The House That Jack Built: The Collected Lectures.* Ed. Peter Gizzi. Middletown, Conn.: Wesleyan University Press, 1998.

———. *One Night Stand & Other Poems.* Ed. Donald Allen. San Francisco: Grey Fox Press, 1980.

Stannard, David E. *American Holocaust: Columbus and the Conquest of the New World.* New York: Oxford University Press, 1992.

Starobinski, Jean. "The Inside and the Outside." Trans. Frederick Brown. *The Hudson Review* 28, no. 3 (autumn 1975): 333–51.

Stein, Charles. "For Gerrit Lansing and His 'Soluble Forest.'" *Talisman* 15 (winter 1995/96): 41.

———. *The Hat Rack Tree: Selected Poems from* theforestforthetrees, *1980–1993.* Barrytown, N.Y.: Station Hill Press, 1994.

Stein, Gertrude. *Lectures in America.* Boston: Beacon Press, 1985.

Stevens, Wallace. *The Palm at the End of the Mind.* Ed. Holly Stevens. New York: Knopf, 1971.

Strickland, Stephanie. *True North.* South Bend, Ind.: University of Notre Dame Press, 1997.

Thompson, Lawrance. *Robert Frost: The Years of Triumph, 1915–1938.* Boston: Henry Holt, 1970.

Thompson, William Irwin, ed. *Gaia, a Way of Knowing: Political Implications of the New Biology.* New York: Lindisfarne, 1987.

———. *The Time Falling Bodies Take to Light.* New York: St. Martin's, 1981.

Thoreau, Henry D. *The Journal.* Ed. Bradford Torrey and Francis H. Allen. New York: Dover, 1962.

———. *Walden and Resistance to Civil Government.* 2nd ed. Ed. William Rossi. New York: Norton, 1992.

Todorov, Tzvetan. *The Conquest of America: The Question of the Other.* Trans. Richard Howard. New York: Harper & Row, 1985.

Valéry, Paul. *Analects* [Collected Works, vol. 14]. Trans. Stuart Gilbert. Princeton: Princeton University Press, 1970.

Vermeule, Emily. *Aspects of Death in Early Greek Art and Poetry.* Berkeley: University of California Press, 1979.

Vico, Giambattista. *The New Science.* 3rd ed. Rev. trans. Thomas Bergin and Max Fisch. Ithaca, N.Y.: Cornell University Press, 1968.

Virilio, Paul. *Speed and Politics: An Essay on Dromology.* Trans. Mark Polizzotti. New York: Semiotext(e), 1986.

Virilio, Paul, and Sylvère Lotringer. *Pure War.* Trans. Mark Polizzotti. New York: Semiotext(e), 1983.

Waldman, Anne. *Helping the Dreamer: New & Selected Poems, 1966–1988.* Minneapolis: Coffee House Press, 1989.

———. *Iovis.* Minneapolis: Coffee House Press, 1993.

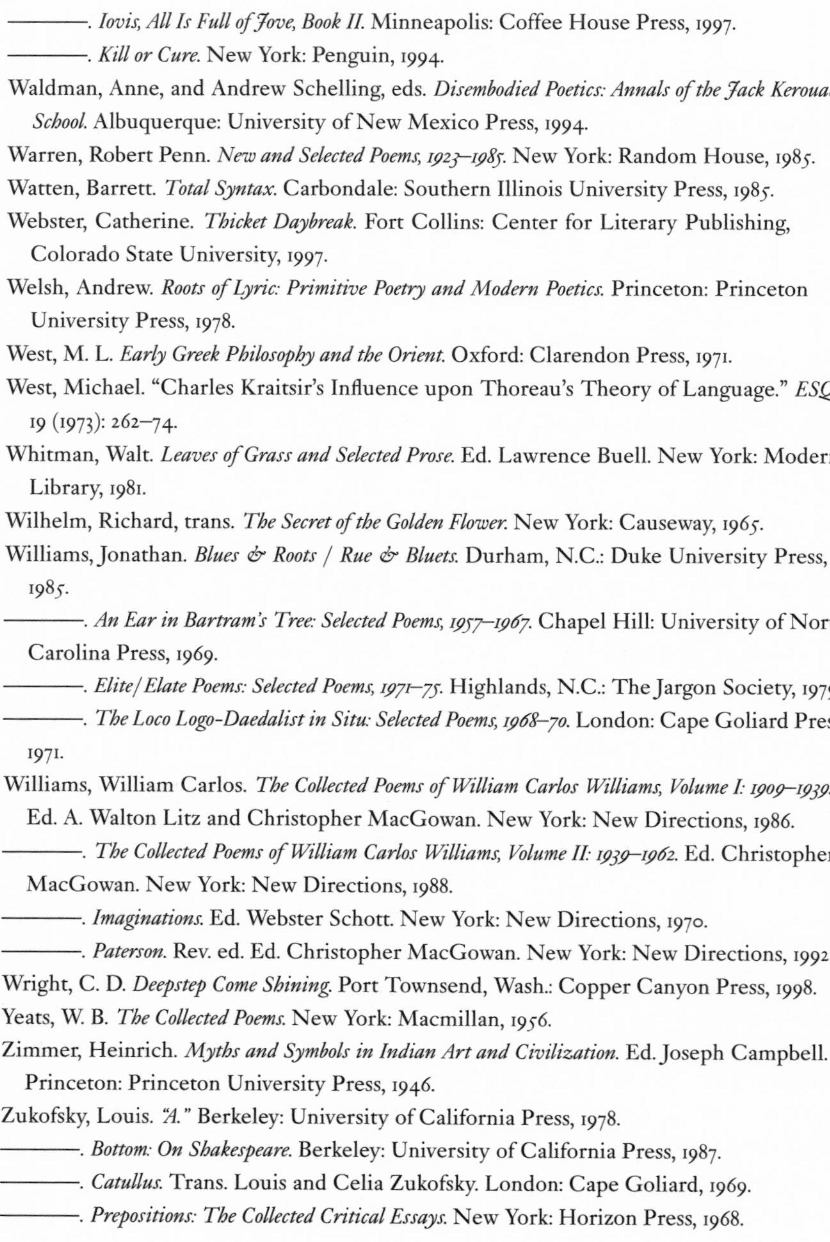

———. *Iovis, All Is Full of Jove, Book II.* Minneapolis: Coffee House Press, 1997.

———. *Kill or Cure.* New York: Penguin, 1994.

Waldman, Anne, and Andrew Schelling, eds. *Disembodied Poetics: Annals of the Jack Kerouac School.* Albuquerque: University of New Mexico Press, 1994.

Warren, Robert Penn. *New and Selected Poems, 1923–1985.* New York: Random House, 1985.

Watten, Barrett. *Total Syntax.* Carbondale: Southern Illinois University Press, 1985.

Webster, Catherine. *Thicket Daybreak.* Fort Collins: Center for Literary Publishing, Colorado State University, 1997.

Welsh, Andrew. *Roots of Lyric: Primitive Poetry and Modern Poetics.* Princeton: Princeton University Press, 1978.

West, M. L. *Early Greek Philosophy and the Orient.* Oxford: Clarendon Press, 1971.

West, Michael. "Charles Kraitsir's Influence upon Thoreau's Theory of Language." *ESQ* 19 (1973): 262–74.

Whitman, Walt. *Leaves of Grass and Selected Prose.* Ed. Lawrence Buell. New York: Modern Library, 1981.

Wilhelm, Richard, trans. *The Secret of the Golden Flower.* New York: Causeway, 1965.

Williams, Jonathan. *Blues & Roots / Rue & Bluets.* Durham, N.C.: Duke University Press, 1985.

———. *An Ear in Bartram's Tree: Selected Poems, 1957–1967.* Chapel Hill: University of North Carolina Press, 1969.

———. *Elite/Elate Poems: Selected Poems, 1971–75.* Highlands, N.C.: The Jargon Society, 1979.

———. *The Loco Logo-Daedalist in Situ: Selected Poems, 1968–70.* London: Cape Goliard Press, 1971.

Williams, William Carlos. *The Collected Poems of William Carlos Williams, Volume I: 1909–1939.* Ed. A. Walton Litz and Christopher MacGowan. New York: New Directions, 1986.

———. *The Collected Poems of William Carlos Williams, Volume II: 1939–1962.* Ed. Christopher MacGowan. New York: New Directions, 1988.

———. *Imaginations.* Ed. Webster Schott. New York: New Directions, 1970.

———. *Paterson.* Rev. ed. Ed. Christopher MacGowan. New York: New Directions, 1992.

Wright, C. D. *Deepstep Come Shining.* Port Townsend, Wash.: Copper Canyon Press, 1998.

Yeats, W. B. *The Collected Poems.* New York: Macmillan, 1956.

Zimmer, Heinrich. *Myths and Symbols in Indian Art and Civilization.* Ed. Joseph Campbell. Princeton: Princeton University Press, 1946.

Zukofsky, Louis. *"A."* Berkeley: University of California Press, 1978.

———. *Bottom: On Shakespeare.* Berkeley: University of California Press, 1987.

———. *Catullus.* Trans. Louis and Celia Zukofsky. London: Cape Goliard, 1969.

———. *Prepositions: The Collected Critical Essays.* New York: Horizon Press, 1968.

Biographical Glossary

Because many of the poets most prominent in *This Compost* have not been widely anthologized or received much critical attention, the following entries provide rudimentary contextual data. Excluded are those figures securely canonized, from Whitman to the generation of modernists (Pound, H.D., et al.), and others who are cited only in passing.

Ammons, A. R. (1926–2001)

Though Ammons is rarely considered in relation to open field poetics, his work nonetheless shares an improvisatory openness with the poetics of Olson, Duncan, and others. See, in particular, the long poems *Tape for the Turn of the Year* (1965, written on a continuous roll of adding-machine paper), *Sphere,* (1974), and *Garbage* (1993).

Ashbery, John (b. 1927)

His fame in recent decades has obscured the fact that Ashbery was first anthologized by Donald Allen in *The New American Poetry* (1960), a context that had extensive implications for readers of the early innovative books *The Tennis Court Oath* (1962), *Rivers and Mountains* (1966), *The Double Dream of Spring* (1970), and *Three Poems* (1972). Ashbery's unorthodox tastes are nicely on display in his Charles Eliot Norton lectures at Harvard, *Other Traditions* (2000), and have informed his prodigious output (twenty-one volumes of poetry through 2000), which includes many long poems (e.g., "Litany" in *As We Know* [1979], *Flow Chart* [1991], and *Girls on the Run* [1999]). "Self Portrait in a Convex Mirror" is Ashbery's most widely known poem, although it is not typical of his work in general.

Blaser, Robin (b. 1925)

Associated with Duncan and Spicer in Berkeley in the late 1940s, Blaser moved in 1966 to Vancouver, where a major symposium honoring his lifework was held in 1995 (published as *The Recovery of the Public World,* edited by Charles Watts and Edward Byrne). His various books of poetry were always conceived as part of a unified field, finally published as *The Holy Forest* (1993). Blaser is also literary executor for Jack Spicer, whose *Collected Books* he edited (1975).

Brandi, John (b. 1943)

Like Ginsberg and Waldman, Brandi is an indefatigable traveling poet, though he takes special care in his work to illuminate a specific geographical continuum from the American Southwest down to South America. *Diary from a Journey to the Middle of the World* (1979) is a characteristic title. The numerous chapbooks have been culled for *That Back Road In: Selected Poems, 1972–1983* and *Heartbeat Geography: Selected & Uncollected Poems, 1966–1994*. In each of his books Brandi's calligraphic realizations (which sometimes incorporate poems) provide a handsome visual complement to the writing. There is also a collection of essays and memoirs, *Reflections in the Lizard's Eye: Notes from the High Desert* (2000).

Clarke, John (1933–92)

A Blake scholar, Clarke was a colleague at the University of Buffalo when Olson was there, and after Olson's death he convened the chapbook series "A Curriculum of the Soul," the titles of which were based on Olson's outline (contributors include Joanne Kyger, Duncan McNaughton, Robin Blaser, Michael McClure, and many more). Clarke's immersion in the cosmological manifold of Olsonian bibliographies is abundantly evident not only in his lectures, *From Feathers to Iron* (1987), but in his sonnet sequences, which include *The End of This Side* (1979) and the posthumous *In the Analogy* (1997).

Creeley, Robert (b. 1926)

A teacher at Black Mountain College and editor of *Black Mountain Review* (1954–57), Creeley has since been associated indelibly with Olson and Duncan. His voluminous correspondence with Olson fills nine volumes. Creeley is a generous promoter and astute chronicler of the work of his peers, and his *Collected Essays* (1989) is an invaluable document. The *Collected Poems, 1945–1975* gathers the work for which he is most famous (including the books *For Love* and *Words*, among the best-selling poetry titles of the 1960s), and it has been followed by a half dozen other collections. Creeley has often collaborated with visual artists—the subject of an extensive exhibition in the New York Public Library (1999).

Dorn, Edward (1929–99)

A student of Olson's at Black Mountain, in the late 1960s Dorn lived in England, where Fulcrum Press published *Geography* (1965), *The North Atlantic Turbine* (1967), and the first installment of his mock epic *Gunslinger* (1969, completed 1975). *Gunslinger* and later work made it clear that Dorn was unique among his peers in being a poet of wit. He also had a keen sense of the underdog, evident in his stories *Some Business Recently Transacted in the White World;* his documentary study, *The Shoshoneans;* and the poetic lament *Recollections of Gran Apacheria* (1974). As coeditor of the gazette *Rolling Stock,* and in the poetry collection *Abhorrences* (1990), Dorn became a chronicler of decades as psychohistorical complexes. *Way West* (1993) offers a selection from thirty years of stories, poems, and essays.

Duncan, Robert (1919–88)

Collaborator with Spicer and Blaser in the Berkeley "Poetry Renaissance" of the 1940s, Duncan briefly taught at Black Mountain College before returning to San Francisco, where he lived the rest of his life. His openly "derivative" stance as a poet is abundantly evident throughout his work, the key collections being *The First Decade, Derivations, The Opening of the Field, Roots and Branches, Bending the Bow,* and the two volumes of *Ground Work.* His nuanced prose expositions of his poetics, and occasional comments on other poets, can be found in *Fictive Certainties* (which reprints *The Truth and Life of Myth*) and *Selected Prose.* Despite thirty years' work on a major prose project, *The H.D. Book,* it was never completed, though most of the chapters appeared in small magazines during the 60s and 70s.

DuPlessis, Rachel Blau (b. 1942)

A friendship with George and Mary Oppen had a decisive impact on DuPlessis's career as a poet and as a scholar. Her scholarly works include an edition of Oppen's correspondence, books on objectivism, H. D., and other twentieth-century writers, and *The Pink Guitar: Writing as Feminist Practice* (1990). Installments of her long serial poem *Drafts* first appeared in *Tabula Rosa* (1987), were expanded throughout the 1990s, and were gathered into a single volume in 2001. DuPlessis also served on the editorial board of Eshleman's journal *Sulfur.*

Eshleman, Clayton (b. 1935)

While living in Japan from 1961 to 1964 Eshleman developed an ongoing association with Gary Snyder. A highly influential promoter of open field poetries as editor of *Caterpillar* (1967–73) and *Sulfur* (1981–2000), Eshleman has also received acclaim as a translator (of Césaire, Artaud, and Vallejo, among others). His own poetry began as psychoactive autobiography and grew to include complex meditations on the prehistory of the human imagination, notably in the Paleolithic cave art of the Dordogne (a major prose study, synthesizing decades of firsthand research, is in press). The Paleolithic focus is most concentrated in the poems gathered in *Hades in Manganese* (1981), *Fracture* (1983), and *Hotel Cro-Magnon* (1989)—though the theme continues intermittently in later collections—and there is a useful selection, *The Name Encanyoned River: Selected Poems, 1960–1985.* There are two substantial collections of essays: *Antiphonal Swing* (1989) and *Companion Spider* (2001).

Howe, Susan (b. 1937)

Initially a visual artist, Howe came to poetry later, with *Hinge Picture* (1974) and *The Western Borders* (1976). She has maintained a steadfast historical and geographical orientation (colonial New England), explicitly claiming allegiance to Olson's precedent. Her imaginative critical prose consists of *My Emily Dickinson* (1985) and *The Birth-mark* (1993). New Directions began publishing her poetry in 1993 *(The Nonconformist's Memorial)* and has issued several volumes since, including a reprint of her earliest titles, *Frame Structures* (1996). Sun & Moon also reprinted several books in *The Europe of Trusts* (1990).

Irby, Kenneth (b. 1936)

Kansas informs much of Irby's poetry, which is intellectually oriented to a sense of open form and geographical space by way of Olson and Dorn. His interest in hermetica has been nourished by his association with Duncan, Kelly, and Lansing, among others. Most of his work has been issued in ephemeral form, from mimeo editions like *The Roadrunner Poem* (1964), *Movements/Sequences* (1965), *The Flower of Having Passed through Paradise in a Dream* (1968), to fine letterpress works like *Archipelago* (1976), *A Set* (1983), and *Antiphonal and Fall to Fall* (1994). The larger collections are *Relation* (1970), *To Max Douglas* (1974), *Catalpa* (1977), *Call Steps* (1992), and *Ridge to Ridge* (2001).

Johnson, Ronald (1935–98)

Published early by Jonathan Williams's Jargon Society, Johnson's work was issued by a large trade publisher in the 1960s *(The Book of the Green Man* and *The Valley of the Many-Colored Grasses).* The Black Mountain link is less pronounced than his debt to Zukofsky, particularly evident in the epic *Ark* (published in 1996, after book-length installments in 1980 and 1984). *RADI OS*—Johnson's sculptural retrieval of a new configuration from *Paradise Lost*—is evidence of his keen eye, along with his books of concrete poetry *Songs of the Earth* (1970) and *Eyes & Objects* (1976). He also wrote five cookbooks. At present, little is available except for Peter O'Leary's thoughtful selection *To Do As Adam Did* (Talisman House, 2000).

Kelly, Robert (b. 1935)

An early theorist, with Rothenberg, of "deep image," and a vigorous participant in the post–Black Mountain open field poetry of the 1960s (as editor of *Trobar* and *Matter* and contributing editor of *Caterpillar*), Kelly was also among the most prolific, publishing over twenty books by the time he was forty. His involvement in hermetic lore is notable in *Finding the Measure* (1967), *Songs I–XXX* (1968), *Flesh Dream Book* (1971), as well as in the long narrative poems in *The Mill of Particulars* (1973) and *The Loom* (1975), a four-hundred-page culmination of Kelly's preoccupations to that point. Kelly was among the first poets published by Black Sparrow Press. Publications have continued apace—and in the 80s and 90s Kelly turned increasingly to fiction—but a convenient sampler and overview is *Red Actions: Selected Poems, 1960–1993* (1995). A stimulating bibliographic *mappa mundi* in the Olsonian vein is *In Time*

(1971). Kelly had considerable influence in the late 1960s through a younger generation of writers, many of whom were his students at Bard College, including Charles Stein, Harvey Bialy, Richard Grossinger, Thomas Meyer, Bruce McClelland, George Quasha, and Pierre Joris.

Lansing, Gerrit (b. 1929)

A resident, like Olson, of Gloucester, Lansing is a thoroughly and deliberately esoteric poet. His work has appeared, on the precedent of Whitman's *Leaves of Grass,* in successive editions of the same book: *The Heavenly Tree Grows Downward* (1966 and 1977), transformed into *Heavenly Tree Soluble Forest* (1995). His theoretical provocation, "The Burden of Set," first issued in Lansing's magazine *Set,* was reprinted in *Caterpillar* in 1970 and *Io* in 1972.

Loy, Mina (1882–1966)

The rehabilitation of Loy's work—a unique amalgam spanning her association with the Italian Futurists and subsequent participation in New York Dada—is due to Roger Conover, but in this context it's worth noting that Jargon Society issued *Lunar Baedeker and Time Tables* in 1958, as well as Conover's edition of *The Last Lunar Baedeker* in 1982.

Mackey, Nathaniel (b. 1947)

Much of Mackey's dissertation, "Call Me Tantra: Open Field Poetics as Muse" (1975), was on Robert Duncan, and his allegiance to Duncan and Olson is evident in *Discrepant Engagement* (1993), a scholarly work uniquely combining open field poetics with cross-cultural figures like Wilson Harris and Kamau Brathwaite. Coeditor of an anthology on jazz, *Moment's Notice,* Mackey's orientation to African American music is most emphatically addressed in a series of epistolary fictions, *Bedouin Hornbook* (1986), *Djbot Baghostus's Run* (1993), and *Atet A.D.* (2001). His demanding poetry is polymathically informed, most of it consisting of the ongoing serial works "Songs of the Andoumboulou" and "mu." Several of the "Songs" are performed on a Strick CD with accompanying instrumentalists.

McClure, Michael (b. 1932)

The youngest of the original Beat poets, McClure embodied 1960s counterculture in his poems, plays, and activism and has continued to perform his work in a musical setting with Ray Manzarek of The Doors. The early *Meat Science Essays,* along with the sound/performance text *Ghost Tantras,* epitomize McClure's bio-poetic perspective of the 1960s. Further prose reflections on Beat culture, poetry, ecology, animal rights, and other topics can be found in *Scratching the Beat Surface* (1982) and *Lighting the Corners* (1993). New Directions has published his poetry since 1975, and in 1995 Penguin reissued some long poems, including *Rare Angel* (in *Three Poems*).

McCord, Howard (b. 1932)

A notable figure of the small press scene, McCord is synecdoche in *This Compost* for a host of others who, like him, have disappeared from literary sight since the 1970s (Drummond Hadley, James Koller, Keith Wilson, John Oliver Simon, and many more): poets and trekkers, often associated with Gary Snyder or his influence. In a letter appended to *Gnomonology* (1971), Snyder cautions McCord about his Olsonian bibliomania. His poetry, on the other hand, never belabors his learning. A *Selected Poems, 1955–1971* appeared in 1975, culling from collections going back to *The Spanish Dark* (1964).

Metcalf, Paul (1917–99)

Metcalf was a teen when he met Charles Olson, who was then researching Metcalf's great-grandfather, Herman Melville, for *Call Me Ishmael.* Metcalf later attended Black Mountain College, and Jonathan Williams published many of his books at Jargon, all of which are pioneering infusions of copious research and a rich paratactic sensibility. Inexplicably taken to be a writer of fiction, Metcalf often uses line breaks as focal orientation, begging the difference between poetry and prose. A handsome three-volume edition by Coffee House (1996–97) made all the work conveniently available shortly before Metcalf died.

Niedecker, Lorine (1903–70)

Completely removed from any literary scene, Niedecker lived in rural Wisconsin all her life. A lengthy and substantial correspondence with Zukofsky and Cid Corman led to her publication. *My Life by Water: Collected Poems, 1936–1968* appeared the year she died. Since then the textual state of her work has been in dispute: collections include Cid Corman's selection, *The Granite Pail* (1985, rev. 1986), and Robert Bertholf's, *From This Condensary* (1985).

Olson, Charles (1910–70)

Information on Olson is readily available elsewhere. Originally involved in politics, Olson turned to poetry after World War II. His impact on American letters stems from his years at Black Mountain College (1951–56). His polymathic stance as poet-educator continued to inspire younger poets until his death, including George Butterick, thanks to whom the final text of *The Maximus Poems* was realized, and whose *Guide* is an exemplary instance of the compost library as habitat.

Oppen, George (1908–84)

With Zukofsky and Reznikoff, Oppen was a member of the "Objectivist" Press collective that published his first book, *Discrete Series*, in 1934. Oppen wrote nothing for several decades, reconvening his poetry career with *The Materials* (1962) and periodic collections until his death. *Of Being Numerous* (1968) won the Pulitzer, briefly giving Oppen a notoriety withheld from his peers. His scrupulously moral attention to the balance of words and concepts is evident not only in his poems but in his correspondence (edited by Rachel Blau DuPlessis, 1990).

Palmer, Michael (b. 1943)

Long a resident of San Francisco, where he was close to Robert Duncan, Palmer has more often been cited as a fellow traveler of the Language poetry movement. However, the real range of affiliations is evident in *Code of Signals: Recent Writings in Poetics*, edited by Palmer in 1983. His earliest books were published by Black Sparrow; and when Jack Shoemaker (of Sand Dollar Books) started North Point Press, the initial poetry publications were by Palmer, Ronald Johnson, and Leslie Scalapino. Palmer's work has been published by New Directions in the 1990s, including *Lion's Gate* (selected poems), *At Passages* (1994), and *The Promises of Glass* (2000).

Rexroth, Kenneth (1905–82)

Autodidact supreme and literary jack-of-all-trades, Rexroth became a resident patron of the Beats in San Francisco in the 1950s and a pioneer of the poetry/jazz performance scene. New Directions published most of his work, including many volumes of essays, poems, and translations (from Japanese and Chinese as well as Greek and French). Rexroth authored a feisty history of American poetry and was an invariably astute observer of literary and other politics. His keen mountaineering outlook and experience, along with his Asian researches, made Rexroth a role model of sorts for Gary Snyder.

Reznikoff, Charles (1894–1976)

Associated with the Objectivists in the 1930s—Oppen, Zukofsky, Rakosi—Reznikoff was a lifelong New Yorker, trained as a lawyer. Jewish heritage contributes much to his work, not only *Holocaust* (1975) but the shorter work gathered in *The Complete Poems* (two volumes, 1976–77). Reznikoff's investigative epic, *Testimony*, also fills two volumes (over five hundred pages). The scope of his achievement became apparent only at the end of his life when Black Sparrow Press published these titles along with his novels, although New Directions had issued two selections in the 1960s.

Rich, Adrienne (b. 1929)

Along with Ashbery, Rich is the most esteemed living American poet. Conspicuously associated with political causes, and highly influential as a feminist theorist and activist, her poetry of the past twenty years has integrated her social concerns into a complex ecological and historical vision, and in the process come very far from the first-person formalism of her early work.

Rothenberg, Jerome (b. 1931)

Early associated in New York with Jackson Mac Low, David Antin, Armand Schwerner, and Robert Kelly, Rothenberg pioneered a unique blend of the international metropolitan avant-garde and primitive lore and ritual, tendencies that came together in his concept of "ethnopoetics." He spent several years living on a Seneca reservation, giving pragmatic focus to his interest in Native American culture and serving as immediate background to his anthologies *Technicians of the Sacred* (1968) and *Shaking the Pumpkin* (1972). His editorial labors have been extensive, including the magazines *Poems from the Floating World* (1960–64), *Some/Thing* (1965–68), *Alcheringa* (1970–76), and *New Wilderness Letter* (1976–85) and nine anthologies, most recent being a two-volume compendium of the twentieth-century avant-garde, *Poems for the Millennium,* coedited with Pierre Joris. *America a Prophecy,* coedited with George Quasha, was a fertilizing event in the generation of *This Compost.* Rothenberg has translated extensively (García Lorca, Schwitters, Picasso, and others), made numerous recordings of collaborative performances, and has published twenty substantial collections of poetry, most of them with New Directions since 1974. A useful gathering of position papers and other prose is *Pre-Faces* (1981).

Rukeyser, Muriel (1913–80)

Her early success as winner of the Yale Younger Poets prize in 1935 led to a misleading prominence in the postwar period, when she was one of the few consistently anthologized female poets in the United States. But the astutely informed outlook in *The Life of Poetry* (1949) discloses a polymathic intelligence rivaled, among her peers, only by Olson at that point. By the time of her death she was known as a champion of causes (feminism and the antiwar movement), and the achievement of her poetry aroused little interest until recently, when most of it is out of print. An encouraging exception is Cary Nelson's inclusion of the complete "Book of the Dead" in his *Anthology of Modern American Poetry* (Oxford, 2000). Jan Heller Levi's *Muriel Rukeyser Reader* includes much of *The Life of Poetry* in addition to a selection of poems from the whole career.

Sanders, Edward (b. 1938)

A protégé of Olson, Sanders edited *Fuck You, A Magazine of the Arts* (1962–65) and operated Peace Eye Bookstore in New York (1964–70) while maintaining a career as lyricist and singer for his band, The Fugs—whose exorcism of the Pentagon in 1967 was documented by Norman Mailer in *Armies of the Night.* Sanders is an Egyptophile, richly evident in the subjects and the quirky illustrations of his poems. *Investigative Poetry* (1976) theorized, for poetry, what he had practiced as an investigative journalist in *The Family: The Story of Charles Manson's Dune Buggy Attack Battalion* (1971). Sanders's investigative propensities have led to several large poetry projects, including *1968* (a political history of the republic intertwined with a chronicle of The Fugs's travels) and *America: A History in Verse* (two volumes so far).

Schwerner, Armand (1927–99)

With Kelly, Antin, Rothenberg, and Mac Low, Schwerner was originally associated with the New York scene of the early 1960s, a scene notably documented and nurtured by Paul Blackburn. His long-term project *The Tablets* appeared in five editions from 1968 to 1989, as well as two recordings. The final text appeared posthumously, including a compact disc of Schwerner's performances. Other significant collections are *Seaweed* (1969), *The Work, the Joy, and the Triumph of the Will* (1977), and *sounds of the river Naranjana* (1983).

Silliman, Ron (b. 1946)

A central promoter of the Language poetry movement and editor of its definitive anthology, *In the American Tree* (1986), Silliman has consistently made clear his debt to—and preoccupation with—the Black Mountain/New American Poetry heritage. Theoretical speculations can be found in *The Age of Huts* (1986) and *The New Sentence* (1987). He was editor of *Tottel's* (1970–81) and executive editor of *Socialist Review* (1986–89)—a political involvement apparent in his poetry, much of which consists of book-length installments of a huge project called *The Alphabet.* These include *Paradise* (1985), *Lit* (1987), *What* (1988), *Toner* (1992), *Demo to Ink* (1992), and *N/O* (1994).

Snyder, Gary (b. 1930)

Equally famous and influential for his ecological views and his poetry, Snyder's career is amply documented elsewhere. In this context I would note his longtime association with the publishing projects (and outlook, too) of Clayton Eshleman and Jerome Rothenberg, and with Naropa and the poetics program there directed by Anne Waldman. Snyder has also been a constant presence in a nexus of western and southwestern poetry, exemplified by *Coyote's Journal,* among others. The single most convenient resource is *The Gary Snyder Reader* (1999), which includes an abundance of essays, poetry, and translations. *Mountains and Rivers Without End,* his long poem forty years in the making, finally appeared in 1996.

Sobin, Gustaf (b. 1935)

A resident of Provence since 1963, Sobin first published his work under the auspices of Montemora, edited by Eliot Weinberger, a key venture in maintaining some continuity between the New American Poetry impetus of the 60s and its expanding international outlook in the 70s. These were *Wind Crysalid's Rattle* (1980) and *Celebration of the Sound Through* (1982). New Directions subsequently published four books, and Talisman House brought out *By the Bias of Sound: Selected Poems, 1974–1994.* Sobin's archaeological interests, much evident in his poetry, resulted in an extensive study, *Luminous Debris* (1999).

Spicer, Jack (1925–65)

A member of the collaborative Berkeley milieu of the late 40s with Blaser and Duncan, Spicer disavowed his early poetic orientation and undertook the composition of books rather than single poems. The impressive results were gathered posthumously by Blaser in *The Collected Books.* Key publications during Spicer's lifetime were *After Lorca* (1957), *The Heads of the Town Up to the Aether* (1962), *The Holy Grail* (1964), and *Language* (1965). Spicer's Vancouver lectures of 1965 had a stimulating effect on the poetry community, especially after their transcription in *Caterpillar* in 1970. A scholarly edition, *The House That Jack Built,* appeared in 1998, along with a biography by Lewis Ellingham and Kevin Killian, *Poet Be Like God: Jack Spicer and the San Francisco Renaissance.*

Stein, Charles (b. 1944)

Beginning with visits to Olson as a teenager, Stein became part of the circle associated with Robert Kelly in the 60s. Author of a study of Olson's use of Jung, *The Secret of the Black Chrysanthemum,* Stein himself gradually followed the path of serial form: *theforestforthetrees* is the title of this project now underway for two decades, from which *The Hat Rack Tree* (1994) is a selection. Earlier poetry titles include *Poems and Glyphs* (1972), *Witch-Hazel* (1975), *Horse Sacrifice* (1980), and *Parts and Other Parts* (1982). Stein's practice as a Buddhist has been an important feature of his poetry, as it has for other practicing Buddhists like Schwerner, Snyder, and Waldman.

Waldman, Anne (b. 1945)

Director of the St. Mark's Poetry Project from 1968 to 1978, Waldman was also cofounder with Allen Ginsberg of the Jack Kerouac School of Disembodied Poetics at the Naropa Institute in Boulder, Colorado, where she still works. The variety of poetic practices nurtured at Naropa are much in evidence in the two volumes coedited with Marilyn Webb, *Talking Poetics from Naropa Institute* (1978–79), and in *Disembodied Poetics* (1994), coedited with Andrew Schelling. Waldman's own output is prodigious, and after *Fast Talking Woman* (1975) she became widely known for her invigorating performances. The two-volume *Iovis* (1993, 1997) is indebted to Ed Sanders's advocacy of "investigative poetry," transfigured through Waldman's performative sensibility, her richly informed cross-cultural awareness, and her extensive travels.

Williams, Jonathan (b. 1929)

As a student at Black Mountain College, Williams started Jargon Society, publishing the first installment of Olson's *Maximus Poems.* Jargon has continued sporadically over the years, proving particularly supportive of the work of Paul Metcalf. Williams's own poetry is occasional in the best sense, and the occasions can be expansive, as in *Mahler* (1969), his book-length poetic response to the complete symphonies.

Zukofsky, Louis (1904–78)

Famously championed by Ezra Pound, with whom he had an extensive correspondence, Zukofsky edited *An "Objectivists" Anthology* in 1932, including work by George Oppen, Carl Rakosi, Charles Reznikoff, Basil Bunting, and Kenneth Rexroth. The "Objectivists" initially formed to promote and publish the then neglected work of William Carlos Williams. Zukofsky had a fastidious and concise literary career, spending fifty years on the long poem *"A"*; producing a philosophical study of Shakespeare, *Bottom* (1963); a textbook/anthology, *A Test of Poetry* (1948); a translation, with wife Celia, of the complete poems of Catullus (1969); as well as plays and stories. *Complete Short Poetry* (1991) reprints everything outside *"A"* (including *Catullus*). Zukofsky carried on a long correspondence with Lorine Niedecker and has been frequently cited as mentor and role model by other poets, including Creeley, Duncan, Kelly, Johnson, and Silliman.

Index